RECLAIMING READING

In a time when teachers are continually disempowered as intellectual decision-makers in their own classrooms, this text is a welcome relief. . . . Noted scholars in the field take us on a journey . . . to visit where we have been, what NCLB taught us, and what current research is indicating that we need to do next. *Reclaiming Reading* is destined to become a welcome resource for all involved in literacy education.

Lori Norton-Meier, University of Louisville

Inviting teachers back to the role of reflective advocates for thoughtful reading instruction, this book presents theory and pedagogical possibilities to reclaim and build upon the knowledge base that was growing when government mandates, scripted commercial programs, and high-stakes tests took over as the dominant agenda for reading instruction in US public schools. Focusing on literacy learners' and their teachers' lives as literate souls, it examines how the teaching of reading can be reclaimed via an intensive reconsideration of five pillars as central to the teaching and learning of reading: learning, teaching, curriculum, language, and sociocultural contexts.

Reclaiming Reading articulates the knowledge base that was marginalized or disrupted by legislated and policy intrusions into classrooms and provides practical examples for taking good reading instruction out of the cracks and moving it back to the center of the classroom. Explaining what happens in readers' minds as they read and how teachers can design practices to support that process, this book encourages teachers to initiate pedagogy that will help them begin or return to the stance of reflective, knowledgeable, professional decision makers. The specific examples provided in each chapter and the unique chapter extensions are reminders that classrooms can be places of joy when children's interests, new literacies, and critical perspectives are at the heart of students' reading experiences.

Richard J. Meyer is Professor, University of New Mexico, College of Education, Department of Language, Literacy, and Sociocultural Studies.

Kathryn F. Whitmore is Professor, The University of Iowa, College of Education Language, Literacy, and Culture Program.

RECLAIMING READING

Teachers, Students, and Researchers Regaining Spaces for Thinking and Action

Edited by

Richard J. Meyer
University of New Mexico

and Kathryn F. Whitmore
The University of Iowa

Routledge
Taylor & Francis Group

NEW YORK AND LONDON

First published 2011
by Routledge
711 Third Avenue, New York, NY 10017

Simultaneously published in the UK
by Routledge
2 Park Square, Milton Park, Abingdon, Oxon OX14 4RN

Routledge is an imprint of the Taylor & Francis Group, an informa business

Library of Congress Cataloging-in-Publication Data
Reclaiming reading : teachers, students, and researchers regaining spaces
for thinking and action [edited by] Richard J. Meyer, Kathryn F. Whitmore.
    p. cm.
1. Reading—United States. 2. Reflective teaching—United States.
I. Meyer, Richard J., 1949– II. Whitmore, Kathryn F., 1959–
LB1050.R436 2011
372.40973–dc22   2010050085

ISBN 13: 978-0-415-88809-7 (hbk)
ISBN 13: 978-0-415-88810-3 (pbk)
ISBN 13: 978-0-203-83266-0 (ebk)

Typeset in Bembo and Stone Sans
by Keystroke, Station Road, Codsall, Wolverhampton
Printed and bound in the United States of America on acid-free paper
by Walsworth Publishing Company, Marceline, MO

DEDICATION

We dedicate this book to all of the teachers, researchers, and supporters of public education who commit time, energy, and passion to reclaiming reading for children and teachers in schools and beyond.

We rededicate ourselves, as have the contributors to this volume, to reclaiming reading by engaging in the work of the Center for Expansion of Language and Thinking with friends, colleagues, students, families, and communities.

CONTENTS

PREFACE

Imagine your ideal elementary or middle school reading classroom. Close your eyes and put yourself there, invisible to the adult(s) and children. What do you see? What do you hear? What do you feel? Is the physical environment colorful? Are the learners engaged? Is the teacher joyful? What kinds of materials do you see? What is the mood in the air?

In too many contemporary reading classrooms a visitor would find children glued silently to desk chairs, holding identical standardized readers and struggling to maintain their attention, much less excel as readers. Their teacher, in far too many cases, would be agonizing over pushing children to read materials that aren't interesting, worrying about an upcoming assessment, and longing to find joy and pleasure in her or his work.

Our imaginary teacher would be knowledgeable and compassionate, and care deeply about the students. She or he would be a hard worker and have years of advanced professional education. But she or he would also be conflicted, thinking:

> Should I do what I know is best for kids? Should I follow the mandates even though I know better? Should I speak to my administrators about the damage these materials and tests are doing to my students? Should I involve the children's parents and caregivers?

This book is a call to teachers to *reclaim reading*. The authors and editors understand that teaching reading is a political act for students, teachers, and researchers. We recognize that the knowledge base of reading has been marginalized and bracketed. We realize that teachers can find joy in teaching reading once their right to be thoughtful decision makers about reading instruction is reclaimed, restored, and reappropriated. *Reclaiming Reading* offers theoretical help to teachers who need and desire to reclaim knowledge-based decision making. *Reclaiming Reading* offers practical help and applicable examples to teachers to extend sound theory into their own practice in their own classrooms. The book focuses on areas that have been neglected or disrupted by legislated and policy intrusions into classrooms and need to once again take center stage. *Reclaiming Reading* reestablishes the critical importance of children learning to read and using reading to become thoughtful citizens.

Of particular concern to the authors and editors is the status of struggling learners from poor, marginalized, linguistically and economically diverse, and underrepresented groups. Such students are more likely to be forced into programs that make little sense for who they are and the contexts in which they live outside of school than students from more mainstream and privileged backgrounds. Further, their teachers suffer and endure the consequences of rigid, often scripted programs that put children and adolescents (and thus communities) at risk. Such programs leave teachers voiceless, and many leave the profession believing it was not a profession at all but a technical field involving delivery of a narrow, often scripted, curriculum that rarely honors the unique languages, cultures, experiences, and contexts that the students bring and represent. And their students often leave— literally or figuratively—as they realize that success in school is not necessarily related to success in life and that school success has become so narrowly defined as to be meaningless in broader sociocultural contexts. Attention to these learners and teachers is evident throughout *Reclaiming Reading*.

Reclaiming Reading concludes with "reclaiming joy." Think again about the imaginary classroom, where the teacher contemplates professional decisions that will deeply affect the reading lives of his or her students. This book brings imaginary classrooms to reality—places that are colorful, full of lively talk and active bodies, and rich in engaging inquiry about the world. It reminds us that teaching *is* joyful. Reading *is* joyful. Learning *is* joyful. *Reclaiming Reading* paves the way for teachers and their students to once again seek authentic literature that makes readers think (and maybe laugh or cry) and is written in the languages of the community; to respond authentically to all kinds of texts; to learn strategic ways to handle challenging materials; to expand definitions of what counts as reading to include new literacies; and to take up a stance as reading education professionals that is agentic—ready to fight joyfully and determinedly for what we believe in.

Center for Expansion of Language and Thinking: The Authorship

The authorship of *Reclaiming Reading* is truly outstanding. The contributors are members of the Center for Expansion of Language and Thinking (CELT). Founded in 1972, CELT (www.celtlink.org) is a non-profit educational corporation, international in scope, whose members believe in the principles of education for democracy with a focus on natural language learning and inquiry. The contributors include theorists who are known and loved internationally by teachers for their holistic transactional view of the reading process and new voices that are moving the reading field forward in decades to come. We are pleased and it is fitting that *Reclaiming Reading* is being published on the eve of the fortieth anniversary of the founding of CELT.

Organization of the Book

Reclaiming Reading is organized into five sections; each presents a pillar of reading: *learning*, *teaching*, *curriculum*, *language*, and *sociocultural contexts*. Although each chapter is placed in a section that focuses on one pillar, the essence of effective reading instruction simultaneously includes all the pillars, as the authors demonstrate in the research and examples they provide. Chapter 1 provides an overview of the five pillars and the ways in which they are interconnected and essential to the understanding and teaching of reading.

Given that the authors of the specific chapters recount examples and stories from their focused points of view and experiences, and that we intend all chapters to speak to teachers across contexts and age groups, an extension follows each chapter. These extensions are brief vignettes in contexts different from the chapters they follow. They offer possibilities for teachers to imagine the content of a chapter in their particular setting. This unique organization should inspire readers to browse and read as their interests are piqued. A particular extension might draw one's attention and the reading of the full-length chapter might follow. Another reader might prefer to read a specific chapter because of a particular interest in that area, relying on the extension to complement the chapter. We do recommend that readers read Chapter 1 because it offers insights into the umbrella ideas of reclaiming reading presented throughout the book.

ACKNOWLEDGMENTS

We want to acknowledge all the voices that contributed to the content of *Reclaiming Reading*, even if their names are not listed as authors in the table of contents. The book developed over the course of many gatherings of the CELT membership. We sat in clusters, often in the corners of grand ballrooms at national conferences, and imagined reading classrooms "post-No Child Left Behind." We listed concerns, brainstormed solutions, debated priorities, and nominated each other as authors. We returned to our home communities and thought about the work we do with teachers who are pushing against restraints. We submitted drafts and read each other's work. And we met again to finalize the contents and hone the message of the book.

We thank the authors of the chapters and extensions that follow for their passion, commitment, and smart thinking about contemporary issues in reading education. We especially acknowledge CELT members who served as invaluable readers for the contents along the way: Yetta Goodman, Peggy Albers, Nita Schmidt, Mitzi Lewison, and Vivian Vasquez. Debi Goodman, Eric Paulson, and Ruth Davenport, in addition, reviewed and responded to chapters and helped to recruit extension authors. The legacy of CELT members' work as scholars and teachers is the ways in which their ideas will be taken up in future classrooms.

We thank Bobbie Bevins at the University of Iowa for endless hours of skilled formatting and attention to numerous minute and critical details.

And thank you to Naomi Silverman, who is a steadfast support behind the message of *Reclaiming Reading* and behind the efforts of so many members of the CELT family.

Rick and Kathy
November, 2010

1

RECLAIMING READING IS A POLITICAL ACT

Richard J. Meyer and Kathryn F. Whitmore

Our purpose in this book is to reclaim reading from corporations and politicians whose profit-driven motives and oversimplified views of the reading process, reading instruction, and reading research have resulted in teachers and children being forced into ineffective, inappropriate, and sometimes damaging programs. We will not document or reiterate the reading tragedies that have occurred in the past ten years. Instead, we look forward as we present specific research and teaching strategies that support teachers' and children's struggles to reclaim reading during oppressive times.

Reclaiming reading is a political act. The authors and editors of this book have chosen to engage politically as reading professionals and hope to inspire readers to do the same. It is our goal to involve readers in thinking, alongside the scholars in this volume, about what we understand reading is, what it is for, and how we might engage our students and ourselves in the authentic work of reading, reading research, and reading instruction. Our work in reclaiming reading is centered on the reappropriation of our power, reflective natures, research, pedagogy, and relationships with each other, and the families and communities with whom we work.

Reclaiming reading is rooted in an increased drive to support reading research and instruction that is crucial to a democratic nation. We understand that an articulate, curious, inquiring, active, and proactive citizenship must interrogate the work of a government that is at the same time rich and poor, strong and weak, responsive and not listening, and united and divided. Therefore, we examine our own literacy work and interrogate the literacy work of others in the context of these intriguing and apparent dichotomies, to seek out places—third spaces (Gutiérrez, Baquedano-López, & Turner, 1997)—in which multiple voices are heard and multiple avenues for action are embraced. This is work that imagines a better tomorrow (Bomer & Bomer, 2001) and moves from states of hopefulness to states of enactment.

Reclaiming reading is political activity because it involves reflecting, coming to know, and, ultimately, acting upon our knowledge. It means ending the silence that saturates professional development sessions in which content is delivered to teachers as the one and only truth, until the next year when a new one and only truth is delivered. It means ending the disenfranchised and marginalized status of researchers whose work positively transformed classrooms and students' lives but was subsequently repressed by narrow and erroneous definitions of what constitutes research. Reclaiming is not exclusively about challenging programs that teachers are forced to use, although that might be one action taken; it includes regaining access to prior and important work done by teachers and researchers. It also involves a dramatic change in the current perception of reading being perpetrated by special interest groups, such as corporations, right-wing organizations, and some legislators who are convinced that schools are chronically failing. It may be more accurate to suggest that they are busy convincing the public that schools are failing because, for some, that *failure* means profit from more fix-it programs; for others, that *failure* means the end of public schools and the privatization of our children's education (Altwerger, 2005).

One part of our reclaiming effort is to inform teachers who were acculturated into the profession in recent years that they have been misled into believing that the five pillars of reading are phonemic awareness, phonics, fluency, vocabulary, and text comprehension. There are ways to think about reading that are much more inclusive, robust, and accurate. Another part of our effort is to support (and, in some cases, reawaken) teachers whose considerable teaching experiences and pedagogic intuitions find fault with what they are being told to do, including the use of high-stakes assessments that claim to measure, but actually reify, their teaching and their students' learning. This book will help teachers reach a deeper understanding of reading, including the process within the learner's mind, the nature of teaching reading (including the importance of relationships in teaching), the complexity (and wonder) of language learning, the substance of reading curriculum, and the relevance of and responsiveness to local contexts in which children and teachers live.

Reclaiming *Predictable Text*: An Illustration

A brief example illustrates our intention to reclaim reading. Consider the term *predictable text*. Ten years ago, teachers discussed the complexity of these words in terms of meanings, contexts, words, and sounds. A predictable text was one that sufficiently engaged the students' prior knowledge to make their reading of the text both effective and efficient (see Goodman & Goodman, this volume, Chapter 2). When Halloween approached and a teacher decided to read *It Didn't Frighten Me* (Goss & Harste, 1981) in her kindergarten class, she knew the children were excited about Halloween and liked to experiment with and explore what *fear* is all about. She relied upon texts like *It Didn't Frighten Me* as vehicles for engaging her students simultaneously in both reading to learn and learning to read. The repetitive nature of the text was meaning based, as on each page the children joined the teacher to chant, "One pitch black, very dark night, right after my mother turned out the light, I looked out my window only to see a ———— up in my tree," and the name of an improbable or fictional creature of a specific color (e.g., a green gremlin) was inserted. The subsequent lines challenged being afraid, as the text states: "But, that green gremlin didn't frighten me!" The colorful illustrations supported the readers' meaning making through the specific color and the animal itself (a brightly colored polka-dotted snake, for example).

With each passing page, the children were increasingly involved as they were swept into the colors, illustrations, rhythm of the text, and a growing sense of excitement and wonder about how fears (both their own and the character's fears) would be resolved. At the end of the book, a real and very probable animal for the context of a tree—an owl—really is up in the tree and actually does scare the child in the story. But, it's clearly a playful kind of scaring, and following the reading the children and their teacher talked about the differences between real fears and ones made up to tickle the imagination.

Predictable, then, refers to drawing upon prior knowledge, using that knowledge to make sense of new experiences, bringing theories to the floor (in this case, about fear), confirming or challenging those theories with a group of thinkers, and experiencing the joy that comes with engaging with a text. The knowledge that is drawn upon also applies to the children's expectation of the use of language in a meaningful way (semantics), the use of certain linguistic structures (syntax), specific words (lexicon), and sounds (phonics). Eventually, the children will study the color words in the book, then the animals, and some will use the repetitive "One pitch black, very dark night . . ." to frame some of their own writing and drawing. In the process of learning to make meaning, they learn words and sounds because those help with their subsequent reading and writing. They reread the text many times, feigning fear, and using expressive voices similar to their teacher's.

The concept *predictable*, which we understand to be a complex cognitive, social, and linguistic process, was appropriated when strongly phonics-based programs for reading were introduced (see Altwerger, 2005). *Predictable* was reduced to phonetically regular words, such as *fat*, *cat*, *rat*, *sat*, and *mat*, squeezed into stories that neither make sense nor resemble real language, and have no rhythm or rhyme, as does good literature. The joy of reading was drowned in a litany of rules, sounds, and words that strained to fit into awkward and meaning-hollow texts. Later, the term "decodable texts" was assigned to this type of book, but such books are neither predictable nor decodable (because decoding means that meaning has been made).

Predictable texts, then, are part of reading that we reclaim in this book. In the example, young children are reclaimed as learners because their teacher knows their experiences matter and the learning process is consistent with complex **learning** theory. Teachers and **teaching** are reclaimed as the teacher makes numerous decisions for reading instruction based on her knowledge of learning, the reading process, the specific children in her specific learning space, and the literature she independently selects. The teacher thereby reclaims **curriculum,** knowing her curricular decisions mean her students will move forward in their learning, individually and socially transacting with a relevant text. **Language** is reclaimed as well—from taking back the theoretical essence of the term *predictable text* to the children's reclaiming of the language of reading, as they learn about words, sounds, grammatical constructions, the parts of a book or text, and the relationships between each other, other texts, and other contexts. As a result, the **sociocultural contexts** of this particular classroom community are reclaimed—brought to their right footing in the children's lives, emotions, and existing knowledge of the world and the word. We organize the remainder of the book around these five pillars of reading, which have a much more informed and scholarly history than those named earlier (Paulson, personal communication): teaching, learning, curriculum, language, and sociocultural contexts.

Five Pillars for Reclaiming Reading

In 1991, Ken Goodman wrote about pillars of whole language and, although we've adapted them slightly in this book, they remain essential to our understanding of reading. With deep, refreshed, and invigorated understanding we can actively reclaim what we know is best for children and be equipped to interrogate, challenge, and actively resist the narrow views of reading inflicted upon teachers and children. By reclaiming the five pillars, we reappropriate and reinvigorate ideas and practices that have been pushed to the sides, shoved into the cracks, or redesigned in ways far from their original intents. We are not suggesting a move backwards, however. We are taking up once again the abandoned (by some) paths that guided how we once taught—for the sake of our children, our democracy, and our futures.

We find the use of *pillars* to be a wonderful metaphor for our reclaiming work. A pillar supports the structures and functions that go both within and above a building. By holding up the roof and defining walls, a pillar creates an interior space in which events may occur. We ask the readers of this book (teachers and researchers) to consider what it is that supports and defines their work.

We hope that it is evident from the predictable text example that the individual pillars rely upon each other to articulate spaces for thinking and action within classroom life as well as in research studies about reading. Each of the chapters in this book includes all five pillars, but explicates one particular pillar in significant depth for two reasons: first, to articulate that pillar in a way that helps readers understand its breadth and depth; and second, to explain ways in which the chapter will help readers reclaim that pillar with a renewed and intensified understanding.

To reclaim reading—to reappropriate how we talk about reading, teach reading, and research reading—we need to engage in actions with our students. The chapters offer ideas for practice that are often "in the cracks" of what is presently required, but we are confident that any individual actions toward reclaiming will become part of a larger movement as we talk to each other, attend conferences, read, and write about our lives with learners.

Reclaiming Learning

Reclaiming reading means reclaiming our foundational knowledge about what learning is, how learning happens, and who learners are. We know that learning to read, like oral language development, occurs in the tension between a personal, inventive force within an individual and the strong social need for individuals to communicate with, and belong to, identity groups. According to Goodman's language development theory, children's language is shaped "through the myriad language transactions that involve children with others. The language is generated by the child, but it is changed in transactions with others by their comprehension or lack of comprehension and by their responses" (Goodman, Smith, Meredith, & Goodman, 1987, p. 34). We know this process continues throughout a literate lifetime.

We know that reading is social, cultural, and political. Young children want to be active literacy participants in their families and social groups, and are

> positioned in groups and in society by their existing cultural identities. [They are also] acquiring cultural identity through reading, writing and participating in school. Therefore, children embody their cultural, racial, linguistic, class, labor, ideological and gendered positions in society. . . .These identities are evident in their relationships with others, in their discourse patterns and linguistic practices and in their constructions of texts.
>
> *(Whitmore, Goodman, Martens, & Owocki, 2003, p. 316)*

We know that learning to read means taking up an identity as a reader, as expressed in the concepts of joining a literacy club (Smith, 1987), being apprenticed into a community of practice (Lave & Wenger, 1991), belonging to an affinity group (Fernie, Kantor, & Whaley, 1995), and taking up a Discourse (Gee, 1996). As Smith says, "All learning pivots on who we think we are, and who we see ourselves as capable of becoming" (1998, p. 11).

Given what we know about learning, reclaiming reading means reclaiming our children and our work with them from those who would appropriate children's learning for their own economic or other gain. Altwerger (2005) describes the greed of corporations interested in profiting financially as they sell reading programs. She explains how some groups work to dismantle public education.

> Reading for profit and corporate control of reading instruction is [a] phenomenon that needs to be understood within its social, political, and historical contexts . . . a whole set of conditions had to be in place over a long period of time in order for corporate America to kidnap reading instruction and public education right from under our noses. But as we regain our composure, we must be ready to resist with knowledge and vision.
>
> *(p. 8)*

We have to know and be articulate about what we believe about learning, so that our responses to challenges are clear and far-reaching into the narratives and metaphors (Lakoff, 2002) that drive the way we and others think. It is not sufficient to express our love for children; in our work, loving children means being advocates for them, seeing them as having agency in such ways that their priorities, needs, and interests are respected, celebrated, elaborated, challenged, interrogated, and confirmed (Jones, 2006).

The children in our classrooms are not products, clients, or future workers, as many suggest. Wolk (2007) wonders about our children going to school "to learn to be workers. [Some] believe that [g]oing to school is largely preparation either to punch a time clock or to own the company with the time clock—depending on how lucky you are in the social-class sorting machine" (p. 650). He challenges us to think about why we want learners to attend school. "If school is not helping children to consciously shape their cultural, political, and moral identities, then we are failing to educate our children to reach their greatest potential[s]" (p. 652).

In the Reclaiming Learning part of the book, Kenneth S. and Yetta M. Goodman reclaim learning to read by providing an overview of their decades of remarkable work to understand the reading process. They present a liberatory pedagogy for reclaiming learning, their beliefs about parallels between language learning and learning to read, and a deep look at their comprehensive literacy model. The Goodman model of reading is foundational to this entire volume. Then, to extend the chapter, Richard J. Meyer and Bess Altwerger imagine the Goodman theory into the future as they explain the ways in which twenty-first-century literacies are rooted in the Goodmans' comprehensive model. Prisca Martens and Michelle Doyle describe how retrospective miscue analysis (RMA) enables young readers to reclaim themselves as proficient, capable (even brilliant) readers, and Carol Gilles and Debra Peters extend their ideas by describing work using RMA in a whole-class context.

Reclaiming Teaching

Reclaiming teachers and teaching is the "other side of the coin" of reclaiming learners and learning. Teachers can no longer anxiously but passively listen to professional developers. We need to stand up, with gathered voices, and be proactive for the learners with whom we work, because they typically cannot participate in such sessions. Or perhaps they can, if we work with them to cultivate their voices as agents of action and change.

Reclaiming the teaching of reading means acting upon the idea that well–informed teachers are at the heart of learning to read. Teaching reading is the process by which, day after day, week after week, and year after year, an informed professional makes pedagogical decisions based on research that is solid and well supported, and rests in clearly articulated views of language, learning, curriculum, and sociocultural contexts. Teaching reading is not the funneling of some pre-constructed program through a teacher's hands, particularly when that program discounts the teacher's knowledge of reading and ignores the children present in the room. The use of such a program implies the lack of need for a skilled professional and has the effect of homogenizing children and teachers into an amorphous "bunch" that is well served by what is provided from afar.

Reclaiming teaching means teachers are individuals who need to be free to make professional decisions based upon the children in our classrooms, the contexts in which the children live, the languages and cultures in which they are immersed, and the unique ways in which they learn. We need to be honest and claim ourselves as reading professionals who dedicate our lives to the children of others and the perpetuation of our democratic way of life. We need to be clear as to what the parameters of our jobs are and how willing we are to challenge the parameters that others set out for us. We need to understand reading in order not to defer to another supposed expert, especially those whose faux expertise seems to change with each school year and who desire to sell us something that will "fix" children. Reclaiming teaching means knowing and responding to our students because we are well informed about reading, not because we are compliant.

Reclaiming the teaching of reading involves teachers and researchers assuming agency and becoming advocates. It means a grassroots movement of teachers who meet in living rooms and coffee shops to talk to each other in order engage in what Parker Palmer (1988) knew to be the most powerful (and threatening) form of teacher professional development: teachers engaged in reflective conversation informed by a body of knowledge.

> If we want to grow in our practice, we have two primary places to go: to the inner ground from which good teaching comes and to the community of fellow teachers from whom we can learn more about ourselves and our craft. The resources we need in order to grow as teachers are abundant within the community of colleagues. Good talk about good teaching is what we need—to enhance both our professional practice and the selfhood from which it comes.
>
> *(p. 176)*

In the Reclaiming Teaching part of the book, Dorothy Watson illustrates how teachers' knowledge about miscues (windows into the reading process) led to effective strategy instruction for two middle school boys. Her ideas are extended by M. Ruth Davenport's description of her use of over the shoulder miscue analysis, a procedure that makes miscue analysis very manageable in a classroom setting. Renita Schmidt elaborates on the power of teacher decision making within the context of literature discussion about a novel labeled as controversial. She describes how preparation to teach literature, particularly with books that involve important and substantive content, is essential to reclaiming teaching. Then Rose Casement discusses book selection around contemporary issues as part of teacher decision making, particularly books that include lesbian, gay, bisexual, transgender and questioning characters in real-world stories. Koomi Kim and Yetta M. Goodman suggest teaching strategies that grow from their RMA research with two readers learning to read in their second language, thereby illustrating teachers' roles when informed about reading and linguistic diversity. Carol Lauritzen describes RMA as a means of teaching a young reader to move away from overreliance on print and toward meaning making. Jennifer L. Wilson and Kristen Gillaspy examine the types of reading conferences that humanize assessment in reclaimed middle school classrooms. Their discussion is extended into the elementary classroom by Allen Koshewa.

Reclaiming Curriculum

Reclaiming curriculum can happen when we are smart about reading, learners and learning, and teachers and teaching. We know ourselves and our students, and we know how to create reading curriculum that is authentic (Short, Harste, & Burke, 1996) and critical (Lewison, Leland, & Harste, 2008). Authentic curriculum is rooted in the relationships between reading and writing and life, includes multiple ways of making meaning, and incorporates twenty-first-century literacies (Kress, 2003). Reclaiming reading in a Freirian sense (Freire & Macedo, 1987) means reclaiming the word and the world—and reclaiming classrooms as sites of engagement, inquiry, struggle, and action upon the world.

The current curricular landscape of many classrooms, resulting from No Child Left Behind, Race to the Top, and other initiatives, involves the imposition of artificial curriculum that is disconnected from the lives and meaning making of our students. Artificial curriculum is prepackaged and one size fits all (Ohanian, 1999). It arrives in a slick box with students' texts that make little sense, workbooks, items to photocopy, and short and meaningless assessments. In reading programs for beginning readers, the absurdity of relying upon devices such as DIBELS has been clearly explicated (Goodman, 2006). Ohanian (1999) and others (Coles, 2003) offer in-depth deconstructions of other artificial, yet supposedly "scientific" (see Allington, 2005), measures.

Curriculum cannot be simultaneously authentic and imposed; imposition and authenticity are mutually exclusive, as Freire (see Del Pilar O'Cadiz, Wong, & Torres, 1998) was well aware of three decades ago, Dewey (1938) knew and wrote about more than seven decades ago, and we know today. Responsible curriculum has

> to be based on the realities of the students' lives, be meaningful to their aspirations, bridge disciplinary divides, incorporate assessments that accurately reflect student learning, and be constantly reflected upon by educators. . . . Teachers . . . create [curriculum] with each other, their students and the community.
>
> *(Peterson, 2009, p. 23)*

When we reclaim curriculum, there can be no separation between reading and writing because they are mutually informative processes. A child might write his or her way into reading or read his or her way into writing. A teacher who understands reading–writing relationships also knows that the student–text, teacher–student, student–student, and student–teacher–families–communities relationships are critical facets of curriculum development and enactment. These relationships—not a boxed set—are at the crux of what may unfold when curriculum is a process.

Reclaiming curriculum in this sense is, of course, a deeply political act that may make us feel vulnerable. Compliance with imposed and artificial curriculum means that teachers and learners have no voice or must defer to a voice that is not theirs (Moje, 2007). When we comply with mandated curriculum, we commit as much of a political act as when we dissent with curriculum, but being silent (Fine, 1996) and complying may make us feel less vulnerable than does challenging or interrogating. Teachers are consistently coerced into compliance when their jobs and security are threatened. Teachers are told that their job is not the creation of curriculum but the delivery of it. During an interview at which one teacher described this process, she wept, recalling the days when she was trusted, her classroom was considerably more joyous, and her students were much more active in their reading and writing lives (Meyer, 2001). The collision of knowing about quality reading curriculum and being forced to comply with mandates framed by illusions of "scientific" evidence makes teaching untenable for some.

The authors of chapters in the Reclaiming Curriculum part of the book offer descriptions and ideas that reclaim teachers as curriculum authorities and bring joy back to the classroom as we look to the future. Teachers who reclaim the curriculum are creative and resourceful; they attend to the local issues present in their classrooms and see the sociocultural backgrounds of their students as resources. Jane Baskwill helps us imagine curriculum that affirms who learners are and how learning occurs by describing how to use family storytelling and digital photography to engage children in learning to read. Corey Drake and Lori Norton-Meier also build curriculum centered in community and family resources, and use photography to help stretch teachers' and children's definitions of reading to include mathematics. Kathy G. Short and Lisa Thomas enlist global children's literature to develop intercultural understanding, and Yoo Kyung Sung and Richard J. Meyer consider more specifically the authenticity of children's literature about Korea. Katie Van Sluys and Tasha Tropp Laman show ways teachers can reclaim reading by designing curricular invitations in elementary multiage and multilingual classrooms. Kathryn Mitchell Pierce and Edward Kastner extend their chapter with descriptions of technology invitations that engaged their middle school students in explorations of their school and their identities.

Reclaiming Language

In this book we reclaim the importance of authentic language use in the teaching and studying of reading. Language exists to make meaning (Wells, 1985). Although many researchers offer different views of the functions and uses of language, they all agree that the construction of meaning is the work of language as a tool (Vygotsky, 1978). Our knowledge of language includes what we know about oral and written language acquisition and what we know about how learners come to be readers. We know about learning to read and write in linguistically diverse settings and the importance of funds of knowledge (González, Moll, & Amanti, 2005) as vehicles for integrating home and school linguistic, cultural, teaching, and learning contexts. We know about oral language development (Lindfors, 2008) and the ways in which oral language development influences written language development. Our brief discussion of *predictable text* demonstrates some of the ways in which minds thrive when they are involved with genuine language and steeped in relevant and meaningful text. Reclaiming language means that we can study language use *with* children (Goodman, 2003) so that they may gain insights into understanding how language has power that influences every aspect of our lives (Janks, 2010).

   We also understand the power of language to construct ideology and the energy created by language because it is at the heart of relationships, self-expression, and coming to know self and others. We are well aware of the co-opting of language about reading for political gain, economic profit, and social positioning. Our understanding of language as a tool for meaning construction has been marginalized by government-imposed use of reading programs based on the fallacy of *reliable, replicable research*. We will not recapitulate the policies and legislative actions that have brought about the very limited view of language that saturates reading programs currently sold to schools and families under the guise of being "research based." That important critique has been presented elsewhere (Altwerger, 2005). We will state quite explicitly, however, that the use of authentic languages—oral or written and first and second (or third or fourth) languages—is a crucial facet of all reading programs. Students engaging in conversations that originate within or because of texts (such as the discussion of *fear* presented earlier) learn academic language as they transact (Rosenblatt, 1978) with texts. These transactions support their learning about the efferent, aesthetic, and critical qualities of the specific text at hand and their generalizing of that learning to texts yet to be read.

In an educational climate in which some states and statutes severely restrict bilingual programs, reclaiming language means supporting bilingual reading education because of the large body of substantive research that supports it. Meaning-based programs use the knowledge that learners have gleaned about language more generally to support their learning of a second language, including reading in multilingual contexts (Freeman & Freeman, 2000). First and second language learners moving across and between language worlds at home and in school are moving across Discourses (Gee, 2006) as well. We know that children need varied school experiences (curriculum) reflective of the ways in which language is used at home and what is expected in academic settings.

We reclaim the use of authentic language because the stilted, scripted, unnatural, and too often meaningless language in many reading programs undermines the ultimate goal of developing thoughtful language users. Poorly performing (and likely economically poor) schools are often forced to use reading programs with the least authentic language. We reclaim the rights of teachers and students to engage in the richest, most comprehensive uses of oral and written language possible. Language, then, is a political issue, just as are the other pillars discussed in this introductory chapter and throughout this book.

In the Reclaiming Language section of this volume, Peggy Albers explains that visual texts are critical to the reading process and shows us how, through visual discourse analysis, we can reclaim visual texts as legitimate parts of the language of reading, composing, and thinking. Jerome C. Harste applies Peggy's ideas to curricular engagement recommendations that infuse the arts seamlessly into the curriculum. Jeanne Gilliam Fain and Robin Horn illustrate how language in school, particularly talk about literature that shares US border stories, offers opportunities to discuss racism, power, and social injustice in a bilingual classroom. Andrea García and Kathryn F. Whitmore extend their ideas with examples of bilingual literature study in community settings. Yvonne and David Freeman and Ann Ebe offer ways to evaluate bilingual books for emerging bilingual readers so that teachers may make informed decisions about book selection. Then Carmen M. Martínez-Roldán provides examples of young children talking critically about such books.

Reclaiming Sociocultural Contexts

Reclaiming the sociocultural contexts in which learners learn and live involves knowing students' homes, communities, and identities, and being willing to make the realities of students' lives more central to what happens in school. Reclaiming sociocultural contexts is political work. It involves interrogating and challenging high-stakes test scores, economic figures, and other demographic data that are used to oppress and position teachers and learners.

A reflective progressive teacher looks forward to the responsibility of designing localized and individualized instruction, as discussed by Meier (1997, p. 97):

> But school reform will only be truly valuable and long-lasting if it matches the specific contexts and situations of teachers, students, and families in their day-to-day school lives. Changing schools can only go so far, for schooling is a way of life, not a static thing to manipulate and fix. All too dynamic, too human, too slippery, schooling is more like an organism evolving over time. . . . Real and lasting educational change, then, comes from the inside out.

In the current evaluation landscape, most US schools worry about making adequate yearly progress (AYP) as outlined by the Elementary and Secondary Education Act. The results of high-stakes tests, with money and jobs in jeopardy, coerce schools to defer to specific reading programs that prepare students for those tests. Failure to achieve AYP results in punitive measures like rigid programs and more (and often absurd) testing and reporting. Although test data are disaggregated once each year, showing proficiency or the lack of it for groups such as English language learners, economically poor students, special education students, etc., the reality is that schools receive one marker of status. Either they have "met" AYP or they have not. Meyer (2010) refers to this as broad-stroke portraits of schools because the status is determined and posted, regardless of the intricacies and specificities at a given school site. The community is homogenized as the individuality of students and teachers fade into two words: failing school.

As a result, legislators develop policies and publishing companies profit. Although some materials claim to address differences in reading achievement, most programs require that teachers address all of the students at one time. All of the children hear or read the same text, are asked the same questions, are taught the same skills, and must do the same independent work. The children's first languages, their home cultures, their communities, and all the complexities of their lives beyond the walls of the program are systematically excluded from their learning to read and write. Although the prominence of a Black, Asian, or Hispanic family in some texts might be pointed out when the program is pitched to district administrators, the specificity reflecting the realities of the students' sociocultural contexts is absent. The program trumps the realities of the children's lives.

The students whose lives (and school achievements) are most consistently reported by the media, and compose the narratives of many legislators and publisher representatives, are the ones who live lives farthest from the stereotypic American dream. These are the families that are often described as not "pulling themselves up by their bootstraps." Of course they can't pull themselves up by bootstraps when they don't have boots and sometimes no longer have homes. Too often, the official portraits of such children and their families are negative pictures of gloom, disparity, and lack of possibilities. One goal of this book is to help deconstruct these "official portraits" (Meyer, 2010) by demonstrating that counterportraits exist; counterportraits become visible when the specificity of the sociocultural context is central to what happens with learners and teachers in school.

In the Reclaiming Sociocultural Contexts part of the book, Karen E. Wohlwend and Pam Hubbard examine the potential of toys as texts for young children's learning to read and teachers' understanding of how they make meaning. Debbie Smith draws connections between toys and texts in the kindergarten classroom and her experience engaging adolescent students in reading and writing tags as texts. Vivian Vasquez and Carol Felderman describe the use of podcasting to identify children's cultural and symbolic resources, and to deconstruct and design texts of varied modalities. Chuck Jurich and Richard J. Meyer examine the intersection of technology, reading and writing, identity exploration, and critical literacy with an example of engaging children in moviemaking during an after-school video club.

Searching for Joy

Reading teachers, teacher educators, and researchers increasingly know that the past decade has placed them in a position of helplessness, frustration, anger, and outrage. Many reading professionals are in the impossible predicament of having to comply with mandates they know are damaging—or surviving in the margins, out of step with their colleagues and in never-ending defensive arguments with authorities and manufactured public perceptions. The isolation that is a byproduct of mandated, test-driven reading curriculum and narrow, inaccurate definitions of reading research further silences teachers into compliance. The title of this book announces that we intend to *reclaim*, or to claim back, that which "has been taken away or temporarily given to another." The word "reclaim" is further defined as "to cause somebody to return to a more moral way of life" (Encarta, 2009); synonyms include the concepts of regaining, recovering, salvaging, and even rescuing—all words that fit the imperative need for reclaiming sensible, ethical, knowledgeable, and productive positions as reading experts and educators. The final chapter of this book is about reclaiming the joy that we once knew as reading teachers. This is a complex view of joy that rests in critical literacy strategies, such as challenging, interrogating, and moving to action. Further, it is about finding, celebrating, and including the many possibilities for joy that learners bring to school.

The authors in the chapters that follow present theoretically grounded and real research that involves real teachers and readers with real texts in real classrooms. They provide specific examples and strategies for the initiation of the work of reclaiming as well as for continuing that work as a sustained effort. Their voices and stories are a point of origin for the work of reclaiming reading, and it falls to the many teachers, researchers, families, and children beyond this text to carry the stories and ideas presented within to other contexts.

References

Allington, R. (2005, February). Ideology is still trumping evidence. *Phi Delta Kappan, 86*(6), 462–468.

Altwerger, B. (2005). *Reading for profit: How the bottom line leaves kids behind.* Portsmouth, NH: Heinemann.

Bomer, R., & Bomer, K. (2001). *For a better world: Reading and writing for social action.* Portsmouth, NH: Heinemann.

Coles, G. (2003). *Reading the naked truth: Literacy, legislation, and lies.* Portsmouth, NH: Heinemann.

Del Pilar O'Cadiz, M., Wong, P. L., & Torres, C. A. (1998). *Education and democracy: Paulo Freire, social movements, and educational reform in São Paulo.* Boulder, CO: Westview Press.

Dewey, J. (1938). *Experience and education.* New York: Collier Books, Macmillan.

Encarta. (2009). Definition of "reclaim." Microsoft. Retrieved from http://encarta.msn.com/encnet/features/dictionary/DictionaryResults.aspx?lextype=3&search=Reclaim

Fernie, D. E., Kantor, R., & Whaley, K. L. (1995). Learning from classroom ethnographies: Same places, different times. In J. A. Hatch (Ed.), *Qualitative research in early childhood settings* (pp. 156–172). Westport, CT: Praeger.

Fine, M. (1996). Silencing in public schools. In B. Power & R. Hubbard (Eds.), *Language development: A reader for teachers* (pp. 243–254). Englewood Cliffs, NJ: Merrill/Prentice Hall.

Freeman, D. E., & Freeman, Y. S. (2000). *Teaching reading in multilingual classrooms.* Portsmouth, NH: Heinemann.

Freire, P. (1970). *Pedagogy of the oppressed.* New York: Seabury Press.

Freire, P., & Macedo, D. (1987). *Literacy: Reading the word and the world.* South Hadley, MA: Bergen & Garvey.

Gee, J. P. (1996). *Social linguistics and literacies: Ideology in discourses* (2nd ed.). London: RoutledgeFalmer.

Gee, J. P. (2006). *An introduction to discourse analysis: Theory and method.* New York: Routledge.

González, N., Moll, L. C., & Amanti, C. (2005). *Funds of knowledge: Theorizing practices in households and classrooms.* Mahwah, NJ: Lawrence Erlbaum.

Goodman, K. S. (1991). *The whole language catalog.* Santa Rosa, CA: American School Publishers.

Goodman, K. S. (2006). *The truth about DIBELS: What it is. What it does.* Portsmouth, NH: Heinemann.

Goodman, K. S., Smith, E. B., Meredith, R., & Goodman, Y. M. (1987). *Language and thinking in school: A whole-language curriculum* (3rd ed.). New York: Richard C. Owen.

Goodman, Y. M. (2003). *Valuing language study.* Urbana, IL: National Council of Teachers of English.

Goss, J., & Harste, J. (1985). *It didn't frighten me.* Worthington, OH: Willowisp Press.

Gutiérrez, K., Baquedano-López, P., & Turner, M. G. (1997). Putting language back into language arts: When the radical middle meets the third space. *Language Arts, 74*(5), 368–378.

Janks, H. (2010). *Literacy and power.* New York: Routledge.

Jones, S. (2006). *Girls, social class and literacy: What teachers can do to make a difference.* Portsmouth, NH: Heinemann.

Kress, G. (2003). *Literacy in the new media age.* London: Routledge.

Lakoff, G. (2002). *Moral politics: How liberals and conservatives think* (2nd ed.). Chicago: University of Chicago Press.

Lave, J., & Wenger, E. (1991). *Situated learning: Legitimate peripheral participation.* New York: Cambridge University Press.

Lewison, M., Leland, C., & Harste, J. C. (2008). *Creating critical classrooms: K–8 reading and writing with an edge.* New York: Erlbaum.

Lindfors, J. W. (2008). *Children's language: Connecting reading, writing, and talk.* New York: Teachers College Press.

Meier, D. (1997). *Learning in small moments: Life in an urban classroom.* New York: Teachers College Press.

Meyer, R. J. (2001). *Phonics exposed: Understanding and resisting systematic direct intense phonics instruction.* Mahwah, NJ: Lawrence Erlbaum.

Meyer, R. J. (2010). *Official portraits and unofficial counterportraits of "at risk" students: Writing spaces in hard times.* New York: Routledge.

Moje, E. (2007). Developing socially just subject-matter instruction: A review of the literature on disciplinary literacy. In L. Parker (Ed.), *Review of research in education* (pp. 1–44). Washington, DC: American Educational Research Association.

Ohanian, S. (1999). *One size fits few: The folly of educational standards.* Portsmouth, NH: Heinemann.

Palmer, P. (1988). *The courage to teach: Exploring the inner landscape of a teacher's life.* San Francisco, CA: Jossey-Bass.

Peterson, B. (2009). Big city superintendents: Dictatorship or democracy: Lessons from Paulo Freire. *Rethinking Schools, 24*(1), 20–25.

Rosenblatt, L. (1978). *The reader, the text, the poem: The transactional theory of the literary work.* Carbondale, IL: Southern Illinois University Press.

Short, K., Harste, J., & Burke, C. (1996). *Creating classrooms for authors and inquirers.* Portsmouth, NH: Heinemann.

Smith, F. (1987). *Joining the literacy club: Further essays into education.* Portsmouth, NH: Heinemann.

Smith, F. (1998). *The book of learning and forgetting.* New York: Teachers College Press.

Vygotsky, L. (1978). *Mind in society: The development of higher psychological processes.* Cambridge, MA: Harvard University Press.

Wells, G. (1985). *The meaning makers: Children learning language and using language to learn.* Portsmouth, NH: Heinemann.

Whitmore, K. F., Goodman, Y. M., Martens, P., & Owocki, G. (2004). Critical lessons from the transactional perspective on early literacy research. *Journal of Early Childhood Literacy, 4*(3), 291–325.

Wolk, S. (2007, May). Why go to school? *Kappan, 88*(9), 648–658.

PILLAR I

Reclaiming Learning

2

LEARNING TO READ

A Comprehensive Model

Kenneth S. Goodman and Yetta M. Goodman

It is essential for teachers to have a theory of learning from which they can draw as they make decisions about what to teach. Teaching and learning cannot be separated from each other, and reclaiming learning is related to each of the other pillars that reclaim reading, as was discussed in Chapter 1. For almost a half-century we have worked toward a comprehensive theory of literacy and an understanding of reading development as compatible with that theory. In this chapter we provide the most current iteration of our comprehensive theory. This includes a shift in our terminology from cuing systems to language levels, more attention to non-alphabetic symbol systems, and what we have learned from eye movement research. To begin, we explain key elements in a liberatory pedagogy that support reading and learning to read, and discuss the foundations of learning and language learning theories that ground our work. We also present what we believe about the relationship between language learning and learning to read. We devote much of this chapter to a close look at our comprehensive theory of reading, a theory intended to serve teachers and the learners they encounter.

Whole Language as a Liberatory Pedagogy for Reclaiming Learning

In order to reclaim learning, we must reclaim pedagogical strategies that support learners in coming to be effective and efficient readers of texts, contexts, and their worlds. Methods and materials for teaching reading need to be rooted in a view of research and a theory of the reading process and reading development to truly support learning. Whole language was developed by teachers who understood the nature of the reading process and who rejected reading instruction that is preoccupied with words, phonics, and skill sequences. In fact, the term "whole language" contrasts with teaching parts of language outside of the context of meaningful use of language.

The widespread interest in whole language in developing nations, and the attacks on it in developed nations, are evidence that whole language is a liberatory pedagogy. It is, by design, democratizing, empowering for teachers and learners, and flexible enough to be adapted to a full range of languages, cultures, and circumstances. It is an instructional philosophy, a pedagogy, that is not dependent on didactic materials, standardized curriculum, high-stakes tests or explicit instruction out of context for only instructional purposes.

Whole language is holistic for learners in two ways: first, it is complete, bringing all aspects of successful education together; and second, it is integrated, unifying what is learned with how it is learned. Language is learned as it is used. Language is learned as children develop concepts and ideas. Understandings from math, science, social studies, and the arts (see Albers and others in this volume) are constructed together, using language in the context of problem solving and interdisciplinary projects.

A major concept in whole language is valuing or, when necessary, revaluing learners. Many of the researchers and teachers whose chapters follow tell detailed stories about how they worked to revalue readers. Some students arrive at school with a privileged set of experiences that fit the typical expectations of school. Others arrive at the classroom feeling as if they don't belong and encounter experiences that don't honor their identities, curious minds, and ways with words; these are the students that whole language teachers work to revalue. Whole language teachers and researchers also use the richness of the many languages that children bring to school in sign systems other than oral and written language—dance, play, song, story, art, etc. Drawing from the pillars introduced by Meyer & Whitmore in Chapter 1, we suggest that there are multiple "respects" that are central to reclaiming learning:

- *Respect for learners:* Building on the language and experience of the learners, whole language teachers start where learners are; linguistic and cultural diversity are valued. Multilingualism and multiliteracy are encouraged.
- *Respect for teachers:* Success in education depends on informed, committed, professionals. Policies can enable teachers but only teachers can turn them into realities that support learners. That's a lesson that politicians must learn.
- *Respect for curriculum:* The curriculum is one that builds on what the learners know, values their cultures, and moves toward broader content necessary for participation in the many realities of the world. In a real sense in whole language, each learner has a unique curriculum.
- *Respect for language:* Language and literacy are valued not just for themselves but for what they do. Language is learned within and as a result of being used for authentic purposes.

- *Respect for society:* Classrooms and schools are democratic communities with respect for both teachers and students. The focus is on collaboration and problem solving.

Through these aspects of respect, reading can be reclaimed, teaching will once again be an honorable and valued profession, and authentic learning will drive the curriculum.

The Scientific and Humanistic Sources of Whole Language: Authentic Learning First

Whole language is both scientific and humanistic. It is based on scientific understandings of how people learn and the role of language in human learning, and incorporates knowledge of human development and how learning is shaped by culture and community. It also is based on valuing and understanding the fact that education is a human endeavor. The role of education is not to replace one culture, way of knowing, or set of values with another. It is to enable learners to expand on all of these and integrate what they know with what they are coming to know.

Elements of the work of John Dewey and Jean Piaget, and Lev Vygotsky's theories about learning and Michael Halliday's theory about language learning, are particularly relevant to whole language teaching; some of these are summarized below.

John Dewey

From John Dewey (1916), the progressive educational philosopher, we gained several key principles:

Starting where the learners are: All human beings, from the moment they are born, are learning; they learn the languages, customs, beliefs, and cultures of their communities. When they come to school, whether as young children or as adults, they bring with them all that they have learned. Successful education builds on what students already know.

Adjusting school to the learners: Schools can take one of two alternative views. They can force learners to adjust to schools that are rigid and have the same expectations for all learners, or they can accept all learners and adjust the school to them, accepting their strengths and starting where they are.

Learning by doing: Humans learn in the process of doing things. In traditional cultures, adults involve children in the activities necessary for survival and participation in their societies. They learn to weave, hunt, plant, dance, and prepare food by working along with parents and grandparents, watching at first and then gradually becoming participants. Learning in school should also involve children in learning through doing.

Problem posing and solving: Learning is not answering other people's questions with other people's answers. It is considering real problems and solving them by posing questions and then seeking answers.

School is life, not just preparation for living: What we learn in school should make an immediate difference in our lives. We learn things that are useful now, not because at some indefinite time in the future they might be useful. Learning in school is no different than learning outside of school, except that in school there is a professional teacher with important knowledge, strategies, and resources to support learning.

Jean Piaget

From the Swiss developmental psychologist Jean Piaget (1978), whole language takes important understandings about human learning.

Constructing meaning: Children expect the world to be a sensible place and they construct meaning as they transact with the world. Meaning is not transmitted; each of us must learn ourselves by constructing our own meanings by inventing them within social conventions.

Assimilation and accommodation: Piaget started his career as a biologist. He believed that just as our bodies change in our transactions with our environment, so too learning changes our brains to accommodate our experiences. Some experiences involve assimilation: new ideas fit well with the schemas deriving from what learners already know. But sometimes there is a conflict between what is known or believed and new experiences. Such experiences may lead to accommodation, a change in schemas to fit new concepts.

Disequilibrium: Often the processes of assimilation and accommodation bring learners to a state of disequilibrium. The process of accommodation involves rethinking what they understand and believe. Disequilibrium, while it can be upsetting, is an important part of human learning. Teachers provide challenging experiences and then support the accommodations the experiences require. When there are broad gaps between the culture of the learners and the ideas they encounter in school, teachers help learners bridge these gaps in a context that is not threatening.

Lev Vygotsky

Russian psychologist Lev Vygotsky (1978) put learning and education in a social context and contributed many concepts to our ideas about school as a social institution and each classroom as a community of learners.

Knowledge is socially constructed: In the course of growing up in a community, as children learn language they also acquire a way of viewing the world their community shares. The ways in which a family and community interact enhance learning in school when a teacher embraces and builds upon the social practices that children bring to the classroom.

Schools as social institutions: What young people learn about how to participate in a democratic school is as important to the future of developing democracies as any academic concepts they acquire. *How* students learn is as important as *what* they learn.

Teaching as mediation: Teaching is not intervention, but mediation. The teacher supports the learning, provides new experiences, and mediates the transactions between the learner and what is being learned, but it is the learners who own the learning. The teacher supports them in constructing new understandings that expand on their existing knowledge.

The zone of proximal development: There is a "zone" beyond what learners know now: it is what they are capable of learning with support from the teacher, a peer, a family member, a text, or the social group. In whole language, the teacher is a "kidwatcher," a term made popular by Yetta Goodman (1978). It means the teacher knows how to observe learners, to document what they know and interpret their observations. Then the teacher provides a question, problem, or task within the ongoing curriculum that mediates the student's learning, taking advantage of what the learner is already reaching toward.

Rooting the classroom in the community and school as a social institution: For schools to be successful in meeting the needs of the learners and the communities they serve, they need to be responsive to the community. Schools and teachers need to treat sociocultural contexts as resources. To expand their horizons, learners must understand where they are in time and space, including the local history, geography, flora and fauna, culture, beliefs and values. Math, physical and social science, literature, language, and the arts must begin with an appreciation of the home and the community. Learners must come to understand that their education must serve their communities as well as themselves.

Michael Halliday

Michael Halliday is a British linguist who studied oral language development, most notably in his work investigating his son's language use and growth over time (1975). From that and subsequent studies, Halliday wrote about the social construction of language development in a theory he called systemic functional grammar.

Language needs to be functional to be learned: There are many functions of language. We use language to get what we want, regulate others, interact, represent, imagine, and much more. Not only at the beginning but throughout life, new language uses and functions form, and even new languages are learned as they are needed. That's why so many people worldwide grow up as multilingual—because of the need to function socially, economically, and personally.

Whenever humans use language, they learn language, they learn through language and they learn about language (Halliday, 2004): Therefore, we argue that conscious learning of the functions, rules, and exceptions to rules of language is a result of learning language, not a prerequisite. Systematically teaching language rules and functions gets in the way of learning, rather than supporting it.

Language involves both social and personal meaning making: Language use is typically at the nexus of the social and personal. We use language that we understand to fit within the context (*field*), as appropriate to the individual(s) with whom we are engaging (*tenor*), and via certain *modes* (oral, digital, writing with a pencil, etc.). The explosion of language use as part of digital technology is a good case in point of the expansion of language in response to cultural innovations (see Meyer & Altwerger's discussion in the extension to this chapter).

Language Learning and Learning to Read

We believe that all children become literate easily if given access to written materials and opportunities to write and read within relevant literacy experiences in homes, communities, and classrooms. Written and oral language are both language. They are parallel processes. We refer to learning these processes as "natural" because they appear effortless when children are supported in learning them in authentic and meaningful contexts. Under such conditions, reading occurs very early for most children. The beginnings of reading go unnoticed by others in the child's world in the same way as when children begin listening. Smith (1976) says, "children begin to read from the moment they become aware of print in any meaningful way and the roots of reading are discernible whenever children strive to make sense of print before they are using cues from the print" (p. 297).

Children learn to read and write for the same reason that they learn to speak and listen: to communicate with others as they actively participate in the language events of their family and the community. In neither case is the user required to have a high level of conscious awareness of the units and systems of language in order to learn or use language effectively. In both cases, control over language comes through preoccupation with communicating. Awareness of the uses of language is needed, but in reading, as in listening, preoccupation with language itself detracts from meaning and produces inefficient and ineffective language use.

Children use the same linguistic resources in reading and writing development as in oral language development. They comprehend in relation to what they already know. They expand their knowledge about the language in their linguistic pool that includes their knowledge of the systems of the sounds, the orthography, the syntax, and meanings of language, and they bring this knowledge to their reading and writing as they transact with text. Through experiences with print in varied sociocultural contexts, children make sense of written language. As they drive down a highway, walk down a street or through a shopping center, or watch television, they are bombarded with print. They become aware that written texts have specific meanings in specific contexts. They know that street signs are organized and occur in different ways than written stories or newspaper articles.

We have studied children's responses to print for decades and know that young children use written language whenever it is functional and significant. As a result, they learn about how written language works. Children demonstrate that they are more concerned with the meaning of a graphic unit than with the specifics of its representation. For example, one 3-year-old responded to Burger Chef, Burger King, and McDonald's signs by calling them all McDonald's. But when he was shown the logo of a local hamburger place that was more distinctly a place to sit down and be served at a table, as opposed to a takeout place, the child said, "That says, 'restaurant'." Ari, at age 2, drew a bicycle with large concentric circles. He then drew a triangle shape in the middle of the circles, pointed to it and said, "That's Ari riding his bicycle." He was reading his own writing. Children categorize using associations in addition to significant graphic features to read. It is not surprising, therefore, that Jimmy responded to each graphic alternative of his name by saying, "That says Jimmy," whether the name was written as Jimmy, Jim, James, James Jones, or Junior.

A number of researchers have made important contributions to understanding literacy development in young children. Clay describes children reading a book in her study of 5-year-old school entrants in New Zealand. They were obviously not following the print, but used written language patterns such as *Once upon a time* or *Mother said, "Do you want a piece of cake?"* She suggests that reading is not talk written down; rather, children indicate that "books talk in a special way" (1972, p. 29). Dyson (2003) documents literacy events in the classroom environment to show how young authors express their meanings in social communities with peers and teachers as they write, read, talk, draw, and play with each other. Reyes' (2006) research provides evidence of the influences of biliterate environments on the biliteracy development of young children. She shows how children know when to switch codes as a function of the context, such as shifting from one language to another as they move between home and school. Lee's (1988) research on children in Taiwan describes how literacy learning in Chinese, a non-alphabetic language, is more similar to than different from literacy learning in English. All young readers are seekers of meaning, motivated by the need to comprehend and be comprehensible, aware of the functions of print, and adaptive to print characteristics.

Children have been making predictions and inferences about the contexts in which they learn since birth, and they confirm what they are learning all the time. If they get confused or are uncertain, they reconfirm or self-correct their predictions and inferences. Reading involves these same universal strategies. Children sample and select the cues from the text as they need them in order to comprehend meaning. Some children learn to read and write before they come to school because of the books in their homes and being read to. But children also initially learn literacy in other modes and venues. Some children learn literacy by writing, and bringing that knowledge to their reading. Others become literate by sitting on the laps of parents engaged with computers; they learn to read in response to signs in their environment; or as they play store or doctor or gas station attendant (Genishi & Goodwin, 2007; Goodman & Martens, 2007; Hall, Larson, & Marsh, 2003). Young children thrive on their inventions of knowledge, concepts, and language. Children are in no more need of being taught to read than they are of being taught to listen. But literacy learning and development are influenced by the social community in both positive and negative ways; therefore, literacy instruction is an important mediator in children's literacy learning.

Thus, reading instruction, particularly beginning reading instruction, has a vital role to play in creating and enhancing the conditions that bring the reader's natural language-learning competence into play. Children must be among people who talk in order to learn to speak and listen. But that's not enough. Their need to communicate must be present and supported by the social community in which their communication takes place. This is also the case in developing literacy. We believe that literacy is learned only once. Children learn written language on the basis of what they have already learned about oral language and the conventions of written language in their world.

Commonsense Beliefs about How People Make Sense of Print Are Wrong

Some widely believed commonsense views of how reading works are wrong. Here are five of them that we know it is important to debunk as we reclaim reading.

Commonsense belief 1: Learning to read centers on reading as word recognition. In this widespread view, language is a set of words that readers identify and then comprehension follows. This belief has led to instructional materials in which vocabulary is controlled to the point that word choice is unnatural. Learners need natural and real language to learn most effectively and efficiently.

Commonsense belief 2: Word recognition depends on phonics. Another very widespread view is that recognizing words depends on matching letters in written words to the sounds of oral words. Readers are taught how to "sound out" each new word and it is believed that if they learn the letter–sound correspondences, loosely called phonics, they can read anything written in their home language. In extreme forms this leads to reduced "decodable" materials in which only words that fit phonics rules already taught are used. This results in strange-sounding materials that are difficult to read.

Commonsense belief 3: Phonemic awareness is central to learning to read. A more recent misconception is that readers must be "aware," in some abstract sense, of the rules by which letters represent sounds. Such instruction is focused on having children learn to read by listening for the sounds in their speech and learning rules for mapping them to the spellings. It is impossible for anyone to understand oral language without the ability to make sense of sequences of sounds since the brain forms its perceptions from listening to the sounds that the ear transmits. All speakers who have hearing are phonemically aware.

Commonsense belief 4: Reading is the accurate identification of words. Also widespread is the belief that reading must be accurate and that learners must say exactly what is written on the page. This is an extension of the view that language is a set of words and that comprehension depends on getting all the words right. Like all the other misconceptions, there is a commonsense base to this view. How can we make sense of what we read if we are not accurately "reading" each word? We've put "reading" in quotes here to indicate the circularity in this way of thinking, because it states that *reading requires the accurate identification of words because reading is the accurate identification of words.* Our research shows that readers construct meaning while using cues from the text selectively and non-linearly. As readers construct meaning, they miscue as they read, reflecting what they *perceive* will be in the text, not what they *see.* In the most extreme form of this belief there is an assertion that readers read every letter in every word. Yet 100 years of eye-tracking research has consistently shown that about one-third of all words are not fixated in reading (Huey, 1907/1968; Paulson & Freeman, 2003).

Commonsense belief 5: Writing is a code for oral language. It is an enduring belief that only oral language, which is easy to learn, is real language, while writing is not language itself but a code for language that is hard to learn. In this view, oral language is innate and not learned. But all language is code. Oral language uses abstract sound sequences to encode meaning, just as written language uses abstract shapes. All forms of language use abstract symbols that have the power to encode meaning.

Too often, instructional programs in reading and writing are what we call one-legged models. They control word frequency. Or they control phonics (most often poorly understood). Or they focus on direct instruction of skill sequences. Or they attempt to use narrowly defined ability groupings based on test scores. Our view is that language works as an integrated whole. Instruction that takes that into account can make learning to read and write as "natural" as learning to speak and listen. We'll discuss why we reject these widespread beliefs as we continue to present these understandings in our comprehensive theory about learning to read.

A Comprehensive Theory Includes All Aspects of Reading

Edmund Huey (1907/1968) over a century ago said that if we understood reading, we would understand the human brain. To that we add that we would also understand the centrality of language in how the brain makes sense of the world. Since reading is a receptive language process, any theory of how reading works must be consistent with theories of how the brain works to make sense of the world. Reading is a process through which the brain makes sense of written language. Therefore, our theory must be consistent with the theories about learning and language learning described above. It must be applicable to all writing systems (i.e., all languages), both alphabetic and non-alphabetic; it must apply to readers of all ages; it must apply to all kinds of texts.

Our theory has been built through in-depth analyses of the miscues of readers of all ages. Miscues occur in oral reading when the observed response (what a reader says) is different from the expected response (what the observer expects to hear). We analyzed actual reading—real readers reading real texts—to develop a theory of the structures and processes of real reading. In recent decades our colleagues have combined miscue analysis with eye tracking to provide another level of actual evidence as we bring together analyses of what the eye is doing while the reader is producing oral reading. We call this research eye movement miscue analysis (EMMA).

Though languages vary widely in almost every characteristic (cultural meanings, orthographies, phonology, grammar, etc.), they all are complex systems of representing meaning. Because they represent meaning they have many commonalities. Our research, involving both alphabetic and non-alphabetic languages, shows that the reading process is essentially the same in all languages and all orthographies. The process, of course, must be flexible to allow for these variabilities, but all reading is the construction of meaning, and the same strategies for use of cues are at work in all languages.

The brain uses the eyes to provide the input necessary to construct meaning. For blind readers, this sensory information comes through their fingertips. Anything that happens in effective reading is subsidiary to meaning construction. The brain is so good at this that it tells the eyes not to bother to fixate on about a third of the words in the written text it is comprehending. To reiterate, reading is not word identification, sounding out words, looking for main ideas, or parsing grammar. The brain makes sense of print with the least amount of time, energy, and cues from the published text. The more readers know about the content of what they are reading, the more efficient their fixations become. The human brain is admirably suited to doing that. Modern brain theory shows that the cortex sends instructions to the eyes and other sensory organs based on predictions of what they will find. The brain is always learning, efficiently making sense of the world. Its perceptions are intelligent constructions that select useful information out of visual and other input and ignore the rest. There is a basic difference between vision and perception. Perception is what the brain makes of the visual images the eyes transmit (Strauss, Goodman, & Paulson, 2009). In order to reclaim the learning of reading, we must understand and draw from a comprehensive model for what happens when we read. The comprehensive reading model takes into account the following concepts.

Concepts of Proficiency

There is a common belief that rapid reading increases comprehension. In fact, there is indeed a correlation in most research between speed of reading and comprehension. Proficient readers by definition have high comprehension. But to be proficient, the reader must be both effective and efficient. Effective reading produces coherent meaning. Efficient reading selectively uses just enough input from the text to be effective. Speed of reading is the result of efficient reading, not its cause. Instruction that focuses on speed can be counterproductive if the reader is not concentrating on making sense.

As Meek (1988) has said, texts teach what readers learn. Making sense of the text involves learners in continuous problem solving as long as the texts are authentic and not artificially constructed. Just as oral language is learned in the process of using it, development of reading proficiency happens in the course of using reading. That requires meaningful texts from the beginning. Only if the texts beginners read are authentic and complete can they learn to efficiently use the strategies necessary to make sense.

Concepts of Transactions with Texts and Reading Strategies

Language and thought work together to make sense, so we call the strategies readers use *psycholinguistic.* As readers construct meaning, they make predictions and draw inferences. They sample selectively and tentatively from the cues in the text. Authors expect their readers to make inferences as they read. No text is ever completely explicit, nor does it need to be. Readers use the same cues to make inferences and predictions and also to confirm or disconfirm their predictions and inferences. They correct when they need to. Whether just learning to read or experienced, readers use these psycholinguistic strategies—prediction and inference, sampling and selection, confirmation and disconfirmation, and correction—as needed.

Each reading event is a transaction between a reader and the text. A transaction is more than an interaction (Dewey & Bentley, 1949/1989). In a transaction, both the reader and the text are changed. Readers, as they read, construct their own texts parallel to the published text with which they are transacting. The reader's text makes use of the reader's experiences, values, culture, background knowledge, insights, and language. It is this reader's text that the reader comprehends. The reader is changed by assimilating or accommodating new knowledge. In Piaget's terms, the reader has a set of schemas, which are ways of organizing ideas. New experiences that fit these schemas are assimilated easily. But if new knowledge contradicts what is known, the reader must reject it, reinterpret it to fit the existing schema, or change the schema to accommodate the new information. In accommodating to the new information, the reader is changed.

Concepts of Language Levels

Earlier, we said that one of the most common misconceptions about language is that it is basically a set of words, which leads to thinking of reading as depending on knowing a lot of words. If language were only words, we could not use it to represent and manipulate the complex ideas we must express to ourselves and to each other. To communicate, we must have language structure, which is the grammatical system, and we must have coherent thoughts to express and understand.

We can think of language as a sphere composed of three layers or strata. The surface level is all that can be sensed directly. In oral language, it is sounds heard; in written language, it is the graphic letters or characters that are visible. In sign languages, it is the set of gestures or hand shapes, sign system symbols that represent meaning. In the core of the sphere is the semantic (meaning) system. Between the surface and the core is what Halliday (1985) calls the lexico-grammar. It is the level where the surface signs are organized into grammatical structures and wordings. All three levels work together simultaneously. Any focus on one level, and not all three, turns language into something less than language.

An author starts with meaning and generates a written text by assigning a grammatical structure and the wording. What is written, the letters or the characters, can only come after the choices in wording and grammar. But word choices bring with them grammatical choices, and grammatical choices limit wordings. The writer, like the speaker, must produce a complete written text that includes all three levels that are comprehensible to the intended audience. "Complete" here does not mean totally explicit on any level. Text never is that. But it must be sufficiently complete to give the reader the cues necessary to construct meaning.

A reader moves from the surface print as efficiently as possible, assigning grammatical structures and creating the wording and meaning structures to build a parallel text that has meaning to the reader. Since the goal is to comprehend, none of the intermediate steps from printed text to meaning needs to be complete. It would simply take a reader far too long to give attention to all of those details; learners' minds seek to make meaning. Having achieved meaning, the reader has the sense of having seen all the letters in all the words, but our thousands of records of miscues, together with more recent records of eye movements, show that that is never so.

In our earlier work we referred to the three levels as cuing systems and called them *graphophonic, syntactic*, and *semantic*, roughly corresponding to Halliday's *sign, lexico-grammar*, and *semantic* systems as labels for the three strata. We prefer his terms because they make clear these are the necessary components of texts. We'll discuss each level of linguistic texts as it is involved with reading, keeping in mind that they are inseparable in language use.

The Sign Level (Formerly Graphophonics)

The universal human ability to think symbolically makes language possible because it allows us to represent reality with meaningless symbols. But it is in the context of the lexico-grammar and semantic levels that any letter or character sequence represents complex meaning. Further, the value of any symbol can change even in a single context. To give a simple example, if you write "ll," it appears to be a numeral sequence with the value eleven. Add "0" and it becomes "ll0." In the decimal system this represents the value one hundred ten, but when it is written as "T0ll" it is *toll*.

All written language displays graphic sequences over two-dimensional space in arbitrary directions. In alphabetic systems the units are letters. Letters are perceptual units, graphemes, with varied forms, allographs. So, the letter A may be written A, 𝒜, a, a, 𝛼 Cursive forms and individual handwriting also vary. Capital letters are different than minuscule letters. What we see in reading is less important than what the brain makes of it. Here's an experiment. Show readers this sentence:

I saw 4 horses.

Then hide it and say, "Write down what you remember reading." The readers will write in their usual handwriting, not in the print form, and they won't be able say whether the "4" was closed or open. That's because the forms of the letters and numerals are perceptual abstractions. Readers remember they saw a four but not the form of it. And they remember the meaning, not the particular letter fonts.

Concepts of Alphabetic and Non-alphabetic Writing

Alphabetic systems relate the phonology of oral language to the orthography of written language, but the constraints on each system make it impossible to do so on a simplistic one-to-one basis. Sounds are produced in time sequence by organs of the mouth and throat, and they are modified by the sounds that precede and follow them. As babies learn to talk in English, they learn to treat a range of sounds as the same, even though they are quite varied. And they learn to treat very small differences such as those between d and t (walked/planned), or l and r (long/wrong) as very important.

In fact the oral and written forms of language connect best through meaning, and even there they serve different purposes. For example, written language can represent large, accessible quantities of data in tables and charts. Oral language is well suited for informal conversation, though email and texting on cell phones have extended that function. The grammar of oral language is more complex because intonation disambiguates clausal relationships that are too complex for expression in writing. You can notice this if you tape a conversation and then transcribe it. The ways in which people speak place different demands on language than when language is written.

Even in cultures where writing is alphabetic, there are limitations that require non-alphabetic writing. Computer users may think they use the alphabet with the computer but the computer actually replaces letters with numeric codes and operates on digital input. Computers also use icons to control a series of complex operations with a single input key. Above your page as you type on a computer is a row of icons. Typically, there's one that looks like a computer disk; another resembles a printer. A curved arrow will undo whatever you just did. A smart phone has dozens of icons that bring up whole functions with a single key press. A clock can show both digital and analog time. These are all non-alphabetic symbols that we read using the same process as when we read alphabetic text.

In math and science, numerals and signs are more easily manipulated than the same ideas written out alphabetically. Numerals, which are used almost universally across languages, are abstract symbols that represent number concepts. The numerals work very much like Chinese characters. They mean the same thing regardless of the oral language of the users. Scientific notations create formulas in which Greek letters or particular letters of the Roman alphabet combine with numerals to represent complex relationships like $A = \pi r^2$.

Chinese characters are signs that represent meaning directly. When the Chinese writing system was developed many centuries ago, a system was needed to unify a vast nation that spoke many different dialects that were not mutually understandable. The system of characters served that need very well. All Chinese characters are produced by combining only eight different strokes into radicals that represent related meanings across characters. So *door, window, in, out,* and *mouth* all have a radical that looks like an opening. Characters that represent various fruits all contain the fruit radical. Some Chinese characters contain a pattern that looks like another character and suggests that it might be pronounced similarly.

When Japan, Korea, and other Asian nations began using writing, they naturally turned to the Chinese writing system (Goodman et al., 2011). It was available, and literate Chinese scribes and teachers could teach them how to write their languages using the Chinese characters, since they represented meaning—not the oral language. Over time, each country made adaptations to fit its own language. In Japan, two added systems were derived for representing the function words (noun determiners, verb auxiliaries, conjunctions, and prepositions) of Japanese. In modern Japanese, a single text uses Chinese characters for the content words and syllabic characters for the function words. The Koreans developed a syllabic writing system in which each component has a consonant and vowel. They still retain use of Chinese characters in many situations. The Chinese writing system works well for the hundreds of millions of people who use it. It is not true that thousands of characters have to be memorized individually. The structure of the character and the context cue meaning in a similar way to alphabetic systems.

Research about the reading process and how readers transact with various texts has shown that the reading process we describe for English readers works for all readers. In Japan, Taiwan, Hong Kong, and Mainland China, many children are already reading when they come to school. They live in a print-rich society and they begin to make sense of the print in their environment, just as those in alphabetic societies do. Ultimately, *all written language represents meaning,* an idea that is simple to say and easy to accept but often forgotten in planning literacy instruction for those learning to read.

Concepts of Phonics

Ken Goodman (1993) defines phonics as the set of relationships between the orthography of a language and someone's phonology. The reasoning for this definition is that spelling in most languages is standardized. But every language is a family of related dialects that vary in every aspect from each other in minor and major ways. For example, *help* is pronounced /help/, /he'p/, or /hey ulp/ in American English dialects. So phonology varies considerably from dialect to dialect. And, within dialect communities there are variations from family to family and person to person. You know immediately who is calling when you hear a familiar voice on the phone.

When printing became important, it was expensive and impractical to have separate versions for each dialect, so spelling was standardized by printers. In the early decades of the United States a group of writers encouraged Noah Webster to differentiate spelling in his dictionary from the British spelling for political reasons. Their motivation was to make American literature easily recognized. So there are (at least) two sets of spelling standards in written English. Spelling standards are arbitrary. The printers who standardized spelling had to make some choices. Should *situation* be spelled *sichuashun*? That would lose the semantic connection between *site*, *situate*, and *situation*. And no spelling of *almond* would suit all those who say /amǝnd/, /almǝnd/, /ahmǝnd/.

From a linguist's point of view, rules are part of the natural system of language. But since spelling was arbitrarily standardized, the spelling rules that exist in school books are not the natural rules of other aspects of language. And as dialects change and drift apart, and language as a dynamic organic system evolves, the rules stay the same, making them a bad fit for the changing sounds. Because of its multiple origins, English spelling is complex, and spelling rules are far from a simple alphabetic–sound correspondence.

If phonics is the relationship between phonology, which varies, and orthography, which is constant, then phonics is variable, too. Many invented spellings are closer representations of the way individuals hear themselves say words than are their conventional counterparts. Reading plays a major part in learning spelling, but only if the learners are involved in writing. That's because they learn to read like a writer; as they read, they note the spellings of words they use in their writing. When people are learning to read, they are most efficient and effective when they do not over-rely upon phonics.

The Lexico-Grammar Level (Formerly Syntax)

Grammar, the structure of language, is what makes it possible to express complex ideas and meanings. Halliday calls this middle level of language the lexicogrammar, because the speaker or writer assigns a grammatical structure and the wording of what is being said at the same time. *Lexis* (as in "lexicon") is a linguistic term for meaning units, although we like the term *wording* because it suggests a dynamic process rather than a memory search.

Concepts of Grammar

On the basis of miscue research, we have learned that readers make use of the knowledge of language structure to a much greater degree than most reading researchers have recognized. Listeners or readers assign a tentative grammatical structure at the beginning of each sentence or clause as the construction of meaning begins, and they also predict what the likely wording will be. For example, when listeners hear a "wh" word at the beginning of a sentence, they expect to hear the intonational pattern that accompanies a question. Grammatical cues include patterns, inflections (mostly word endings), and function words. The wording of the text is assigned at the same time as the grammatical structure because each depends on the other. As sentences are produced, choice of grammar carries with it certain word patterns, and choice of wording requires particular grammar.

Predictions and inferences are used to construct meaning and to make choices among the ambiguous meanings of the wording. It is the grammar that makes it possible to comprehend. For example, the author Roald Dahl chose to use a single long sentence with a complex grammatical structure to start his story "Poison" (1969). We'll delve into this short text several times to explore how readers engage the lexico-grammatical and semantic levels as they read.

> It must have been around midnight
> when I drove home, and as I approached
> the gates of the bungalow I switched off
> the headlamps of the car so the beam
> wouldn't swing in through the window
> of the side bedroom and wake Harry Pope.

Dahl wants his readers to be propelled into the story. His use of *must have been around midnight* is formulaic. He could have said more simply, "It was around midnight." His choice makes the time more important. Combining a series of independent and dependent clauses requires the reader to use the clausal relationships to get at the meaning. *And* as a conjunction can only be used between equivalent grammatical units, such as nouns (*Tom and Mary*) or verbs (*run and play*). In this passage, *and* joins two independent clauses:

> *It must have been around midnight* and *I switched off the headlamps*

But these are separated by two dependent clauses. *When I drove home* goes with the preceding independent clause, and *as I approached the gate* goes with the following independent clause. In the latter case, the reader must suspend comprehending until the following clause is read. The final two clauses are also dependent on the clause that precedes them.

The *beam* is the subject of both clauses, but it is left out of the second clause, so the reader must infer that it is the beam that might *wake Harry Pope*. These two dependent clauses are also joined by *and*. Leaving the subject out of the clause follows the rule of economy (Grice, 1989) that exists in language: it is unnecessary to repeat information that is already given.

In the Dahl passage, as with any piece that learners read, the grammatical patterns limit the word choices in predictable ways. We cannot express even the simplest idea without grammar. In the sentence *The boy likes the girl*, we know *he likes her* only because of the pattern. *Boy* comes before the verb, so it is the subject. *Girl* comes after, so it is the object of the transitive verb *likes*. Word order matters, not just the words or the sounds within them. Learning to read must involve all of the cueing systems so that meaning can be constructed.

Concepts of Wording

Wording is the other part of lexico-grammar. Words in alphabetic systems are usually evident units because alphabetic writing systems have a convention of separating words with a space. Chinese and Japanese don't use word space. Each character gets equal space. These languages are composed of characters that the reader needs to group together in a given context to make sense. There are complexities in alphabetic languages in relation to what is a word. Compound English words lose the word space, as in *cupboard*. But should *cup cake* be two words or one? Perhaps it should have a hyphen? In English, there is uncertainty about what determines when two words should be written as a compound. How is *wallboard* different than *shuffle board*? When a clause turns into a noun modifier it is often hyphenated, as in *blood-curdling scream* or *award-winning play*.

Words in English have inflected forms such as *walk, walks, walked, walking* or *do, does, doing, did, done*. Some behavioral psychologists believe each of these different word forms has to be taught separately. But miscue analysis shows that the reader assigns the sentence syntax and the appropriate form of the word to fit the grammar at the same time.

English has a vast set of verb and particle combinations and they have different meanings than the verb by itself. For example, the verb *make* occurs in many combinations with different meanings: *make up, make out, make over, make off*. A young woman can *make up* her mind to *make up* her exam. She can put on her *make-up* to look her best and then *make up* an excuse for her teacher.

In early basal readers, where vocabulary control was the key organizing factor, the editors counted the number of times a word occurred but not how many meanings it had. So words were often used as proper names: Mr. Green, Mrs. Vine, Puff the cat, and Spot the dog. In our early miscue research, we documented that readers had more difficulty with such uses than when words were used in meaningful ways. Nouns used as noun modifiers were also harder to read than when they were in noun positions: *the circus man* caused more miscues than *he went to the circus*.

The Semantic Level (Formerly Semantics)

Reading is ultimately about *making sense*. *Comprehending* is the Latin-based way of saying the same thing. To consider meaning, we draw again on Halliday's (1985) systemic functional view of language to see how the reader makes sense. First we need to get rid of a common notion. As we explained earlier in our discussion of transaction, the meaning is *not* in the text. The text the author produces has a *meaning potential*, and the author uses patterns of oral and written language symbols to represent the intended meaning. The reader, who shares knowledge about the same language patterns, constructs an independent meaning for the text.

If both the author and the reader are successful, there is relatively good communication. But the meaning the author expressed is never exactly what the reader comprehends. The reader constructs meaning that is not found in the text. That's because there is no way that one mind can project meaning into another. However, language makes communication possible. Both the writer and the reader actively construct meaning based on their own schemas; those schemas are composed of what they bring to their reading and writing based on what they know. Grice (1989) calls this reader–writer relationship a cooperative principle. The writer tries to be comprehensible and the reader tries to comprehend.

We return to Dahl's passage to demonstrate this process and to illustrate several semantic principles Halliday (1985) delineated.

Dahl's text is cohesive—it hangs together into a unified whole—in part because of the syntactic factors discussed in the lexico-grammatical subsection. But in Halliday's view, three kinds of meaning, present at the same time, are important semantic factors: experiential meaning, interpersonal meaning, and text meaning.

Experiential meaning includes the factual experiences that the writer is trying to convey. In this passage we know that someone (the unnamed narrator):

- had been away from home
- and is returning.
- That person is driving.
- It is a car that is being driven.
- It was near midnight.
- There is a bungalow involved.
- The bungalow has gates.
- Another character, Harry Pope, is home.

We can also make some inferences that are not explicit:

- The car approaches on some type of driveway
- which causes the beams of the head lamps to swing as the car approaches.
- The bungalow is some kind of home.

However, each reader's experience with bungalows influences how the fact that a bungalow is a home is understood. Across the United States, most readers say a bungalow is like a cottage or cabin. In Canada, a bungalow has three bedrooms on one floor. Only a student from India knew that, at the time period in which this story is set, British officials in India lived in bungalows which were in fact substantial houses, big enough to have gates.

Interpersonal meaning, a second kind of meaning, includes both the relationships between characters and the relationship between the author and the reader. There are two characters in the story and it appears that the narrator either is being considerate, or is concerned about how Harry Pope will react to his or her being out so late, or is planning some kind of trick or harm toward Harry. By his choice of language, Dahl manipulates his reader into being curious about what sinister events are coming. We wonder why the narrator is careful not to wake Harry and what the relationship between them might be. Dahl's choice of first person is important because it makes the reader much closer to the perspective of the narrator. The reader sees the story as the "I" character sees it. In fact, the name and gender of the narrator are not provided, although many readers do predict such information when talking about the passage. Dahl has also not provided any information about whether the driver is alone in the car. We assume that as a successful author he is deliberately delaying certain information and teasing his reader to speculate about what is not yet known.

Textual meaning is meaning conveyed through how the text itself is used. The author's use of this long, complex single sentence is surely deliberate. He does not allow his readers a chance to pause for breath until he has hooked them into wanting to know what will happen when the narrator is actually in the house.

Dahl chose to sequence his clauses so that some information is made subordinate to other information. He could have written *I drove home around midnight* and conveyed the same information. Separate clauses related to time to start the story make the reader aware that the time is somehow significant. On the other hand, Dahl conveys a lot about the scene while keeping the reader's focus on the narrator coming home. There must be at least two bedrooms because he embedded in the text *a side bedroom*. The bungalow has gates, which must stretch across a driveway, and the driveway must curve, or how could the light swing into the window? Readers infer a driveway, though none is mentioned.

Of course, the reader brings to this story a sense of how such stories are constructed. Readers know that the narrator is not going to quietly enter the house, go to his or her room and go to sleep. Something else is going to happen, most likely involving Harry. So in just the beginning of this short story we see three kinds of meaning and the storyteller, with a strong sense of his intended audience, carefully manipulating readers into his narrative.

The Set for Ambiguity

With so much variation in forms and meanings of words, the concept of word recognition is clearly inadequate to explain how the reader gets to the meaning of written language. We call readers' ability to deal with complexities *a set for ambiguity*. The existence of multiple meanings for the same word or set of symbols raises the issue of how and why this phenomenon continues in language. The simple answer is that language is always changing. One way it changes is that words acquire new meanings by abduction. For example, the meaning of *sharp* is carried from a degree of fineness of a knife to a keen eye, as in *sharpshooter*, to a fancy dresser in *sharp dresser*, and so forth. The result is that English has a rich stock of words, phrases, and formulaic language that make it possible to express meanings and emotions with subtle shades of difference that fit moods and intentions.

What makes it possible for readers to make sense of such variability? How do readers deal with such ambiguity? Do readers sort through all the possible meanings to select the right one? That can't be true, because if so, readers would never get to the end of the first sentence. Nor do readers simply "sound out" words to identify them, since they can't know how to pronounce them until they know their function in context. And that explanation doesn't allow for the homophones that would still sound alike. Nor could readers recognize all the words and later decide on the meaning of the whole. That would take far too much time.

It comes back to the universal human ability to think symbolically. Our ability to attach meaning to an abstraction is so powerful that language users are able to change the value of the symbol within the same utterance. Each of us has a set for ambiguity: we expect and can make sense of ambiguous language. We make sense of written language by using cues from the written text which depend for their symbolic value on the sense of the whole, on the wording and the structure that create the context. We can easily choose among alternative values for words as we construct the meaning within the context of the whole. In most cases we are not aware of the ambiguity. The context disambiguates the language. Rarely is more than one meaning possible in a given context. So our brain constructs the meaning that best fits. When there is too much ambiguity, if we should choose wrongly we become aware of our miscue as we continue to read and we regress to review what we have read and correct ourselves. Or we realize our miscue and shift to an alternative that makes sense without regressing.

This set for ambiguity explains why language can be effective and still be so complex. It is precisely because we are constructing meaning and not simply recognizing words. We use the cues available in the text efficiently to get to the meaning.

Here's an example from Paulson and Freeman (2003, p. 35) of a record of eye movements on a text as read by one reader.

Text (what was on the page):

At that time, near the end of a barge canal, there lived a carpenter.

Fixation sequence (the words that the reader's eyes stopped on, in the order of each stop):

that At time the of barge canal , barge lived carpenter carpenter

Words not fixated (words that the reader *could not* focus on because his eye did not fixate on or near enough that word):

near end a canal (fixation on following comma) *a*

The record of the reader's eye movements shows that the reader did not read each word from left to right accurately and in sequence. Four words had no direct fixation. The fixations did not flow sequentially from left to right. The reader, for example, fixated on *barge*, then his eyes moved to the comma after *canal* and then regressed to repeat a fixation on *barge*. It seems likely that he was trying to make sense of *barge* and *canal* together. Yet the oral reading of the sentence **was without miscues**.

The reader's repeated fixation on *carpenter* may have been to confirm the first reading or just to note the end of the sentence. We cannot know exactly what was going on in this reader's mind. What we do know is that he was using cues from the text and constructing meaning. And in doing so he was sampling from the print, skipping some cues such as the two *a*'s and reading words he didn't fixate on. In other words, he constructed both a text and meaning. And we don't know whether he knew what a barge canal is, even though he read the words correctly.

Reclaiming Learning to Read

Whole language recognizes that the best materials for learning to read are authentic ones, those that already have authentic functions in society. Such materials make it possible for learners to use all their already learned strategies for comprehending. Didactic materials with syllables, word lists, or letter practice are not suitable for literacy development. From the beginning, materials being read and written must be authentic; they must have real meaning and real purposes for the learners. And they must be worth reading. Real books, stories, newspapers, labels, signs, menus, and digital means of making meaning are examples of such authentic materials. The classroom should be a literate environment, rich in authentic print.

We live in an era in which policies and laws mandate absurd tests, methods, and materials. In this chapter we described a comprehensive view of literacy, how reading works and is learned, and how such a view can be the basis for a liberatory pedagogy that provides access to literacy for all learners. If this knowledge isn't valued, it is because there are powerful, moneyed, vested interests who have manufactured a crisis in education centered on imputed schools' failure to teach children to read. This crisis then is used to marginalize truth and substitute for it simplistic pseudoscience.

In the long term we are optimists. Those who understand and use our comprehensive model will be successful. We know that from the success of whole language teachers before laws made it difficult and dangerous for teachers to do what they knew best. Success will stimulate new interest in why these teachers are successful. When the absurdity of what is currently mandated becomes evident, teachers and researchers will continue or start again and go beyond what we now know. Our dedication to reclaiming reading is celebrated in the chapters of this book and the work presented herein; these moments for celebration will hopefully inspire others to reclaim spaces in which learning is authentic, holistic, and truly dedicated to participation and multiple voices in our democracy.

References

Clay, M. (1972). *Reading: The patterning of complex behavior*. Auckland, New Zealand: Heinemann Educational Books.

Dahl, R. (1969). Poison. In *Twenty nine kisses* (p. 259). London: Michael Joseph.

Dewey, J. (1916). *Democracy and education*. London: Macmillan.

Dewey, J., & Bentley, A. (1949/1989). *Knowing and the known*. Boston, MA: Beacon.

Dyson, A. (2003). *The brothers and sisters learn to write: Popular literacies in childhood and school cultures*. New York: Teachers College Press.

Genishi, C., & Goodwin, A. L. (2007). *Diversities in early childhood education: Rethinking and doing*. New York: Routledge

Goodman, K. S. (1993). *Phonics phacts*. Portsmouth, NH: Heinemann.

Goodman, K. S., Wang, S., Iventosh, M., & Goodman, Y. M. (Eds.) *Reading in Asian languages: Making sense of written texts in Chinese, Japanese, and Korean*. New York: Routledge.

Goodman, Y. M. (1978). Kidwatching: An alternative to testing. *National Elementary School Principal, 57*(4), 41–45.

Goodman, Y. M., & Martens, P. (2007). *Critical issues in early literacy: Research and pedagogy*. Mahwah, NJ: Lawrence Erlbaum.

Grice, H. (Ed.). (1989). *Studies in the way of words*. Cambridge, MA: Harvard University Press.

Hall, N., Larson, J., & Marsh J. (2003). *Handbook of early childhood literacy*. London: Sage.

Halliday, M. A. K. (1975). *Learning how to mean*. London: Edward Arnold.

Halliday, M. A. K. (1985). *An introduction to functional grammar*. London: Edward Arnold.

Halliday, M. A. K. (2004). Three aspects of children's language development: Learning language, learning through language, learning about language. In J. Webster (Ed.), *The collected works of Michael Halliday: Vol. 4. The language of early childhood* (pp. 28–59). New York: Continuum.

Huey, E. (1907/1968). *The psychology and pedagogy of reading*. Cambridge, MA: MIT Press.

Lee, L. (1988). *Developing control of reading and writing in Chinese*. Occasional Paper 20.

Program in Language and Literacy, College of Education, University of Arizona. Tucson, AZ.

Meek, M. (1988). How texts teach what readers learn. In M. Lightfoot & N. Martin (Eds.), *The word for teaching is learning: Language and learning today: Essays for James Britton* (pp. 82–106). Portsmouth, NH: Heinemann.

Paulson, E. J., & Freeman, A. E. (2003). *Insight from the eyes: The science of effective reading instruction*. Portsmouth, NH: Heinemann.

Piaget, J. (1978). *The development of thought: Equilibration of cognitive structures*. New York: Viking Press.

Reyes, I. (2006, December). Exploring connections between emergent biliteracy and bilingualism. *Journal of Early Childhood Literacy, 6*, 267–292.

Smith, F. (1976). Learning to read by reading. *Language Arts, 53*, 297–299, 322.

Strauss, S. L., Goodman, K.S., & Paulson, E. J. (2009, February). Brain research and reading: How emerging concepts in neuroscience support a meaning construction view of the reading process. *Educational Research and Reviews, 4*(2), 21–22.

Vygotsky, L. (1978). *Mind in society*. Cambridge, MA: Harvard University Press.

CHAPTER 2 EXTENSION

Goodman 2.0

Richard J. Meyer and Bess Altwerger

Goodman and Goodman present a model of reading that extends to the many different literacies in our lives and the lives of our students. Even though their model originates in the twentieth century, it serves us well as literacy learning is expanded and redefined in the twenty-first century. Since their model is comprehensive and involves readers actively constructing meaning, we refer to it as Goodman 2.0, using a metaphor from the development of the World Wide Web. When the web was first available, it was a one-way communication in that people could read the sites that others created. There could be email between people, but that involved one person writing, another reading and responding, that second person sending their thoughts back, and so on. Meaning was like a tennis match in which individuals put their own spins on each ball. Web 2.0 is much more interactive, involves active collaboration, is multimodal, and deals with critical issues. Goodman 2.0 parallels this in that the reading process remains the same fundamental way of dealing with text. There is still one reading process, although texts are now multimodal and increasingly complex, composed by, for, and with others, and have different conventions than those found on the printed page. Reading in the twenty-first century is still reading *and* it is enhanced by the multiplicity of options now available for those privileged enough to have access.

Many children in our classrooms are digital natives, meaning that they were born into a world rich in digital technologies such as cell phones, computers, video games, other computerized "toys," and much more. Let's follow an imaginary 15-year-old girl as she makes her way through just part of her day, reading her world. As soon as she is wakened in the morning, her world is saturated with texts and technologies, all of which she has learned to read and uses to write.

Wendy wakes up when her "clock" plays a piece of music that she selected the previous night as she readied herself for bed. That clock actually connects to her phone, which she inserts into the clock. She "read" the clock–phone interface as she set the time on the alarm, the music, and the volume. That phone is no simple phone, either. It is packed with music, games, texting capabilities, and is a small computer. If she or her parents were to pay the fee, the phone could be linked to her home computer and she could read files from that computer while she was away at almost any location.

Once out of bed, Wendy immediately begins to read her world: checking for text messages, looking at emails, reading her blog and writing responses, checking her pages on the social networks to which she belongs, and reading others' pages (sometimes called "walls") on those networks. She makes sure to carry some form of mobile digital memory with her because that memory contains various assignments due, in progress, or planned. At breakfast, she uses a laptop to read a teen version of the news on a website that she frequents. Her day is merely 15 minutes into its morning and she has had many active reading moments.

As a reader, Wendy has already engaged in the process described by Goodman and Goodman. She sampled, predicted, confirmed, etc., as described in their chapter. The beauty of the Goodman and Goodman comprehensive model is that it extends so easily into Wendy's lived experiences. The model acknowledges the varied social practices in which Wendy is involved as a literate person. Further, Wendy transacts with texts, creating her own meaning within the various conventions with which she is faced; and she transacts collaboratively as she and her friends negotiate meanings and intentions between each other and various texts. She can easily read a text on her phone from her friend, "C U L8R," as *see you later*. In fact, if we used eye movement technology to track her reading, we'd be witness to just how few of these "words" she actually focuses on. She predicts and confirms quickly, relying as little as possible on the actual text. The meaning is constructed in her mind.

As Wendy checks her various social networks, she navigates and constructs meaning using various icons, which she clicks to make certain things happen. She predicts what she will find, and confirms her predictions when a certain friend agrees to meet for lunch as planned, or disconfirms when she is forced to cancel because of an orthodontist appointment. She may originally miscue part of what she reads, and regress with her eyes to read again in order to make meaning. She does all of this within modes of text that were non-existent ten years before her birth.

Wendy takes the school bus to her high school and during the ride there is much conversation between the students. Some students on the bus text each other because they are too far away to talk or because they don't want others to overhear. The decision to text is in keeping with Goodman and Goodman's discussion about Halliday. Readers and writers make decisions about how text will be created and what text means based on where they are, what language is used, and their relationships with others. For Wendy, the complexity of reading transactions in the twenty-first century is simply part of the literacy world into which she was born and is a contributor.

Let's follow Wendy a bit longer as she enters her social studies class, the first period of her very packed day. In this classroom, true to the critical literacy nature of instruction across disciplines, Wendy's English and social studies teachers are collaborating on curriculum. The class has been comparing how history is told over time in various texts to learn about US history and how it is represented in print. The students notice and discuss the ways in which authors wrote about events differently and realize that some voices are missing (those of women and various ethnic groups) while others are strongly represented and assigned prestige (men and Eurocentric perspectives.) As the class continues to interrogate their own beliefs about various groups, the teachers shift to a more critical perspective and make the decision to study particular themes over and across time. The teachers decide to help themselves and their students consider the dialectics or tensions between *revolution*, *uprising*, and *riot* as these themes present themselves in different time periods. For example, the class considers whether the Boston Tea Party was an uprising, part of a revolution (or perhaps a fuse-igniting event for a revolution), or a riot. Points of view become an important part of this discussion, and the students research whose points of view are represented within different historical documents and whose are not. The students search various websites for primary source documents, write blogs from different points of view, and argue about what really happened.

The teachers work to provide the students with a more global perspective. They challenge the students to find out what was occurring in Africa, the Middle East, central and far-western parts of the United States, and Asia during the moments in history that they are studying thematically. Indeed, how many readers of this chapter extension know what was occurring in Asia during 1776?

The critical theme study is extended into more recent history with a consideration of key moments in Los Angeles, Wendy's home town, when different groups engaged in protests. The students find newspaper articles, interviews, movie clips from news reports, and many other sources that reported these events. They find that the same events were reported as riots by one group and as uprisings by another. The teachers work to incorporate reading and composing activities that reflect the students' interests, emerging passions, and growing understanding of various historical events as part of the inquiry. They refer to writing as *composing* because the students work on blogs, web pages, podcasts, movies, documentaries, reenactments, and more. They write (compose) scripts for these events, engage in multiple takes (which are twenty-first-century revisions), and produce texts that are read, interpreted, and discussed by each other, other students in the school, and more broadly as decisions are made to release their compositions to the public in various forums. Discussions of their own safety and the safety of the Internet are part of the many conversations and arguments in which they engage. Thus, the multiple modes available to them are interrogated as spaces that are not (and could never be) neutral.

The teachers include and challenge the students with issues of race, gender, age, sexual orientation, wealth, power, and prestige as integral facets of who and what they study. When footage of the 1992 activity in Los Angeles following the release of the video of Rodney King being beaten is shown alongside video of activity in the city following the shooting death of Manuel Jamines in 2010, the students raise many questions. They want to know what each man was doing, their ethnicity, their socioeconomic status, and more. They hunger to read the details, find different perspectives, and discuss. The teachers also help the students consider their own ethnicities, socioeconomic status, and other critical factors that seem to consistently affect representations of history over time. These *differences that made a difference* become a growing set of lenses through which the students view, read, write about, and represent historical moments and events. Wendy considers her own blackness, the friends she keeps, her view of others, and more as she works in a safe environment to explore these issues.

After social studies, Wendy's day continues as she texts friends between classes, checks email, presents an interactive lesson to her colleagues in math class, and works on a self-portrait in the art studio. Her day is a fictional account of the multiple engagements available in today's technologically complex environment, yet it certainly resonates with many of today's students. A comprehensive model of literacy accounts for and incorporates the limitless ways in which meaning can potentially be constructed in an ever-changing, complex society.

Thus, Goodman 2.0, as an extension of Goodman and Goodman's comprehensive model for the twenty-first century, must account for:

- situated literacies embedded within an expanded range of social practices;
- multimodal literacies and semiotic systems;
- new literacies in digital, web-based, online domains;
- critical literacies embodying relationships of power and ideology.

Goodman 2.0 extends the principles and processes underlying a comprehensive model of proficient reading, as presented in Chapter 2, to include the following.

- Meaning construction is simultaneously individual and social, stable and responsive, enacted within and across situated literacy practices.
- Meaning-makers utilize the unique affordances, constraints and resources (linguistic, visual, spatial, temporal) available within and across modalities and sign systems.
- Meaning-makers efficiently and effectively sample, select and orchestrate multiple resources across modalities and sign systems in pursuit of meaning making.
- Meaning making in digital domains requires the flexible and coordinated use of cognitive strategies and the efficient use of relevant resources specific to the purposes of the reader as well as the affordances of the medium.
- Individuals have power and agency over the act of meaning making. They are free to read the world in the act of reading the word despite the ideology and intention of the author.

- Across literacy practices, multiple modalities, and digital domains, meaning makers can exercise power and agency in recognizing, critiquing, and contesting ideological content and dominant narratives and to design and redesign alternative visions of existing and possible worlds.

3

REVALUING READERS AND READING

Learning from the "Mighty Readers"

Prisca Martens and Michelle Doyle

Nate, Ron, Ben, Kyle (third graders), and Prisca are in the library workroom for a retrospective miscue analysis (RMA) session. They are listening to sections of the audiotape of their readings and discussing miscues they each made while reading *Miss Nelson Is Missing!* (Allard, 1977) earlier that week.

Prisca: Let's read this sentence together. [All read: *I'm sure it won't happen again.*] Now listen to the brilliant, brilliant, brilliant, brilliant thing Ron did.

Ron: (on the tape) I'm *sorry*, it won't happen again.

Prisca: What did you say that was brilliant, Ron? (On Ron's face was total shock!)

Ron: sorry

Prisca: Does that make sense to say *I'm sorry, it won't happen again*?

All: Yes, it does.

Prisca: It makes perfect sense. It's brilliant!

Nate: I'm sorry, it won't happen again and *I'm sure it won't happen again.*

Prisca: Sorry begins with an *s* and has an *r* in it like *sure* so he was using the clues that were in the text. . . . And usually people say *I'm sorry.* . . . These were all brilliant miscues because you were making substitutions that made sense. And if you can't think of a substitution that makes sense, what is another option you have?

Nate: To skip it.

Prisca: Skip it. Saying something that *doesn't* make sense is not a good option.

(The office called on the intercom for another teacher. Prisca replied that she wasn't there.)

Kyle: (to the intercom) This is Miss Martens and the Brilliant Readers!

Nate: Four Mighty Readers!

Prisca: The Brilliant Readers or the Mighty Readers?
All: Mighty Readers!
Prisca: The Mighty Readers!
Kyle: And their teacher!

This conversation took place during session 13 of 17 RMA sessions that Prisca had with four boys. The goal was for the boys to read and discuss effective and efficient strategies that support making sense. Kyle (African American), Nate (Hispanic), and Ron (African American) had been in Michelle's classroom all year; Ben (White) had joined in January when his family moved to the United States from England. Kyle and Nate had Individualized Education Plans. The school, in a large metropolitan area, served about 577 students with 30 heritage cultures and a range of socioeconomic levels (22 percent free and reduced lunches).

In this chapter we describe the Mighty Readers' collaborative RMA experience and how through it the boys reclaimed their own learning and revalued reading, themselves, and each other as capable readers and learners. Several factors prompted us to use RMA with these students. An evaluation of the boys' reading using the Reading Miscue Inventory (RMI) (Goodman, Watson, & Burke, 2005) showed that they generally comprehended what they read but they were not efficient readers. Their oral reading was labored and included long pauses, numerous attempts to "sound out" unfamiliar text, and a frequent lack of correction when their predictions did not make sense. In addition, the boys had increasing difficulty reading and completing assignments and assessments in the basal anthology Michelle was required to use. Despite increased difficulty in orally reading the stories, their comprehension as evaluated through retellings and district and school assessments had not decreased. We hypothesized that the boys compensated for difficult text by drawing on visual clues in the stories and using effective strategies inconsistently to support their comprehension. We were concerned because in fourth grade they would need to consistently use a range of effective strategies.

All four boys had been selected by the school reading specialist to participate in a remedial program for fluency, based on their DIBELS (Good & Kaminski, 2002) assessments. During 30 minutes of remediation daily (part of their two-hour reading block), the boys participated in activities such as working on phonics skills, playing word games, and reading. We knew from the boys' RMI graphophonic scores that they attended strongly to phonics. We believed these remediation experiences (other than actually reading) did not support their use of strategies focused on constructing meaning across a text, which RMA would do.

Retrospective Miscue Analysis Sessions

Retrospective miscue analysis (RMA) grows out of the transactional socio-psycholinguistic theory (see Goodman & Goodman, this volume, Chapter 2).

Readers look through the miscue "window" with another reader, or for collaborative RMA, a group of readers, to examine their own reading process and evaluate, understand, and learn from it. The readers are actively involved in their learning, a process that is essential to reclaiming reading. RMA readers learn to appreciate their strengths as meaning makers, revalue themselves as competent and capable readers, and revalue reading as a meaningful, constructive process (Moore & Gilles, 2005; Paulson, 2001). As readers gain confidence, they lose their negative perceptions of reading and themselves as readers, and increase their reading proficiency (Almazroui, 2007; Flurkey & Goodman, 2000; Martens, 1998), thereby reclaiming themselves as learners.

The typical RMA sequence begins with a session in which the student is audio-recorded reading and retelling a text, following RMI procedures. Then, the student listens to portions of the tape and participates in analyzing particular miscues to understand the strengths he or she already demonstrates so he or she can use these effective strategies more consistently (Goodman & Marek, 1996). Collaborative RMA sessions with groups of students sometimes involve a teacher leading the discussion and other times the students listening to the tape and selecting the miscues they want to discuss (Costello, 1996; Moore & Gilles, 2005).

When teachers/researchers meet for RMA with readers who are struggling, they often select high-quality miscues (i.e., meaningful substitutions or insertions or omissions that maintain meaning) for these discussions because these miscues show the readers' effective strategies and meaning construction processes. The discussion focuses on whether the miscue makes sense, the language cues and strategies the student drew on to make the miscues, whether the miscue was corrected, and whether or not it should have been corrected. The teacher/researcher emphasizes that the reader is already using effective strategies, that all readers make miscues, and that proficient readers use these same strategies. Over a number of RMA sessions the goal is for readers to revalue reading as a meaningful, constructive process and reclaim themselves as competent and capable learners (Goodman, 2003; Goodman & Marek, 1996).

RMA sessions with the Mighty Readers were of 30–45 minutes in three parts. They began with a review of the reading process, followed by listening to portions of audiotapes and discussing the miscues. Before listening to the recording, Prisca gave each boy a pencil and a copy of the text, and they marked the miscues. The miscues were chosen from readings recorded by Mighty Readers in a previous session, as well as miscues made by students from Prisca's earlier studies. While Prisca only selected high-quality miscues to discuss, she used portions of recordings that included high- and low-quality miscues the other readers made to facilitate discussions of the more effective and efficient strategies that a reader *could* have used. Lastly, the Mighty Readers worked together to read a new text.

Two "ground rules" guided the sessions. First, no one interrupted to correct, or provide a word if a reader was having difficulty. Prisca made it clear that it was the reader's responsibility to make sense while reading and the group needed to honor and respect the reader by staying out of the way and letting him work. Second, when the reader finished, he talked first about his reading. (Occasionally, one of the listeners was excited by what he heard and jumped in first, however.) After that, others could talk about the brilliant strategies the reader used.

In the two weeks before the sessions began, each boy individually read and retold *Willy the Wizard* (Browne, 1995) (*Willy*) with Prisca, following miscue analysis procedures. After the 17 RMA sessions concluded, they individually read and retold *Willy* with Prisca again and, in an additional session, read and retold *The Biggest House in the World* (Lionni, 1968) (*House*). According to the Children's Literature Comprehensive Database (2007), Accelerated Reader levels *Willy* at a 3.7 grade level and *House* at 4.0. (Stories used in miscue analysis are complete stories that are unfamiliar and somewhat challenging to the reader to allow teachers/researchers to learn how the reader deals with difficulties across a whole text.)

These readings were analyzed quantitatively through the RMI Classroom Procedure and qualitatively by analyzing the typescripts (a copy of the text read) for patterns in the miscues and to learn more specifically the strategies the readers used. Since analysis in the Classroom Procedure is on the sentence level, we looked at each individual miscue to determine whether it was a high-quality miscue that supported the constructing of meaning (i.e., a correction, an uncorrected substitution that made sense, etc.) or a low-quality miscue that resulted in meaning change (i.e., an uncorrected substitution or omission that didn't make sense). We then calculated the percentage of miscues in each story that were high quality and low quality. The retellings were quantitatively analyzed with retelling guides for information related to story events.

We constructed profiles of the boys' reading of each text using their comprehending and comprehension scores. Comprehending is the reader's process of constructing meaning *as* they read. In the RMI Classroom Procedure, it is the percentage of sentences the reader produces that make sense (semantics) and sound like grammatical structures (syntax), including the reader's pattern of self-correction. Since we selected challenging stories, we didn't expect the boys' comprehending scores to be 100 percent. The comprehension score, based on the retelling, indicates the understanding readers shared when they finish reading.

The Mighty Readers Grow in Reading Proficiency

We first analyzed the boys' RMI Classroom Procedure scores as evidence of growth in comprehension and proficiency. With a few exceptions, the Mighty Readers' comprehending, comprehension, and high-quality miscues increased from their first reading of *Willy* to their second reading of *Willy* and their reading of *House*. (Kyle was experiencing a stressful situation outside of school, which we believe influenced his reading and learning in school.) Examined collectively, the boys' comprehending while they were reading *Willy* grew from a mean of

57 percent to 70 percent, and their comprehension increased from 63 percent to 66 percent. Ben's readings of the same sections of *Willy* (Figure 3.1) demonstrate the kinds of shifts the Mighty Readers made to using more effective and efficient strategies.

In April (see Figure 3.1A), Ben's high-quality miscues included substituting the names *William* (0201 and 0301) and *Will* (0304) for *Willy*, both of which make

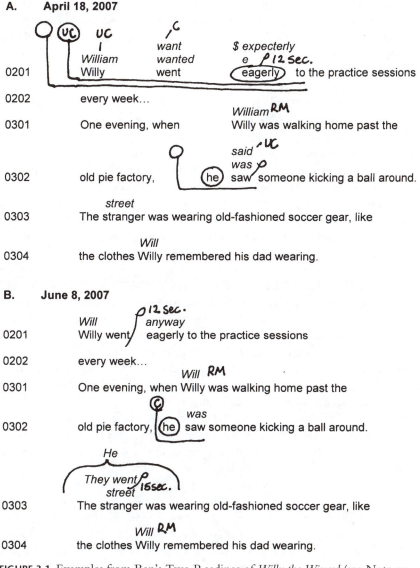

FIGURE 3.1 Examples from Ben's Two Readings of *Willy the Wizard* (see Note on p. 59)

sense; correcting predictions to construct meaning (*wanted* and *want* for *went* in 0201; and omitting *he* in 0302). He also integrated graphophonic and syntactic cues to predict and produce miscues that didn't make sense. In 0201, after first omitting *eagerly* (which would not have affected the meaning of the sentence), he gave the non-word *expecterly*, substituting something that looked similar to the text and retained the syntactic structure. Ben made two other substitutions which fitted the grammatical structure and looked and sounded similar to the text, but didn't make sense in the story. In 0302 he first predicted *was* for *saw*, then paused and substituted *said*, which began like *saw*. In 0303 he substituted *street* for *stranger*.

In June (see Figure 3.1B), Ben made miscues in almost all of the same places, but with very different results. This time all of his miscues made sense. He again made name substitutions (0201, 0301, 0304). After a pause in 0201, he substituted *anyway* for *eagerly*, which made sense and fitted the grammatical structure of the sentence. (Ben said: Willy wants to play soccer. Even though he can't afford to purchase the equipment he needs, he goes to practice *anyway*.) In 0302 he corrected his omission of *he* and substitution of *was* (which would not make sense) for *saw* to produce a meaningful sentence. In 0303 he substituted *street* for *stranger*, then read *They went*, paused for 15 seconds, and substituted *He* for the noun phrase *The stranger* to create a syntactically and semantically acceptable sentence. During the retelling, Ben referred back to that miscue, saying, "It was *The* and I couldn't figure out a word after it . . . I ended up calling it *He* because it [*stranger*] didn't make sense." His comment revealed that he had learned to give himself permission to revise the printed text to construct a meaningful text.

Generally, and not surprisingly, the Mighty Readers found *House* more challenging than *Willy*. Like all readers who encounter challenges while reading, they tended to work on smaller pieces of text and were not as flexible in their use of strategies. Their mean comprehending score was 55 percent and their mean comprehension score was 72 percent. While their comprehending score was lower than that for their second reading of *Willy* (70 percent), their comprehension mean was 6 points higher, showing that the more difficult text did not constrain their understanding. Despite the difficulties, the boys showed a more consistent use of efficient and effective strategies, as in Figure 3.2.

Both boys were unsure of *cousins* (1802), paused, and decided to deliberately omit it, using one of the strategies we discussed that readers have available when they are unsure. As Nate reminded us numerous times, "If something is important to the meaning, it'll come up in the text again and there will be other clues." Ben also omitted *awe* and *later* (1802), but these omissions have only minor impacts on meaning. Both boys also corrected predictions that weren't going to make sense, Ben in 1802 (*that* for *they*) and Nate in 1801 (*farm* for *family* and *were* for *way*). And both made high-quality substitutions for *an amazing sight* (1803). In the story, a snail works to grow his shell so he'll have the biggest house in the world. In that context, Ben's substitution of *a enormous size* and Nate's substitution of *a magnificent sight* make sense.

Ben

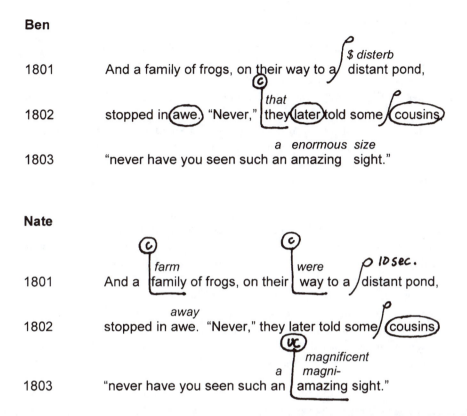

Nate

FIGURE 3.2 Miscue Examples from Ben's and Nate's Readings of *The Biggest House in the World*

Ben and Nate used less efficient and effective strategies when they encountered difficulties, however. Ben paused briefly and substituted the non-word *disterb* for *distant* (1801) and Nate substituted *away* for *awe* (1802), graphically similar substitutions that did not make sense.

Our analysis of the quality of the boys' miscues showed that overall their percentage of high-quality miscues for *House* (mean: 51 percent) was similar to the percentage of their high-quality miscues for their second reading of *Willy* (mean: 54 percent) and higher than in their first reading of *Willy* (mean: 40 percent). In other words, even though they had difficulty, they were still concerned with constructing meaning. They used meaning-making strategies more consistently while reading the challenging text *House* than they had in their first reading of *Willy*. Their stronger retelling scores for *House* (72 percent compared to 63 percent) further supported their increased attention to constructing meaning.

Learning from and with the Mighty Readers

Our RMA conversations were critical dialogues (Goodman, Martens, & Flurkey, 2008) that empowered the Mighty Readers to reclaim their own learning, revalue reading as a process of meaning construction, and view themselves as capable, competent readers. We grew also to understand how RMA discussions create environments and communities that support teachers and readers in reclaiming learning. We now share our insights, which may be applied to other learning contexts in which reclaiming the learning of reading is the focus. Our "big reclaiming ideas" are presented in *italics* and then substantiated through examples.

In RMA discussions, **all** *group members experience revaluing during discussions of miscues and contribute to the revaluing process of each other, thereby doing the work of reclaiming themselves as learners.* RMA discussions focus on the miscues of a particular reader, and in our initial sessions the primary discussion was often between the reader and Prisca. The boys needed time to understand the concept of miscues and how to identify and analyze them. Though not active in the discussions, the other boys listened and deepened their understandings. They heard the strategies they use legitimized as strategies all good readers use. In the third session, conversation focused on Ben's miscues from a section of *Gregory, the Terrible Eater* (Sharmat, 1980). Earlier in the session, we had decided that substituting *George* for *Gregory* was a good strategy when the reader was unsure of a name. The text read: *After Gregory went to bed, Mother Goat said, "I'm afraid Gregory will eat my clothes hamper."*

Ben: (on the recording) "After *George* went to bed, Mother Goat said, *"I'm after, I'm afraid George* will eat my clothes hamper."
Prisca: So what did you do well?
Ben: Well, I got stuck on that word [*afraid*] but when I said, *"I'm after George will eat my clothes . . ."* then I knew it was *"I'm afraid George will eat my clothes . . ."*
Prisca: Excellent! So Ben was thinking, "What's going to make sense? *I'm after George will eat my clothes?* That's strange!" And then he thinks, "Oh, *afraid!*" What else did he do?

In the next portion of this RMA session, the text reads: *He's eating too much.*

Ben: (on tape) *"He eats* too much."
Ben: I don't even know what I did! (giggles)
Prisca: . . . Read this line, Ben.
Ben: *"He's eating too much."*
Prisca: Do you know what you said? (Ben indicates he doesn't.) You said, *"He eats too much."*
Kyle: He did, yeah, he did!
Ben: I did?
Prisca: Ben said, *"He eats too much"* and he kept going. Now why did you keep reading?

Ben: Because I made sense!

Prisca: It made sense! And that's what good readers do! If it makes sense, you think, "Hm, that's fine! Let's keep rolling." But here, *I'm after George* didn't make sense, so he did what good readers do: he went back and corrected it. So he goes back when he's supposed to go back and fix it and he keeps reading when it makes sense! Outstanding!

While Prisca and Ben were the two to discuss Ben's miscues, Kyle's interjection of "He did, yeah, he did!" indicates his attentiveness. Kyle, Nate, and Ron heard Ben talk about a miscue he realized didn't make sense and then corrected; they heard Ben say he wasn't aware he even made a miscue that did make sense; and they heard Prisca state that Ben's miscues and strategies were similar to those of "good" readers. They witnessed Ben's revaluing and Ben had witnesses hear about his strengths as a reader. Together, the boys reclaimed their learning of reading.

As the boys gained understanding of the reading and revaluing process, they took more ownership of the discussions, gradually became more vocal and affirmed each other's strengths and strategies, and experienced their own continuing reclaiming. The following discussion of Ron's miscues in a sentence from *Alexander and the Terrible, Horrible, No Good, Very Bad Day* (Viorst, 1972) occurred three sessions after the previous discussion of Ben's miscues. The text reads: *He also said to watch out for the books on his desk . . .*

Ron: (on tape) He also said to *which* (pause) watch out for *his* books on his desk . . .

Ben: He said *which.*

Prisca: He said *which. He also said to which . . .* and then he stopped.

Nate: He stopped and he thought.

Prisca: And what do you think he was thinking about?

Nate: Like *which* doesn't make sense. *Which out for the books on his . . .*

Prisca: Good. Do you remember what you were thinking, Ron?

Ron: I think I was thinking *which* doesn't sound too much better and *watch* sounds a little bit more better than *which.*

Prisca: Right, 'cause *watch* makes sense. Now do you know how to spell *which*?

All: w-h-i-c-h

Prisca: And see how you spell *watch* [points to *watch* in the book]? You can see how much *which* and *watch* look alike. You were doing a good job of picking up on those clues of what was there but then you thought, "Wait a minute! Something's not right!" And, you did the brilliant thing good readers do. You stopped and you thought about what's going to make sense and you corrected. What's the next thing that happens? (Prisca plays the tape again.)

Nate: Watch out.

Prisca: He said *watch out for his books . . .* And what does the book say?

All: Watch out for the books.

Prisca: Now, that's brilliant! Why is that brilliant?

Kyle: That makes sense! It makes better sense than the book!

Prisca: I agree. It's talking about his dad and it's his dad's books. . . . Ron, why did you go back and correct *which* but you didn't go back and correct *his?*

Ron: *His* sounds kind of better than *the*.

Prisca: Yeah! *His* makes perfect sense! And we had to play the tape extra times to even hear it because it was sooo brilliant! When it makes sense, you keep reading but if it doesn't, like *which*, you stop and correct it. That's the brilliant thing good readers do!

Ron and his peers shifted from being passive observers to actively reclaiming their learning of reading as young researchers and colleagues. In this instance Ben was so excited that he immediately started the conversation. Nate jumped in with his hypothesis on why Ron paused, namely, to think. Ron, meanwhile, listened to his peers affirm him as a reader, with comments like Kyle's "That makes sense! It makes better sense than the book!" Now Ron knows the respect the Mighty Readers have for him as a competent reader.

Through the RMA sessions the Mighty Readers gained (claimed and reclaimed) confidence in their abilities to analyze the miscues they and the others made. Comments such as "I did that too in the last story we read!" were evidence the boys were classifying types of miscues, understanding the miscues they made and why they made them, and identifying the reading process as one they shared. Most importantly, the boys were experiencing revaluing themselves—a process critical to reclaiming their learning—long after the session that focused on their own miscues (Martens & Arya, 2004).

In an ongoing collaborative RMA community, readers develop a history together that they draw on to support their own and others' reading development and revaluing; relationships are part of reclaiming learning. As each session and each miscue discussion built on previous sessions, the Mighty Readers developed a history of working together. When the talk related to a previous discussion, Prisca made the connection visible. The following example is from the third RMA session and focuses on one of Kyle's miscues in *Gregory* that was discussed immediately after he finished reading. The discussion was primarily between Kyle and Prisca, while the others listened in. The text read: *Vegetable soup. But there is one condition. You also have to eat the can.*

Kyle: (on tape) Vegetable soup. But there is one *cot-, canditch, twist.* You also have to eat the can.

Prisca: (after Kyle finished reading) Now what did you do well, Kyle?

Kyle: I said *There's one twist* on this one but it wasn't really *twist.*

Prisca: So why did you substitute *twist?*

Kyle: Because it's like there's one, one, one condition. (Kyle immediately looked at the book and it was clear on his face that he knew he'd said what was in the text.)

Prisca: How do you know it's *condition?*

Kyle: Because that's *condition*, the word . . .

Prisca: . . . So you all of a sudden figured out *condition*. . . . He's doing what Ben did when he was reading before. . . . All the way across the text as he's reading and thinking, "What can that be? What can that be?" and he figures it out! Even if he didn't figure it out, *twist* makes good sense! He says, *"There is one twist. You also have to eat the can."* Outstanding!

Earlier in the session we had discussed how, while reading, Ben had paused and then regressed two lines to correct four miscues that hadn't made sense. Ben had shared that he kept thinking about what would make sense and went back to correct the miscues. Prisca connected Kyle's substitution of *twist* and later correction (even though *twist* made sense) with Ben's correction strategy. Connecting these miscues, as both boys demonstrated thinking and meaning construction across the text, contributed to the revaluing of both boys.

Threads of understandings like these connected one conversation to the next. The transcript below occurred during the first part of the fifth session and focused on the miscues Valerie, a third grader, made while reading "The Man Who Kept House" (McInnes, 1962). The text read: *She hurried up the path.*

Valerie: (on tape) She *heard* up *to practice.*

Prisca: What does she say?

Ben: She heard up to practice!

Prisca: So . . . does that make sense?

All: No!

Prisca: . . . It doesn't make any sense at all. What should she have done?

Ron: She should have thought what makes sense.

Prisca: Right, Ron, she should have thought, "What's going to make sense here?" *She heard* is a good prediction, but . . .

Kyle: (interrupting) It doesn't make sense . . .

Ben: She should have said, "Oh, that doesn't make sense" and stopped and thought and read it in her head to see if she can get any different words . . . that make sense.

Prisca: Right, Ben! She should have stopped and read it in her head, but . . .

Ben: (interrupting) Like Nate did when he was stuck on the first page of that other book.

Prisca: Right! You stop and think about it in your head, and if you can't get it, if you can't figure it out, what do you do?

Ron: You go on.

The Mighty Readers' reading community and their common experiences, built over numerous RMA sessions, allowed them to thread connections between their own and each other's revaluing throughout all of the sessions, and such revaluing is at the heart of their reclaiming their learning to read.

Through RMA, the Mighty Readers assumed agency—which is essential for reclaiming as an active process—for themselves outside, as well as inside, the session as they shared revaluing with others. As the boys worked with Prisca, they developed a sense of agency over their own reading process and gained a confidence in themselves as readers that was not previously apparent. This confidence carried over into the classroom. Michelle noticed changes in the boys' interactions with their classmates and in their reading. Ben, who had rarely participated in large- or small-group discussions before this, began sharing and contributing his personal thoughts and connections related to what he was reading and writing. Ben's awareness that he needed to make meaning when he read was also evident. One day while Michelle was circulating to observe students partner-read, she heard Ben say, "That doesn't make sense," then watched Ben make an acceptable substitution. Michelle complimented him for focusing so intently on making meaning. Ben said that that was what he had been working on with Ms. Martens. Another time, when Michelle had a mini-refresher lesson with the class, Kyle chimed in, stating, "You have to learn to do it on your own because you won't always have someone there to help you when you are having troubles." The boys assumed responsibility for their own reading process.

The importance of a safe community environment, where readers may take risks and respect and value the knowledge and strengths they each DO have, cannot be overstated. The Mighty Readers experienced an environment in which the boys felt accepted for who they were as readers, safe, valued, and free to respond. None of the discussions the Mighty Readers had with Prisca or Michelle would have occurred in contexts where they were inhibited, told what they did wrong, or believed their reading wasn't "good" because it wasn't accurate. This underscores the importance of a safe social community in which learners are respected for who they are and the strengths they have.

The safe community for the Mighty Readers' RMA sessions needed to be built; it was not there immediately. While Michelle continually fostered respect and created a safe environment in her classroom, the RMA sessions with Prisca were a new context for the boys. The first miscues the Mighty Readers discussed with Prisca were made by Donna, a reader in a previous study. Some of Donna's miscues were high quality and supported constructing meaning, and some weren't. The discussion focused on distinguishing which miscues made sense and sounded like language and which didn't and what Donna could have done in those non-meaning-making instances. The discussion was good and the boys seemed to understand. Towards the end, though, Kyle said, "It's kind of like we're making fun of her." Prisca responded, "No, we're not making fun of her. We're trying to understand what readers do and can do to make meaning. Donna did what we're doing. She thought and talked about what she could do to be a better reader." In the next session, after RMA discussions of miscues Nate made, Prisca referred back to Kyle's comment:

Prisca: Yesterday Kyle thought that maybe we were making fun of Donna. If we were really making fun, what would we do?

Kyle: We would say, "Ha, ha, ha!"

Prisca: Yes, we'd be laughing and saying she's not a very good reader. But when we listened to the brilliant strategy Nate used when he paused to think, were we making fun of Nate?

All: No.

Prisca: No, Nate was helping us learn and helping us think . . . and so was Donna . . . so we learn from what other readers do so we can become better readers.

In a safe RMA community where the boys felt valued and respected and discussions focused on authentic content, the Mighty Readers grew to assume agency, reclaim learning, and revalue reading, themselves, and each other. Through the discussions about the "brilliant" strategies they and all good readers use, they came to understand the one reading process all readers share and the critical importance of always focusing on constructing meaning. As teachers and students engage in similar discussions, they too will find themselves empowered to reclaim learning and reading.

Note

Following are miscue analysis markings used in the text excerpts in Figure 3.1 and Figure 3.2: substitutions are written above the text; omissions are circled; RM indicates a repeated miscue, meaning that an identical miscue occurred earlier in the story; $ indicates a non-word; an enlarged "P" indicates a 5-second pause (or longer as indicated). A circle connected to a line(s) under a portion of the text marks a regression and the letter(s) in the circle indicates what occurred: C indicates that the miscue was corrected; UC means that an unsuccessful attempt was made to correct the miscue; an empty circle indicates more than one change occurred in the regression and individual miscues are marked for the change made.

References

Almazroui, K. (2007). Learning together through retrospective miscue analysis: Salem's case study. *Reading Improvement, 44*(3), 153–168.

Children's Literature Comprehensive Database. Data retrieved November 14, 2007, from http://clcd.odyssi.com.proxytu.researchport.umd.edu/member/csearch.htm (available only upon payment of joining fee).

Costello, S. (1996). A teacher/researcher uses RMA. In Y. Goodman & A. Marek (Eds.), *Retrospective miscue analysis: Revaluing readers and reading* (pp. 165–175). Katonah, NY: Richard C. Owen.

Flurkey, A., & Goodman, Y. (2000). Andrew, stuck in words: A retrospective miscue analysis case study in revaluing. In L. Denti & P. Cousin (Eds.), *New ways of looking at learning disabilities* (pp. 129–149). Denver, CO: Love Publishing.

Good, R. H., & Kaminski, R. A. (Eds.). (2002). *Dynamic indicators of basic early literacy skills* (6th ed.). Eugene, OR: Institute for the Development of Educational Achievement.

Goodman, K. (2003). Revaluing readers and reading. In A. D. Flurkey & J. Xu (Eds.), *On the revolution of reading: The selected writings of Kenneth S. Goodman* (pp. 421–429). Portsmouth, NH: Heinemann.

Goodman, Y., & Marek, A. (1996). *Retrospective miscue analysis: Revaluing readers and reading.* Katonah, NY: Richard C. Owen.

Goodman, Y. M., Watson, D., & Burke, C. (2005). *Reading miscue inventory: From evaluation to instruction.* Katonah, NY: Richard C. Owen.

Goodman, Y., Martens, P., & Flurkey, A. (2008). Revaluing readers: Learning from Zachary (unpublished manuscript).

Martens, P. (1998). Using retrospective miscue analysis to inquire: Learning from Michael. *The Reading Teacher, 52*(2), 176–184.

Martens, P., & Arya, P. (2004). Strengthening literate identities through retrospective miscue analysis: The process of revaluing readers and reading. *Thinking Classroom: An International Journal of Reading, Writing and Critical Reflection, 5*(3), 23–29.

Moore, R., & Gilles, C. (2005). *Reading conversations: Retrospective miscue analysis with struggling readers, Grades 4–12.* Portsmouth, NH: Heinemann.

Paulson, E. (2001). The discourse of retrospective miscue analysis: Links with adult learning theory. *Journal of College Reading and Learning, 32*(1). Retrieved January 14, 2005, from www.highbeam.com.

Children's Literature References

Allard, H. (1977). *Miss Nelson is missing!* New York: Scholastic.

Browne, A. (1995). *Willy the wizard.* New York: Alfred A. Knopf.

Lionni, L. (1968). *The biggest house in the world.* New York: Alfred A. Knopf.

McInnes, J. (Ed.). (1962). The man who kept house. In *Magic and make believe.* Toronto: Thomas Nelson.

Sharmat, M. (1980). *Gregory, the terrible eater.* New York: Scholastic.

Viorst, J. (1972). *Alexander and the terrible, horrible, no good, very bad day.* New York: Scholastic.

CHAPTER 3 EXTENSION

Extending and Expanding Retrospective Miscue Analysis

Carol Gilles and Debra Peters

Retrospective miscue analysis (RMA) worked well with third graders as described by Martens and Doyle in the main part of their chapter, and we wondered how RMA might work with a whole class of older learners with less direct teacher intervention. Debra Peters, a middle school teacher, and Carol Gilles, a university researcher, collaborated with Debra's entire seventh-grade homeroom class at a suburban school that is about 60 percent Caucasian, 30 percent African American, and 10 percent other races, with about 44 percent who receive free or reduced lunch. Debra's class of 25 mirrored the school's population; most students were Caucasian, with three African Americans, and one student who spoke English as a second language. Debra was concerned that some of her students didn't engage deeply with the texts they read and that they didn't always monitor for meaning. Although they chose books they wanted to read, and completed the books, Debra wondered if there was something that they could do that would teach them more about reading, particularly to promote more engagement and monitoring. Our project, lasting the final five weeks of a school year, was a chance for both of us to dig a little deeper into RMA as a way of helping learners reclaim reading.

The Process

Debra decided that because her students were older than Martens and Doyle's, they could learn the fundamentals of RMA from a more mature perspective. She invited Carol to come in and talk with the students about how reading works, the cuing systems of language, and miscue analysis (Goodman, Watson, & Burke, 2005). Debra introduced them to simple miscue markings (omission, insertion, substitution, repetition, correction) and they practiced marking texts that Debra read to them aloud and that they heard on tape recorders. Carol showed the students the difference between a high-quality miscue (defined for them as one that doesn't change the meaning) and a low-quality miscue (one that does change the meaning). Students practiced marking miscues and sharing the markings with their partners. We circulated as the students practiced, reminding them to listen very carefully and to mark exactly what they heard. We also showed students how to take notes about the retelling of the text.

From the marking, we moved on to teaching students the questions that guide RMA sessions (Moore & Gilles, 2004): (1) Does the miscue make sense? (2) Does it change the meaning of the sentence? (3) Why do you think the reader miscued? (4) What were you thinking?

Since our goal was not student assessment but awareness, Debra chose a passage for the practice session from "Frog Watching" (Harvey & Goudvis, 2007), an accessible text that held students' interest because there was a gigantic puddle outside the classroom that had become a home for noisy frogs. Students listened to their partners read the passage, marked their partners' miscues, asked for a retelling and jotted down notes, and then had the RMA conversation with their partners by asking the above question. Students chose the miscues that they wanted to discuss. The RMA began a deeper discussion about why certain miscues were made, how meaning is made, and the thinking that occurs when one reads. This is the essence of reclaiming learning through student agency.

During the readers workshop, as partners were ready they moved to the listening station, where one person read the text (and was audiotaped). The other partner listened, marked miscues, and then took notes as his or her partner retold the story. They checked each other's miscue markings and filled out an RMA organizer. The organizer is a form on which one partner writes the number of the line of text, the expected response, and the miscue his or her partner made. Both partners decided whether the miscue was self-corrected and whether it changed the meaning or not. Filling out the RMA organizer began the conversation about the miscue. (For more information, see Moore & Gilles, 2004.)

Although we saw that most students were successful at marking the miscues and using the questions to begin deeper discussions with their partners, we noticed that some were having difficulty with the distinction between high- and low-quality miscues. Since the conversations were taped, Carol asked two partners, James and Adam, if we could share with the entire class an excerpt from their larger conversation and discuss it. We heard the following:

James: The word was *expandable* and you said *expadable*. Does this miscue make sense?

Adam: Yes, I think it does.

James: Um, why do you think that?

Adam: Because it sounds a lot like *expandable*.

James: OK. Does it change the meaning of the sentence?

Adam: Um, not really. I would consider it a high-level miscue.

James: Why?
Adam: Because it sounds a lot like *expandable.*
James: OK. Why do you think you miscued?
Adam: Because it sounds a lot like [laughs] *expandable.*
James: Maybe you were reading too fast?
Adam: Yes, I think I was reading way too fast.
James: OK.

As James and Adam read their transcripted conversation aloud, Adam stopped. "Wait," he said, "that word really doesn't make sense! I think it was low level, not high level." As the larger group talked about what had happened in Adam and James's conversation, they came to understand that just because a word *looks* like another word, it doesn't mean that it *makes sense.* Several other classmates shared their excerpts, thus strengthening their knowledge and reclaiming (or claiming for the first time) their learning about reading.

For Round II of RMA, Debra let students choose articles of varying difficulty from topics such as child labor, slavery, schools in Afghanistan, social justice, and women's suffrage. Once again the students marked each other's miscues and then used the RMA Organizer to complete the RMA. To help the students stay organized in the process, we provided a checklist on which they could check off each phase of the process:

1. Read story and partner records miscue.
2. Retell story.
3. Switch. Read story, record miscues, and do retelling.
4. Check to see you marked correctly.
5. Fill out RMA organizer.
6. Have the conversation.
7. "What were you thinking?"

As we listened to the second round of partnerships, we noticed that they discussed unknown words, wondered about particular events in the piece, and moved into more critical conversations about the topics of the pieces.

For Round III, Debra asked students to choose a topic (such as peer pressure) and she provided two articles that offered somewhat differing opinions on the issue. This time, students talked a bit more about the topic (focusing on meaning) and less about their miscues (focusing on words).

What Did These Students Learn?

We interviewed the students and found that nearly all of them noted that when they used RMA, they could "stay with" a piece—that is, they were engaged. They also learned a great deal about themselves as readers. One child said, "I almost always substitute words that make sense; they don't change the meaning. I make those high [quality] miscues." Students learned to self-monitor and correct miscues that changed meaning. In talking about his partner, one boy said, "We both skip words 'cause we're reading ahead, reading too fast." He and his partner learned to vary their speed depending on the text and context, because reading aloud is different from reading silently.

Learning about RMA took the mystery out of assessment. One girl told Carol, "I always thought when I read to the teacher that she was marking down everything that was wrong. Now I know that she is marking down my miscues." She confided that she did much better on her annual reading assessment. Debra found that this process gave her students more agency as they reclaimed themselves as readers. She concluded:

> I realize how powerful that one question, "What were you thinking?" can be. You just need to listen to their answers and realize that kids don't all have to be doing the same thing at the same time. They can be (and are) responsible when we expect it and model it.

Debra's students learned about reading and ended the year with a greater understanding of themselves and others as readers.

References

Goodman, Y. M., Watson, D., & Burke, C. (2005). *Reading miscue inventory: From evaluation to instruction.* Katonah, NY: Richard C. Owen.

Harvey, S. & Goudvis, A. (2007). Frog watching. In *Toolkit texts* (Harvey & Goudvis, Eds.). Portsmouth, NH: Heinemann.

Moore, R. & Gilles, C. (2004). *Reading conversations: Retrospective miscue analysis with students in grades 4–12.* Portsmouth, NH: Heinemann.

PILLAR II
Reclaiming Teaching

4

WHERE DO WE GO FROM HERE?

From Miscues to Strategies

Dorothy Watson

Miscue analysis is at the cornerstone of reclaiming the teaching of reading. Among the first questions many teachers ask as they use miscue analysis to learn about the reading process are: Will all this hard work pay off? Will I learn something that can help my students become better readers? Regular users of miscue analysis have a ready answer: Miscue analysis can inform and guide your teaching as no other evaluation procedure can. The implications for individual and group instruction are numerous.

Moving from miscue analysis that provides information about students' *reading* **process** *strategies* (what they do as readers) to appropriate *reading* **teaching** *strategies* (what we teach) takes an investment of time and intellect on the part of the teacher and students. I'm making a distinction here between the reading strategies readers use to construct meaning and the strategies teachers use in their instruction. Ken Goodman's reading model of *sampling* from the text, *predicting* upcoming text, *inferring* meaning, *confirming* or *rejecting* predictions, and *integrating* new information gained from the text with information readers have in their heads and lives is the basis for understanding both the *process strategies* and the *teaching strategies* (Goodman, 1994). The optimum way of moving from *reader's strategies* to *teaching strategies* is to become involved in the process and progress of the reader by using miscue analysis, as explained in *The Reading Miscue Inventory* (RMI) (Goodman, Watson, & Burke, 2005).

In this chapter, readers meet two students, Blake and Syed, who needed help with their reading. Teachers described Blake as the least proficient reader in his middle school. I worked with Blake during the school year and for one summer. Syed, from Sudan, spent three years in an Ethiopian refugee camp without benefit of schooling before moving to the United States. We began working together his sophomore year; he is now a high school senior.

Although both Blake and Syed were discouraged with their progress in reading, they agreed to try reading classes once again when they were assured their instruction would start with their competencies rather than with their failures. We began with miscue analysis, which included the Burke Reading Interview (BRI) and the Reading Miscue Inventory (Goodman et al., 2005), and conversations about reading—often initiated by Retrospective Miscue Analysis (RMA) (Goodman & Marek, 1996). Miscue analysis was the only evaluation instrument powerful enough to provide detailed information to begin to teach these boys in a way that reclaimed teaching as an informed and thoughtful process. RMA was one facet of such teaching because it provided Blake and Syed with the opportunity to study their miscues and their thinking as meaning makers. RMA and other strategies for reclaiming the teaching of reading are presented by example as the two students learnt to revalue themselves as readers.

Studying a student's beliefs about the reading process, reading instruction, and text helps us become aware of the compatibility or incompatibility of the reader's beliefs with the existing reading program. Studying the student's beliefs also helps us rethink our own beliefs and may lead us to reconfirm or modify long-held opinions about readers and reading. Once data are collected and analyzed, decisions about suitable reading experiences can be made. The following sections summarize Blake's and Syed's curricular stories and explain how reading strategy lessons were arrived at and conducted. I also provide some of the insights I had into my own ever-growing understanding of the reading process.

Blake

Blake's test scores (of which there was an abundance) gave me no hint about his idea of the reading process, nor did the scores indicate how to begin our work. Although I heard a great deal about what Blake could not do (respond in class, read assignments, attempt writing, etc.), I wanted to start with what he could do. After talking with him about his life, interests, and accomplishments ("I can draw and I have a good sense of humor"), we set to work, starting with the BRI, which helped me get to know Blake's beliefs about reading and himself as a reader.

The first question on the BRI addresses strategies the reader believes are most important, "When you're reading and you come to something you don't know, what do you do?" Blake responded with a range of strategies: "Skip it and go on. Read to the end of the sentence and go back to see if it makes sense. Sound it out." In this response, Blake mentioned some strategies that support meaning making. I wondered if he was repeating what teachers had told him, or what he thought I wanted to hear. I was in for a surprise. When I asked, "Do you ever do anything else?" Blake replied, "Well, I don't even do that. They don't work. I can't read if I don't know what it means." I wasn't sure whether "it" referred to meaning found in the entire text or in the individual word.

The next BRI question, "Who is a good reader you know?" was asked to get a sense of what Blake thought made someone a proficient reader. Blake responded, "Mom is a good reader because she reads all the time and she's interested in books." Both of these reasons indicated positive insights into proficient reading. However, Blake felt his mom never came to anything she didn't know, indicating that accuracy, or knowing all the words, was also a part of good reading. We find that non-proficient readers often think capable readers never have a problem. When asked what his mom would do if she had a problem, Blake felt she didn't have trouble; but if she did, she would keep it in the family and "call Grandpa and ask." Blake then announced, perhaps as vindication for his non-proficient reading, "But my whole family has a reading disability. Mom couldn't read till she was in eighth grade." This was just the first of Blake's use of special education language, in this case to excuse himself for not being a successful reader; Blake was a seventh grader, but he had a genetic excuse for another year of not reading!

Although Blake emphasized that he couldn't read, I plowed ahead with the next question, "If you knew someone were having trouble reading, how would you help that person?" Blake spoke emphatically and very slowly—so I, the interviewer, wouldn't miss it, "I WOULDN'T because I – don't – know – how – to – read – myself."

When asked how his teacher would help a troubled reader, Blake responded, "Go line by line. Say the word and keep going." I wondered if this was an indication that Blake thought reading was pronouncing every word, not getting to meaning, as I thought he had indicated earlier.

I asked Blake, "How did you learn to read?" For the third time, he forcefully repeated that he couldn't read: "I haven't! I can't read." He added, as if providing scientific evidence, "I've been in reading class since third grade." Asked what he would like to do better as a reader, Blake answered, "Read. Get all the words right. If I can read, I can write." This response left me with two questions and a revelation. The questions: First, what did he mean by, "Get all the words right"? Was he referring to meaning or to pronunciation? Second, what did he want to write? And, the revelation: Blake possibly saw the connection between reading and writing.

Finally, I asked Blake, "Do you think you're a good reader?" For the fourth time, he persistently announced, "NO. I can't read! I get tongue-tied. That frustrates me and I give up. I CAN'T read." But to cap his argument, he added, "You can check my test scores!"

After we had finished the BRI, my first comment to Blake couldn't be described as encouraging or professional. I said, "Blake, it really irritates me when you say you can't read. Please don't say it again. Don't say it again. Don't say it again." He replied, "Well, I can't . . . [I glared] . . . ever say that again." I agreed, and prompted by his comment about test scores, I followed with a few unkind words about standardized tests. After my speech to a surprised Blake, we moved to our first strategy. I reminded Blake that he had said that *if he could read, he could write*. As it turned out, he wanted to write descriptions of his drawings, "like the ones in magazines and books." We talked about captions, what they were and what they needed to do. I encouraged Blake to tell me about the two drawings he had in his notebook, and to bring to our next meeting captions for each.

It was time to read. I asked Blake to select one of three stories. He looked at the pieces for several minutes, always coming back to Virginia Hamilton's *Time Pieces: The Book of Times* (2005). After a while, to move us along, I said, "Let's try that one." Blake replied, "But I can't re—— [caught himself and grinned]. It looks hard." I was surprised Blake chose a story about a girl. He said, "No problem. I like girls."

After Blake had finished reading, he retold the story as slowly as he had read it, carefully giving details (the dog put his paw on dad's knee), while ignoring important concepts (Valena was extremely curious about stars). When asked about his focus on small things, Blake said, "Well, I'm just a detail man. What can I tell ya?" It wasn't evident if Blake was missing the major meanings of the story or if he was just not expressing them. We talked about how details enrich stories, but it was necessary to get the main points if we wanted to make sense of the piece. From continued discussions, it appeared that Blake did grasp meaning-giving ideas, but didn't always take time to express them. In later sessions, Blake dictated Minute Memos (this strategy, and others throughout the chapter, are capitalized to highlight them as teaching). In one minute he told the story (as if to someone who hadn't read it), making sure the theme or major ideas were highlighted. Later in the semester, Blake wrote, rather than dictated, the Minute (or Two- or Three-Minute) Memos. Composing Bumper Stickers helped Blake focus on a concept important in the story, such as the one, "Girls Can Be Astronauts," that he composed for *Time Pieces*.

All of Blake's miscues were represented using specific markings (Goodman et al., 2005). On the first look at Blake's marked typescript, it was obvious that he was not satisfied with his reading of the girl's name, Valena. His pronunciations included the following nine variations:

Line	Observed Response	Line	Observed Response
2	Valna's	8	Valley
3	Van ella	10	Valna
5	Valley's	13	Val- Valena
6	Valna	17	Velma
		26	Valena

Immediately on finishing the story, Blake asked, "What's that girl's name?" He was surprised when I told him I wasn't quite sure (rather than support his overreliance on outside help in his reading), but that I thought he settled on a good pronunciation, that it was efficient, and that after line 26 he kept the name Valena throughout the remainder of the story. These are the types of discussions that occur during RMA; they are rooted in the miscues the learner or teacher notices. We looked at his substitution of *Lady* for *Laddie*, an efficient use of the Naming Strategy, a strategy in which the reader decides on one substitution for a name or word and sticks with it if it moves the reading along. Blake wasn't immediately convinced that good readers use such a strategy, but later in the semester he benefited from the Naming Strategy, moving from saying "blank" to substituting a suitable synonym for an unknown word or name.

I found Blake's substitutions of two words for contractions curious; readers often do the reverse. Blake's substitutions included *there is* for *there's*, *what is* for *what's*, *do not* for *don't*, etc. He explained that he knew the author used contractions, but added that she could have just been sleepy or in a hurry. He wanted "to make it right." I asked Blake why Virginia Hamilton might have intended to use contractions. He quickly offered, "Well, that's the real way we talk." We discussed the author's responsibility to portray characters realistically; using a character's informal language would help do that. The question of dialect came up later in the semester. We then considered the reader's responsibility of trying to understand *why* authors use certain spellings, words, phrases, and techniques; I suggested that he, as the reader, was not responsible for Virginia Hamilton's choice of words. To which he replied, "Good, I've got enough to worry about as it is!"

At our second RMA session, I called Blake's attention to comments he made after trying to sound out *side* and *have*. He had said, "I know that word" and "Vowels are my enemies." Blake reminded me he had been in reading classes since third grade. He added, "We always worked on vowels, vowels, vowels! I hate them, but I need to get them right." I asked, "If vowels are your enemies, what might make life easier?" Blake thought and replied seriously, "Maybe I should hang out with consonants?" I agreed that consonants *and* meaning are two good teammates in the reading game, and that focusing on vowels provided only a little information and may even distract the reader from constructing meaning. We looked at the following. (Thanks to Debi Goodman for this strategy.) I asked Blake to read: __y __a__e i__ __ __ __ a __ e. Of course, he couldn't read the sentence, no matter how long he worked on the vowels. But after carefully studying the following, and with the hint that it was something he might say to someone he was meeting for the first time, he read the sentence: M__ n__m__ __s Bl__k__. In October, after talking about how background knowledge helped us construct meaning, Blake successfully read: __ pl__dg__ __ll__g__nc__ t__ th__ fl__g __f th__ __n__t__d St__t__s __f __m__r__c__.

In all our sessions we talked first about his high-quality miscues, that is, those that moved him along in making meaning. Blake began to recognize miscues that did not detract from the process of making sense of text. We then discussed miscues that were often neither syntactically nor semantically acceptable, resulting in the destroying of coherence and meaning.

When readers insert something (typically a word) into the text, it is usually taken from the line *above* that text. In Blake's case, the word was always taken from

TABLE 4.1 Examples of Blake's "Looking Ahead" Miscues

Line on Which Miscue Occurs	Expected Response (Printed Text)	Observed Response (Blake Reads)	Blake's Response Occurs in Text Line:
2	close	side	3
3	——	other	4
7	like up there	already	8
9	hear	real	10
26	hanging	twinkling	27

a line *below* where he was reading. To explain such miscues, Blake said he was doing what he had been told to do, predict; and predicting meant "looking ahead." After discussing at length a more accurate and helpful definition of predicting, Blake concluded, "I guess predicting means <u>thinking</u> ahead." Table 4.1 shows some of Blake's other miscues in which he looked ahead and said words that occurred at a later point in the text.

The peripheral field miscues, combined with Blake's comment, "I'm drowning in words," prompted my suggestion that he use a marker under the lines of text. This strategy prevented his eyes from "looking ahead" to the line below where he was reading, as well as limiting the number of words Blake might "drown in." He also read picture books in which there was only one line on each page, for example, Leo and Diane Dillon's (2002) *Rap a Tap Tap: Here's Bojangles—Think of That*. Although he was in seventh grade, Blake said he had "no problem" reading picture books intended for younger children.

Rap a Tap Tap became one of Blake's favorites, as well as his Warm Up Book, a familiar piece that he read at the beginning of each session. Much later in the semester, Blake agreed (it took some persuasion) to read *Rap a Tap Tap* to a small group of children who were labeled "learning disabled." He was afraid that he would get tongue-tied and frustrated. After practicing for days, he nervously read to the group; his performance was flawless. After applause and cheers from his audience, Blake, without prompting, said the group should hear the book again. On the second reading he pointed out that most people loved Bojangles, but that one man was prejudiced and closed his shop when Bojangles danced by. Blake commented, "Isn't that a shame!" The audience enthusiastically agreed.

Near the end of seventh grade, Blake gained enough confidence and courage to join a Literature Study group, but only, he said, "if I don't have to say anything and if I can sit outside the circle." To my surprise, after a few sessions Blake agreed to be the group's ethnographer, taking notes about the discussion. His writing remained full of invented spelling, but he liked the job and felt that he didn't need to talk. The five-member group was reading Avi's (2002) *Crispin: The Cross of Lead*. (Remember that at our first meeting, I emphatically told Blake he was never again to say he couldn't read.) The literature group came to a point in the book in which Crispin talks with his mentor about a particular document. This document is important to Crispin as it might explain why he is being hunted. The text reads: *I wish I knew what the document was that the stranger brought to John Aycliff. Though, even if I had seen it, I couldn't have read it.* At this point Blake broke his silence, "I bet he can read more than he thinks he can! He shouldn't say that!" That one statement was payment in abundance for time spent with a boy who once, but no longer, thought he couldn't read. Blake's story is also the story of a teacher (myself) involved in reclaiming teaching as an active, interactive, and reflective process in which teachers informed about the reading process use that knowledge to develop teaching strategies specific to students' needs.

Syed

For almost three years, Syed, now a high school senior, and I met on a regular basis to work primarily on his reading comprehension. Syed's responses to his first BRI indicated that reading was a matter of sounding out words rather than making meaning; his RMI confirmed this belief.

Two strategies that helped Syed challenge his notion that pronouncing each word was reading were Retrospective Miscue Analysis (RMA) (Goodman & Marek, 1996; Moore & Gilles, 2005) and Reader Selected Miscues (RSM) (Watson, 1978). Both experiences directed us to other strategies that made use of Syed's strengths. Because he selected most of the miscues for discussion, and because we analyzed them together, Syed felt valued as an intelligent student and as a capable reader, but also one who had needs. Syed liked being a "Miscuteer," someone who not only monitored his own meaning-seeking process, but also entered into informed discussions about the process.

A significant reading issue Syed faced was the expectation that he understand materials we both felt were extremely difficult for him. For example, his eleventh-grade reading list included *The Crucible* (Miller, 1953), *The Good Earth* (Buck, 1931), *The Tortilla Curtain* (Boyle, 1996), and *The Things They Carried* (O'Brien, 1998) (a story of American soldiers in the Vietnam War). To support Syed's reading development, as well as to give him some background information that would help him understand concepts addressed in his assigned books, we read some less difficult, but related, materials. But because Syed desperately wanted to keep up with his classmates, we spent the greater part of our time reading (making sense of) the assigned books.

Unfortunately, I initially assumed that Syed had nothing in his background to help him understand the texts. What could this boy from Sudan possibly know about, for example, the Salem witch trials, important in understanding *The Crucible*? I thought there wasn't anything in this story to which he could relate. I was mistaken. The link was made when we talked about how one person in power, Preacher Parris, controlled and influenced the lives of other people. In class, and later when we talked about *The Crucible* as an allegory for McCarthyism, Syed grasped the heart of the story. He told me that his father called this injustice "the theft of power," and that it had happened to his family. Syed's uncle and father had been blacklisted, accused of something they hadn't done, and taken into custody. This explains in part why it took three years for his family to get to the United States. I learned that Syed could read between the lines before reading the lines; that is, reading the world helped him read the word (Freire in Campos, 1990). Syed taught me never to make unexamined assumptions about what a student might or might not know and feel.

Early on, analysis of Syed's miscues on school-assigned materials indicated that his graphophonic similarity scores (miscues that look similar to the text) were almost always high, near 85 percent. Semantic acceptability, or percentage of meaningful sentences, ranged between 65 percent and 70 percent. His retelling scores were generally around 45 percent. However, when reading materials were about soccer or stories of special interest, as found in the newspaper or *Newsweek* about Sudan, his retelling scores were around 80 percent. Later in the semester, as he learned to search text for meaning, and to relate the author's information to his own experiences, Syed's semantic acceptability and no-meaning-change scores rose; these are indicators, in miscue analysis, of greater understanding of the text. His retelling scores were also high, 85–95 percent. Gradually, Syed came to realize that spending time and energy on pronouncing words, rather than on searching for meaning, left him with very little understanding of the text. He also expressed his increasing ability to concentrate (one of his major concerns) when he attended to meaning rather than recoding (going from print to sound).

Some of the strategies I routinely depend on as a reading teacher were not as effective with Syed as with other readers. For example, to suggest that when he came to something he didn't know (understand), to say *blank* or to substitute a word or phrase that made sense and then continue reading, wasn't always helpful; in his assigned texts there were often five or more unknown words in a single paragraph. Syed couldn't uncover enough understandable context for this strategy to be helpful, and he was becoming acutely aware that even standard pronunciation did not provide sufficient needed information, or, as he succinctly commented once, "I just can't get any traction." The challenge became how to support Syed in developing conceptual understandings, how he could get traction.

In one section of *The Crucible*, Syed did not know the meaning of *chant*, *witchcraft*, *afoot*, *confront*, *allude*, *infidelity*, *poppet*, *voodoo*, and *fate*. I was surprised that he did know *confess*, *threaten*, *accuse*, *interrogate*, *warrant*, *vicious*, and *kinfolk*. If I had been presumptuous enough to pre-teach vocabulary, I'm sure I would have chosen as many words from the known-word list as from the unknown.

The following paragraphs summarize some strategies we used to address meaning construction when issues such as vocabulary and complex text constructions loomed as important, yet were discouraging.

We started with Reader-Selected Miscues. As Syed read and came to something he could pronounce, but didn't know the meaning of and thought it important, he made a check mark. At the end of the section, we talked about the checked items. Syed gained the meaning of some words as he read further in the text (Keep Going Strategy), some he guessed at, and occasionally we checked our guesses with the dictionary or Wikipedia. If there were a large quantity of checked words, in order not to get bogged down I did something I seldom do: I provided a definition, but always within the context of the story and with, "Let's see, as we read, if this is right."

RMA was invaluable, and a favorite strategy of Syed. Engaging in RMA, Syed was in charge of his progress as he thought out loud about making meaning. The procedure inevitably led to other strategies, such as determining meaning by understanding who was talking, what that person's agenda was, who else was involved, who was excluded from the conversation, where the talk took place, etc.

Assisted Reading (AR) helped Syed move across difficult passages, gather meaning, and take over the reading. We started AR by reading aloud together; when Syed gained confidence, I faded out, and didn't chime in again until needed.

I introduced Estimate, Read, Respond, Question (ERRQ) (Watson & Gilles in Watson, 1987) when Syed felt more secure as a reader. After scanning the text, he estimated how far he could read with understanding, penciled that spot, read the text aloud or silently, then responded by retelling, expressing his opinion, relating the text to his life or to other texts. Finally, Syed and I questioned each other. When we read about Sudan, Ethiopia, or sports (especially soccer), I always had off-the-page questions (asking for information not provided by the text), and Syed had answers.

Sketch to Stretch (Siegel, 1988) was one of my favorite strategies, because Syed, like Blake, was an artist. After reading about the author, reviewing class discussions, talking about the title and introduction to the piece, Syed made a "sketch prediction." As he progressed in the book, he sketched anything that struck him as interesting and important. A final sketch served as a conclusion or summary expression.

Using Background Knowledge is crucial to understanding and an incentive to read. Syed and I often talked about his knowledge of Sudan and Ethiopia, his interest in soccer, and his willingness to read about them. One day he looked up from his reading to say, "You know, the more I know about something, the more I want to know." On a big Post-it note I wrote, "Information is Motivation." Syed decorated the note and taped it in his notebook.

Reflection on our work was a valuable strategy. At the end of each session I typically asked two questions: (1)What did you learn today? (Often what Syed mentioned was not what I thought we had focused on.) (2) How did you learn it? His answers ranged from "I got it when we talked about it," "As I read on I understood it," "I thought about something else I'd read," "It was something

I already knew and just remembered," "The map helped," to "It just came to me." By reflecting on his reading, Syed made his strategies explicit. As he mentioned these strategies, I jotted them down for later discussion, especially for times when the discussion of the strategy could help with getting to meaning.

Wrapping Up in Order to Start Again

There is no real stopping point if we continue to listen to students and to use miscue analysis to value and evaluate students' competencies as well as their needs. Each experience with learners yields important information, and, inevitably, sensible teaching strategies emerge, sometimes occurring to the student before occurring to the teacher. For example, Blake once asked, "Do I need to read this slow? In my reading classes they always told me to go slow and pronounce every word. I'm thinking that doesn't always help." He knew that a focus on speed would not necessarily lead to meaning making.

At all our meetings, Syed and I spent time reading and talking about Sudan. When the conflict broke out between Chad and the Darfur region of Sudan, there was a great deal about that struggle in the newspapers, and I'm sure there was interested talk in Syed's home. At a session taking place at the time of heated battles, Syed confidently took over our discussion. He ended our talk, before I could pose my routine questions (above), by asking me, "What did you learn today?" Somewhat surprised, but pleased, I replied that I'd learned about possible causes of the conflict between the people of those regions, where exactly the deadly cross-border raids were happening, and how the fighting might turn out. I then expected, "How did you learn that?" but instead, Syed asked, "And who did you learn that from?" I answered honestly, "Syed, I learned it all from you. You're a wonderful teacher." I realized that both Syed and I had taken a tremendously important step. Never before had we challenged the old way of doing business, meaning that I was in charge. Syed, at last, was sure enough of himself to claim his rightful place in the learning experience. And I was sure enough of myself to become a student learning from an informed teacher. The students in this chapter and I reclaimed reading by using miscue analysis to open the door to reflective teaching and learning. We reclaimed teaching as a space in which relationships are built, grow, and are used to support the use of strategies for more effective and efficient reading.

References

Avi. (2002). *Crispin: The cross of lead.* New York: Hyperion Books for Children.
Boyle, T. C. (1996). *The tortilla curtain.* New York: Viking.
Buck, P. (1931). *The good earth.* New York: John Day.
Campos, M. D. (1990). *Reading the world: Interview with Brazilian educator Paulo Freire.* UNESCO: Courier.

Dillon, L., & Dillon, D. (2002). *Rap a tap tap: Here's Bojangles—think of that!* New York: Scholastic.

Goodman, K. S. (1994). Reading, writing, and written texts: A transactional sociopsycholinguistic view. In R. B. Ruddell, M. R. Ruddell, & H. Singer (Eds.), *Theoretical models and processes of reading* (4th ed., pp. 1093–1130). Newark, DE: International Reading Association.

Goodman, Y. M., & Marek, A. (1996). *Retrospective miscue analysis: Revaluing readers and reading.* Katonah, NY: Richard C. Owen.

Goodman, Y. M., Watson, D., & Burke, C. (2005). *Reading miscue inventory: From evaluation to instruction.* Katonah, NY: Richard C. Owen.

Hamilton, V. (2005). *Time pieces: The book of times.* New York: Scholastic.

Miller, A. (1953). *The crucible.* New York: Viking Press.

Moore, R., & Gilles, C. (2005). *Reading conversations: Retrospective miscue analysis with struggling readers.* Portsmouth, NH: Heinemann.

O'Brien, T. (1998). *The things they carried.* New York: Broadway Books.

Siegel, M. (1988). Sketch to stretch. In J. C. Harste & K. G. Short with C. Burke (Eds.), *Creating classrooms for authors: The reading writing connection* (pp. 528–536). Portsmouth, NH: Heinemann.

Watson, D. (1978). Reader selected miscues: Getting more from sustained silent reading. *English Education, 10*(2), 75–85.

Watson, D. (Ed.). (1987). *Ideas and insights: Language arts in the elementary school.* Urbana, IL: National Council of Teachers of English.

CHAPTER 4 EXTENSION

Conversations: From Miscues to Strategies

M. Ruth Davenport

In the main part of the chapter, Dorothy Watson drew upon miscue analysis to learn who Blake and Syed were as individuals, discovered their views of reading and themselves as readers, and then thoughtfully selected strategies that provide the best support to move them forward from the most important starting point for learning: what they are doing well right now. Another miscue analysis procedure, Over the Shoulder (OTS) miscue analysis (Davenport, 2002), also allows teachers to nurture readers.

The Conversations Begin

OTS is an untaped, informal reading assessment based on the principles and theoretical foundations of miscue analysis, and takes place during brief one-on-one conferences between a reader and a teacher. The student reads a brief passage aloud, usually from a self-selected text. The teacher looks over the reader's shoulder at the same text, reading from the reader's text. When the teacher hears a miscue, she writes down what the reader said (the observed response) and what the text said (the expected response). She then quickly determines whether the miscue: (1) was self-corrected; (2) was not corrected but did not significantly change meaning; or (3) was not corrected and did result in a meaning change. Without stopping at the point of miscue, the reader and teacher talk at various points during the session to clarify confusions or to discuss particular meaning-change miscues. At the end of the brief conference, the teacher requests and scribes the reader's retelling, shares what is written on the form (as evidence of smart thinking, meaningful predictions, or appropriate self-corrections), shares something the reader is doing well (Celebration Point) and suggests a strategy to use when reading alone (Teaching Point).

Before starting individual OTS conferences, the teacher has many discussions with the whole class to build students' understandings of the reading process, miscues, reading strategies used by proficient readers, and reading assessment through miscue analysis. This may be done regardless of the age of the students, as even very young children are able to understand such discussions when they are presented in developmentally appropriate ways. This creates a classroom culture in which discussions about miscues are woven into conversations throughout the day in a variety of literacy-learning contexts. The message is clear: talking about reading is valued and supported.

Focus of the Conversations

Whole-class discussions mean students have a chance to become keen observers of readers, reading, and OTS as a reading assessment. When they come to their first OTS session they know what to expect and know the teacher will talk with them about their reading process. The teacher also might conduct OTS conferences in front of the class, first with adults and then with student volunteers. These conversations are demonstrations in which the children learn the mind of proficient readers; teachers and students discuss their observations of the readers' actions, with the focus on the construction of meaning, not just saying all the words on the page.

The conversations continue when students meet with the teacher (me, in this case) individually in OTS conferences. The focus remains on the sense children make of the texts they're reading. Following is an excerpt of a conversation between Josh (a pseudonym), who was a second grader, and me. Josh had been reading Clifford books, stories about a very big red dog. I reminded Josh about what he'd retold in a previous conference with me and then we moved to a brief retelling of what he'd read since then.

Ruth: What was the last part about? We stopped where he was just getting out of the tunnel . . .
Josh: He jumped out onto the street.
Ruth: [Long pause, so I decide to ask a question to help him continue, but not lead him.] OK, then what?
Josh: There was a town he didn't recognize.
Ruth: [After another long pause; these pauses continued throughout the first few moments of the retelling, suggesting Josh's tentativeness in believing in himself as a meaning maker.] OK, good, what else?
Josh: And then he climbed a bunch of buildings and he saw his mom's house and he walked there and he got involved in a football game along the way.
Ruth: OK, you're doing great. After the football game, what did he do?
Josh: He found his mom's house and he, then he went home.
Ruth: What did he do while he was at his mom's house?

Josh: He ate dinner—and then he went home and he saw Emily Elizabeth 'cause
 they got home at the same time.
Ruth: OK, good for you, what a great reader you are, Josh!

(Excerpted from Davenport, 2002, pp. 171–173)

After the reading and retelling, I presented Josh with many Celebration Points.
I showed him the miscues that he self-corrected and told him what a smart reader
he was. I did this by showing him the column for *self-corrections* on my record sheet
of his reading. I said, "OK, remember this one [pointing to the column] is where
you fixed it [a miscue] yourself; look how many times you did that. . . . That means
you were really listening carefully as you were reading." His broad smile suggested
his sense of accomplishment and growing sense of feeling valued as a reader. I
selected two brief Teaching Points that I believed would support Josh in understanding this and future stories. First, we discussed his use of the naming strategy,
in which he substituted "Bone" for "Bonnie":

Ruth: Bonnie—have you ever heard that name? [He shakes his head.]

By telling him Bonnie's name, helping him understand that Bonnie is a name, and
then seeing whether he recalled it in subsequent readings of Clifford books, I
provided Josh with a basic bit of information. It turned out that he did remember
Bonnie as he continued his reading of the books.

The other Teaching Point was Josh's omission of the word "drawbridge."
Skipping the word made the sentence semantically unacceptable. Josh sensed that
something was amiss as he said, "Uh-oh, this can't be good," as he left the word
and continued reading. I brought Josh back to the place in the book at which he
made the decision to skip the word.

Ruth: . . . And this one [miscue] changed the meaning. . . . Look at this again
 [looking at "drawbridge," showing him the word in the text, and pointing to
 the illustration]. Do you know what kind of bridge that is?
Josh: No.
Ruth: Let's look at this word again where it tells you—do you see two words inside
 that word?
Josh: Braaww. [He starts sounding it out with a "b" sound.]
Ruth: It starts with a "d."
Josh: Drawbridge. [He just says it.]
Ruth: Drawbridge—have you ever heard of a drawbridge?
Josh: Yep.
Ruth: OK, what does a drawbridge do?

Josh explained, "It opens when a boat comes, so no cars go, and it breaks and it
lands on the boat and the boat sinks and everybody drowns and then it closed."

I pointed out that he could use some sounds, but that illustrations carry a lot more meaning and may be relied upon to get at that meaning. I ended the session by pointing out more of his self-corrections, another celebration.

The Conversations Continue

So much of what we do with learners is based on trust and our ever-growing relationships. We convey to our students the expectation that they will grow and improve as readers and let them know we have faith in them to apply what they're learning when reading independently. They come to expect that the strategies they're trying will indeed work and support their comprehension. We verbalize our confidence in them and give them evidence of their improvements, such as the information gleaned from OTS. They gain self-assurance as they see the use for the skills they've learned and observe how miscue analysis helps them know what they do now as readers and how to improve.

The opportunity to give kids feedback about our observations can take place within the context of OTS discussions of the Celebration Point and Teaching Point, casual conversations about reading throughout a school day, and through continued whole-group modeling and debriefing. There is "no real stopping point" when it comes to these thoughtful discussions about reading. Miscue analysis is indeed "worth the investment in time and intellect," and we know this to be true when we see our students become more engaged readers, we notice they are more willing to be literacy-learning risk takers, and we find ourselves improving as reflective teachers.

References

Davenport, M. R. (2002). *Miscues not mistakes: Reading assessment in the classroom*. Portsmouth, NH: Heinemann.

5

DECIDING TO USE REAL BOOKS

The Higher Power of Lucky

Renita Schmidt

The current political climate encourages and in many cases requires a return to teaching that demands scripted texts and leveled materials in reading programs that claim to increase achievement in an efficient manner with all children. This insults teachers and students. Long ago, Dewey (1938) challenged educators to make experiences more educative by considering the quality of what we do in school by selecting "the kind of present experiences that live fruitfully and creatively in subsequent experiences" (p. 28). Dewey's understanding of reclaiming curriculum most certainly applies to reading.

In this chapter I focus on what we as teachers can do to reclaim our position as professional decision makers in the classroom. I share an experience I had reading *The Higher Power of Lucky* (Patron, 2006) with a small group of fourth graders to illustrate how to prepare to discuss quality, challenging literature with children. I describe my experiences as a way to demonstrate the kinds of knowledge teachers use to choose a variety of real (trade) books and literature discussion methods for reading that is important in children's lives. I argue that if teachers want to reclaim their proper place as curricular decision makers in the classroom, we must articulate our preparation and decision making so that we are once again trusted as experts.

Decision Making as Preparation Rather than Planning

The decisions teachers make are important keys for being good teachers (Anderson, 2003). Although some decisions appear to happen instantly and others happen over longer periods of time, some involve individual students and others involve groups, some focus on behavior while others focus on academics, all decisions rely on assessments teachers make about how to teach students in school. Effective reading teachers understand that reading involves much more than decoding letters into sounds and answering comprehension questions (Peterson & Eeds, 2007). Elementary teachers, in particular, feel a strong responsibility for decisions that help children become better readers.

I believe *planning* is difficult, even impossible, for teachers until students in the classroom are present as participators. In fact, I suggest that reclaiming reading means conceptualizing teaching decisions as preparation, rather than planning. *Preparation* is the work teachers do prior to teaching during the school day in an attempt to ready the classroom for what may come during learning activity. Preparation for literature discussions includes three components that I make visible in my practice in this discussion: knowledge of the students, knowledge of quality children's literature, and knowledge of sociocultural and transactional reading theories and methods.

As with all teaching, preparation begins with knowledge of the students: who the students are, what interests them, and what they can accomplish. Children in our classrooms often live controversy that is not that different from the characters they meet in *The Higher Power of Lucky*, and all readers bring their identities and experiences into every transaction with text (Rosenblatt, 1978). Some come to school hungry, some come to school sad because of what happened before they arrived, and some know that there isn't enough money to buy food for dinner when they return home. All children are figuring out their places in the world.

The *Lucky* literature discussion group was made up of six fourth graders who participated in an after-school tutoring program in their Title I elementary school in an urban Southern school district. I immediately learned that each student participant was a unique and individual reader. Although labeled as struggling to reach proficiency on the state standardized test, they were motivated to read because they, as Guthrie (2000) suggested, also saw themselves as close to achieving proficiency, a positive label. One girl and two boys were Caucasian, two boys were Latino, and one boy was African American. The majority of students in the school are from a variety of Latin American countries and are native Spanish speakers learning English. The children chose to participate in the group.

Just as important as knowing students, preparation includes accessing our knowledge of the tools of our trade, in this case an awareness of the vast amount of quality children's literature available for school reading. Teachers can find engaging and beautiful children's books for every topic and interest. When teachers reclaim reading and view school as an agent for social change, we select reading materials about important world issues and engage children in discussions about them.

I chose *The Higher Power of Lucky* because I fell in love with its pristine author craft the first time I read it. I saw the literary elements in the book as a way to move readers toward dialogue and help make their literary experiences interesting and motivational. And I believed children could find pleasure in reading it. Plus, *Lucky* is filled with real-life societal issues rarely accessible in materials for reading in school settings, such as unemployment, inadequate support checks, and living in unusual housing like water tanks and welded-together trailers. It is common for teachers to avoid discussions about tough topics (Schmidt, Armstrong, & Everett, 2007), but I knew Patron believed children could handle thinking about these issues. I believed fourth graders could engage in interesting conversations with each other about the book.

Finally, preparation includes considering sociocultural and transactional theories about language and teaching reading that ensure children are co-creators of meaning during literature discussions. Because all texts require readers' transactions to create meaning, teachers can prepare for literature discussion but can never completely plan for what may happen in any teaching setting. I intended the *Lucky* discussions to be student led and not school-like, and similar to discussions people have when they read books outside of school. I saw my role as a mediator for these students and their teacher working in a community of learners (Whitmore, 2005). I wanted to work with the children but also wanted the children to work with one another to transact with the text and expand its potential for meaning through interpretation (Peterson & Eeds, 2007).

The Book, the Plot, the Author, and the Controversy

In 2007 *The Higher Power of Lucky* by Susan Patron won the Newbery Medal for the best children's literature of the year. Almost immediately, people around the United States began to call it "the scrotum book." *Lucky* is the story of a young girl named Lucky whose mother died tragically in an accident. Although Lucky seems to have a happy life living with her guardian, Brigitte, in the California desert, she worries that Brigitte really wants to return to her homeland, France, leaving Lucky homeless and in an orphanage. Patron spent ten years writing this tender story of a little girl struggling to answer life's difficult questions and find her "higher power" (Oleck, 2007).

The book is filled with real-life people and issues. In addition to the tragic death of Lucky's mother, readers learn about Lucky's father, who abandoned her and provides inadequate child support, a town filled with people who receive government surplus food, and what it means to be the member of an "Anonymous" group (such as Alcoholics Anonymous). Lucky's friend Miles is cared for by his grandmother because his mother is in jail for selling marijuana. Although these issues trouble some adult readers, who believe children must be sheltered from life's difficulties, in the end it is Patron's use of the word "scrotum" in the opening lines of her novel that ignited the most controversy about this book. The story says:

> Sammy told of the day when he had drunk half a gallon of rum listening to Johnny Cash all morning in his parked '62 Cadillac, then fallen out of the car when he saw a rattlesnake on the passenger seat biting his dog, Roy, on the scrotum.
>
> *(Patron, 2006, p. 1)*

In her Newbery Medal acceptance speech, Patron (2007) shared the way she dealt with the fallout from her choice of events and word: "In a librarianesque way, I set up a folder: SCROTUM. Soon that folder was inadequate" (p. 8). The folder contained everything from nasty emails and scrotum-inspired products like T-shirts and mouse pads to a listing of *The Higher Power of Lucky* in Wikipedia under the word "scrotum" (no longer active). But Patron also explained her need for readers to respond to the book: "I was interested in relating to readers on a deeply emotional level, in a way that could help them figure out a little about how the world works" (p. 9). Patron believed children could relate to and learn from the text, showing a direct bridge between author's intent and the decisions teachers make in choosing materials for school literature discussions. "Scrotum" was such a "sensitive word and subject, something a little bit taboo" (p. 9) that it showed the reader that Brigitte loved Lucky so much that Lucky could ask her to explain what a scrotum is.

Preparing for *The Higher Power of Lucky* Discussions

I was intentional about preparing rather than planning in order to encourage spontaneity during our discussions. I read the book ahead of time, I listed several words from the text I found interesting (i.e., "anonymous," "splendiferousness," "antivenom," "eavesdropping"), and I thought about possible stopping points within the book that might encourage extended discussions (a discussion of Higher Power, for example). I believed the children would shape these decisions, but I wanted to be ready in case they did not, so I recorded them in my own response journal.

I also gathered an assortment of materials (a kind of text set) that contextualized the setting, language, and characters and I placed these items in a "survival back-pack" like the one Lucky always carries. My backpack held a French–English dictionary; printed pages from the International Guild of Knot Tyers (www.igkt. net); a copy of *Are You My Mother?* by P. D. Eastman (1960); Mojave Desert Wildlife (http://digitaldesert.com) pictures of a Red Racer, a cholla burr, and a chukar; a map of California that showed the Mojave Desert; pictures of the Coso Mountain Range (http://maps.google.com); art materials including colored pencils, markers, assorted pens and pencils, large construction paper; and response journals for the children.

Jane, the children's teacher, had taken both an early literacy and an intermediate-grades literacy course with me. Jane believes her students develop strong literacy from her use of a wide range of transactional literacy methods that includes read-alouds, independent reading, whole-class novel reading, literature discussions, and writer's workshops. Jane was interested in having her students read a new award-winning book, wanted to watch me lead the discussion, and hoped to participate in the discussion herself at least part of the time. We spoke about the controversies associated with *The Higher Power of Lucky*, and Jane did not believe anyone in her classroom community would feel overly concerned or upset by the discussion. She contacted the parents to let them know what we would be reading and doing. Working in a state that has high levels of children living in poverty and some of the lowest test scores in the nation, I entered the classroom hoping the discussions would help the children when it came to testing time. The prohibitive impact of high-stakes testing made me feel responsible for careful use of the time given to me for reading and discussion with these fourth graders.

Our *Lucky* discussions occurred twice a week for eight weeks. I audio-recorded, listened to, and transcribed the discussions for closer analysis. Children read portions of the book on the days I was not in attendance, and most students responded in personal journals that contained space for writing and sketching. Responses were meant to be authentic and personal, not teacher-controlled assignments.

Getting to Know the Students

Initially, I felt concern about having only one girl in the group. Eight of my 18 years of teaching experience were in fourth grade, and I knew that being the only girl in a group of boys could be difficult for some preadolescents. Lily was absent the first time the group met, but approached me the second day with these words: "I play softball. I'm going to get a softball scholarship to go to college. Where are you sitting? I like to sit by the teacher." My fears about this lone girl holding her own with the boys in the group quickly eased. Lily found ways to make her thoughts about the story known. She wrote in her response journal regularly and was excited to talk with me privately about the book every day when I arrived.

Billy, a quiet African American boy, was the soft-spoken connector in the group. When Billy had something to say, he used words like, "I'm thinking about . . ." or "This is like. . . ." The response connections he made were more often oral than written and almost always related to popular culture, especially television programs and video games. Early in the first book discussion, however, he asked an important question pertaining to a character named Short Sammy. "How can Short Sammy drink a half-gallon of rum and still survive?" This difficult question caused immediate but short-lived tension for me as a visiting teacher to this classroom because I wasn't completely sure alcoholism was a sanctioned topic. Over time, however, the topic actually helped me consider how texts can elicit and help young readers discuss controversial issues. I did not shy away from any topic a child broached in our discussions.

James and David quickly established themselves as the leaders of the group. Besides being physically larger than the other children, they were active during discussions and seemed accustomed to hearing their voices as authorities. Jane verified this observation in an email exchange: "As you pointed out in your field notes, James and David are leaders in my classroom. They have many friends and are often chosen first for teams on the playground."

When James (a native Spanish speaker learning English) noticed the frequency of French words in the text early in the discussion sessions, he told me, "I'd like to learn another language." Indeed, his response journal held a special page for storing the list of new French words he discovered as he read. David enjoyed answering questions that others had about the text, typically bringing forth literal facts he felt would be important for discussion. For example, on the second day, David asked, "Can I tell them what 'pop. 43' means?" But this was quickly followed by a question to me: "Don't you think that's important to know?" "Pop. 43" refers to the population of the town where the story takes place. David often saw literal facts as critical, but he was also socially adept and knew ways (like verification from the authority figure) to make certain his ideas were heard and accepted as important by everyone in the group.

Andrew wanted to be a leader in the group and made sure he was always in close proximity to James or David. He often expressed doubts about whether or not he would be able to complete the reading to prepare for discussion: "I have a game tonight. I don't know if I'll have time to read all that." But he always came to discussion prepared with the chapters read ahead of time. Andrew was not confident as a reader and may have wanted me to think he didn't have time, rather than believe him incapable of accomplishing the work.

The sixth participant, Dominic, always had a smile on his face, and although he kept us laughing and often eased tension, his words and questions about the reading were insightful. "How did Lucky's mother get electrocuted?" "What's a meanness gland and do we all have one? . . . I think I do, especially when people break things that belong to me." Dominic was also highly interested in the novel's mention of the word "scrotum."

The Discussions

In the first chapter, Lucky is spying on an Alcoholics Anonymous meeting when she hears Short Sammy talk about drinking a gallon of rum and reaching "rock bottom" when his dog Roy is bitten on the scrotum by a rattlesnake. I knew Patron felt that this was a topic children could understand but I was tense about whether the children were mature enough to handle these ideas. I decided to broach the topic immediately and began our first discussion by telling the children the book had some parts in the story that many people did not consider appropriate for children their age. When one of the children said, "Like what?" I asked them if they knew what "Anonymous" groups were.

"Oh, yeah," said Dominic. "That's when someone drinks or smokes too much. There's Gamblers Anonymous, too." He seemed nonplussed, so I moved ahead with my own self-described weak definition of scrotum.

"Well, there's a word in this first chapter that's part of a male's anatomy, but not a female's." And as the children looked at me inquisitively, I added, "It's called a scrotum. Do you know what that is?"

Their heads nodded assent, but no one said a word. I let the topic drop and we proceeded to read the first two chapters aloud and interact as we read. Students agreed to read the third and fourth chapters during their independent reading time before I returned.

On the second day of discussion several days later, I asked students to draw a sketch of their favorite part in the first four chapters as a way to get them thinking about the book again. The children immediately drew a variety of scenes. Two were interested in Short Sammy's story about Roy being bitten on the scrotum by the rattlesnake, and three were interested in the scene when Lincoln puts graffiti on a sign. After seeing a road sign that read "Slow Children at Play," Lincoln decides that he must add a colon so the sign will read "Slow: Children at Play" to ensure accurate understanding and deter anyone from thinking the children in Hard Pan, California, are "slow."

Dominic's interest lay in his sketch of Short Sammy as he passed out from drinking too much rum (Figure 5.1). Dominic was intent on making the prickly thorns on the cactus, the hot sun beating down on Short Sammy, and red marks emanating out of the dog's body to indicate the dog's pain from the rattlesnake bite on the scrotum. It wasn't clear that he understood which part of the dog is the scrotum, but he realized the dog was in pain. He drew Short Sammy falling out of the car just as he visualized it in the book, and the rattlesnake sneaking away under the black Cadillac. Dominic's sketch shows exquisite detail and good understanding of the story's gist.

FIGURE 5.1 Dominic's Sketch of the Desert Setting and Characters after Drinking the Rum

As the children drew, they talked and altered their sketches to reflect growing understanding that evolved from the dialogue. For example, Billy asked about Sammy's consumption of a gallon of rum, which initiated a serious discussion of alcoholism. Suddenly, Dominic relieved group tension by chuckling loudly as he added Roy (the dog) howling in pain to his picture. The students knew Roy was howling because he had been bitten on the scrotum by a rattlesnake. "Oh, now I know what a scrotum is," said James, and everyone laughed, although it still wasn't clear what they each thought.

David announced that his picture was finished and showed his rendition of an early scene when Lincoln adds graffiti to a road sign. As Dominic listened intently, he added the "Slow Children at Play" sign to his own sketch, almost as an affirmation of David's thinking and an example of the ways both sketching and discussion contributed to the social construction of meaning making (Vygotsky, 1978; Wells, 1999).

Through David's sketch, I also understood his interpretation of the story. He visually created an authentic desert scene, with a broiling orange sun, sand underfoot, blue sky, and a thorny cactus. Central to his picture was the road sign after Lincoln added the colon. David dressed Lucky in a skirt, perhaps to signify the gender differences between Lucky and Lincoln, even though Lucky was never described in the story as wearing a skirt. He placed a hat on Lucky's head, and drew her holding a book or sheet of paper, perhaps to further signify her intelligence. He made sure a smiling Lincoln was holding the pen and Lucky's dog, HMS Beagle, was nearby. The details indicated David's close reading of the first four chapters.

As Dominic's and David's sketches indicated, these fourth graders were struck by the strong characterizations in the story and quickly pointed out that Lucky was the main, although certainly not the only important, character. Their understanding was emphasized throughout our discussions. In the children's words:

> I wish Lucky was in our class. She would know so much about science.
>
> *(Lily)*

> Miles is such a pain. He's just like my little brother, always asking for cookies and wanting someone to read to him.
>
> *(James)*

> I'd never eat Short Sammy's food. It's so greasy and bad for your health.
>
> *(Dominic)*

The children also highlighted the subtle and yet powerful symbolism throughout the book. Lincoln's knots, government surplus food, the urn, Brigitte's red dress, the parsley grinder, and the book *Are You My Mother?* (Eastman, 1960) are important. Although the language used by the children was not sophisticated, the symbolic meaning they gained in reading was inherent in their responses. For instance, the children compared Lincoln's knot tying to problems in the world. One of them said, "Lincoln is smart and he unties the knots. Smart people can figure out the problems in the world too. Just like Lincoln."

Brigitte's dress was another symbol the students related to themselves. "Sometimes I put on my father's Army stuff. It makes me feel grown up," said David.

"Yeah, I think Lucky feels grown up when she puts Brigitte's dress on too," agreed Lily.

The students loved sticky notes and used them to mark favorite parts in the reading, which they often read aloud during our discussions. Everyone scanned the text regularly for answers and clues that proved why we were thinking specific ways about characters and plot.

Sometimes the children's responses surprised me because they were so different from my own. For example, one day when I asked the children if they would like to live in Hard Pan, they immediately said no. When I pressed them to explain why, they said, "It's so hot in the desert. There is nothing there except bugs and snakes. No people live there . . . they only have pop. 43" (a population of 43 people). I wanted them to think more deeply about relationships and suggested that they consider the people who lived in Hard Pan near Lucky. I asked, "But, wouldn't you like to be friends with Lincoln and Miles? And how about Short Sammy . . . wouldn't you like to try his food?"

While the children considered my questions thoughtfully, they were not interested in trying Short Sammy's food. "Too greasy," was Dominic's immediate response.

"Hard Pan is a boring, hot desert where no one would care to live," said David.

"Brigitte is from France," said James. "France is way more interesting than Hard Pan."

In our work together, the response journals served a number of purposes, but I'll readily admit they were not always what I expected, either. For example, I hoped the journals would serve as an effective place for students to write rich narratives in response to the text and I did not immediately see such writing. In fact, I was initially disappointed by what I saw as lack of substance and process, but when I looked more specifically at what students were accomplishing (rather than at what they were not accomplishing), I found evidence of thoughtfulness in sketches, lists, and questions. For instance, several students methodically copied and tried out the pronunciations of the French words in the book. The lists were typically read, reread, and even performed during our discussions. The dramatization of "speaking French" took on a silliness that was perhaps also insecurity about speaking another language.

Students also used the journal as a way to remember questions they wanted to discuss during our time together. James' questions included: "What is a burro?" "What is pop. 42 and pop. 43?" and "What is a *maman*?" His question "How can nail polish kill ants?" spawned talk that both clarified meaning for James and helped him make a connection to his own experience with nail polish remover. "Oh, it's nasty! I have to leave the room when my mom uses that stuff! Now I get it!"

Many people feel topics like the ones mentioned in this chapter are too difficult for elementary-aged readers (Bosman, 2007); however, the interest and sensitivity the children displayed in their discussions prove just the opposite. Because of the way Patron presented Lucky's predicaments, the children were able to make connections to other texts and to their own lives. During the third discussion, the students discussed chapter 6. In this chapter, Brigitte returns to the trailer with government surplus commodities. To begin the discussion I ask, "What are commodities? Brigitte brought home a bag of commodities."

Andrew: They're like food stamps.
Jane: We know about food stamps. Don't we?
Andrew: My mom gets them.
Nita: Brigitte had a letter in her hand when she came back too. What was that? Can you remember? Look on page 46.
Billy: It was a letter from Lucky's dad.
Nita: Yes, and something else too.
Billy: A check.
Nita: Right, and what about the check? We're finding out something else about Lucky's dad here. Right?
Jane: Does he seem very supportive?
Dominic: No. Is that abandonment?
Jane: Well, not really. He hired Brigitte to stay with Lucky.
Nita: He sent money but did he send Lucky a letter?
Dominic: No. She's sad and depressed.
Nita: We don't hear from Lucky's dad's point of view.
Dominic: (making reference to a character in another novel, *Ruby Holler*, by Creech, 2003, that they were reading in their classroom) We heard about another guy being depressed today. Mr. Trepid was depressed in *Ruby Holler*. He got money, but he cheated someone to get it.
Jane: He did kind of cheat him out of money. Didn't he?
Billy: Brigitte and Lucky seem worried about the money situation.
Dominic: They don't have a car.
Billy: Yes, they do.
James: It's a Jeep or a Cadillac.
Billy: They have to have gas, and food, and money to pay the electricity. They need a lot of stuff so they need a lot of money.
Nita: Do you think Lucky's worried about something in particular?
Dominic: Yes, the money.

The students understood that Lucky and Brigitte needed a certain amount of money to live and that Lucky's father didn't always send enough money. The students' talk indicated their knowledge of specific household bills like those for gas, food, and electricity, and connections between food stamps and government surplus food. The children also realized that Lucky's father didn't always send enough money and did not directly communicate with Lucky and Brigitte. Depression is not an easy topic, but students knew that when someone is depressed they are sad. The tone during this segment of the discussion was respectful and inquisitive. Dominic even broached the subject of "abandonment" as he puzzled out his thinking about Lucky, her father, and Brigitte. That word is not used in the text, but Dominic had heard it somewhere and was trying to define it here in relationship to Lucky.

On the last day of our discussions, several of the children approached me with private statements about the book, almost as if they wanted me to know how seriously they were considering things that happened to Lucky. James came first, carrying his open book where I could see sticky notes protruding on one page. "Brigitte told Lucky what a scrotum was. I'm glad she did. She's a good mother."

Next came Billy, the quietest student, who did not often complete written responses in his journal. "What was your favorite part, Billy?" I asked him.

"My favorite part was when Brigitte said, 'If somebody hurts you I'll rip their heart out.' See? It says it right here. She really loves Lucky."

Billy's strong point made me question my own assumptions about what I had initially mistaken for a lack of understanding and perhaps even laziness when he was reluctant to write things down in his journal. His thinking challenged me to remember that children comprehend in different ways and teachers must always think about ways to discover what children know rather than what they don't know.

Reclaiming Teaching

Reclaiming teaching involves teacher decision making that encourages and supports critical conversations about sensitive topics like race, class, sexuality, and religion (Schmidt et al., 2007). Preparing to read controversy and engage in dialogue in a supportive setting such as our literature discussion group gave children time to ponder the problems and fate of book characters not that different from themselves.

Student engagement in dialogue comes more easily when you talk about real-life issues that matter. I was able to give up some of the control I sometimes felt necessary in my past teaching when I watched specifically for times when students took the lead during discussion. My role as a mediator became more obvious when the students needed clarification of a tough issue (why Lucky had an urn that contained her mother's ashes, for instance) or further help finding a good resource (content materials about the desert plant and animal life.)

If we continue to let outside parties like publishers and legislators make decisions about schools, classrooms, and students they do not know, we will not be able to do our work as teachers effectively. Long-range curricular plans required for submission at the beginning of the school year do not contain room for adaptations when current world celebrations and traumas occur. They are not sensitive to special circumstances that cannot be planned for ahead of time. The students in every classroom deserve teacher professionals who prepare for study with them because they know them as unique individuals. Choosing a variety of rich materials, providing lots of time to read, and responding through a variety of means allowed the children who read *Lucky* with me to grow as aesthetic, efferent, and critical readers. *Lucky* was filled with complex knots that gave us opportunities to talk and think about the world. A great text will do that for you, too.

References

Anderson, L. (2003). *Classroom assessment: Enhancing the quality of teacher decision making.* Mahwah, NJ: Lawrence Erlbaum.

Bosman, J. (2007, February 8). With one word children's book sets off uproar. *New York Times.* Retrieved from http://www.nytimes.com/2007/02/18/books/18newb.html

Creech, S. (2003). *Ruby Holler.* New York: HarperCollins.

Dewey, J. (1938). *Experience and education.* New York: Touchstone.

Eastman, P. D. (1960). *Are you my mother?* New York: Random House.

Guthrie, T. (2000). Engagement and motivation in reading. In P. D. Pearson, R. Barr, & P. Mosenthal (Eds.), *Handbook of reading research, Vol. 3* (pp. 403–422). Mahwah, NJ: Lawrence Erlbaum.

Oleck, J. (2007). The higher power of Patron. *School Library Journal, 53*(3), 42–45.

Patron, S. (2006). *The higher power of Lucky.* New York: Atheneum Books.

Patron, S. (2007). Newbery Medal acceptance speech: The bathtub storyteller. *Children and Libraries, 5*(2), 6–9.

Peterson, R. & Eeds, M. (2007). *Grand conversations: Literature groups in action.* Portsmouth, NH: Heinemann.

Rosenblatt, L. (1978). *The reader, the text, the poem: The transactional theory of the literary work.* Carbondale, IL: Southern Illinois University Press.

Schmidt, R., Armstrong, L., & Everett, T. (2007). Teacher resistance to critical conversations: Exploring why teachers avoid critical conversations in their classrooms. *New England Reading Association Journal, 43*(2), 49–55.

Vygotsky, L. S. (1978). *Mind in society: The development of higher psychological processes.* Cambridge, MA: Harvard University Press.

Wells, G. (1999). *Dialogic inquiry: Towards a sociocultural practice and theory of education.* Cambridge: Cambridge University Press.

Whitmore, K. F. (2005). Literature study groups: Support for community building in democratic classrooms. *Talking Points, 17*(1), 13–22.

CHAPTER 5 EXTENSION

Real Books: Including LGBTQ Literature

Rose Casement

By sharing her experience of preparing for and working with a group of fourth graders reading Patron's award-winning book *The Higher Power of Lucky*, Schmidt makes clear that her theoretical beliefs about reading include much more than word decoding skills and superficial comprehension questions of the kind that so often drive the teaching of reading in scripted, leveled reading instruction. The children who read *Lucky* responded to the symbolism in the story, constructed new understandings through discussion, and demonstrated a depth of understanding and growth that clearly reflects Schmidt's confidence in them to understand complex issues in stories.

I agree with Schmidt that *The Higher Power of Lucky* is an excellent piece of writing. Selecting this book for its *real* qualities challenged many assumptions about the ability of children to understand difficult concepts. Authors like Patron weave together tapestries of story that wrap around a reader for just a moment in time, but the experience becomes part of a greater understanding about our human family. As we reclaim reading, we need to think carefully about book selection for the twenty-first century.

Issues in Children's Literature: Bringing Real Voices into the Classroom

Lucky is often not an easy read. But as teachers we know that good literature can be a window for children to become acquainted with children and families both like and unlike their own. Not many children are likely to live in a remote desert in the southwest United States with a population of 43, or live in a welded together string of trailers, or ever know someone who lives in an abandoned water tank, let alone know the owner of a dog that has been bitten on the scrotum by a rattlesnake, but they have an opportunity to read themselves there together.

The real-world concepts that are included in Lucky's story (death, abandonment, child support, alcoholism, and unemployment) would be unlikely subjects for study on their own in a fourth-grade classroom. However, included in the story they support its realism and provide an interesting context for gaining a deeper understanding of characters dealing with real-life issues. To continue to insist that children cannot deal with issues that surround them in daily life feels disingenuous at best and dishonest at worse. Further, a climate of silence can create a hostile environment for children.

Bringing LGBTQ-Inclusive Children's Literature into the Classroom

Lucky's search for her own higher power is much the same as that of young people who are beginning to self-identify as gay or lesbian and are searching for their place in the world while struggling with discovering their own identity. With an estimated 4 million children in the United States living with one or both parents who identify as gay or lesbian (Austin, 2010), it is unlikely that a teacher will not at some point have a student with same-sex parents. And, with gay men and lesbians being more open about their sexual orientation, children are likely to know self-identifying family members and friends. Contemporary lesbian, gay, bisexual, transgender, and questioning (LGBTQ) issues are now ever-present in the media, such as gays in the military, gay marriage, and tragedies associated with anti-gay violence.

Given that more children self-identify as gay or lesbian at an earlier age, teachers are likely to have students who will need their understanding and support as they address their possible concerns and fears. We know that the fate of many students who have gay or lesbian family members or self-identify as gay and lesbian is to be harassed and bullied, sometimes for years. Gay slurs are one of bullies' best tools, and children perceived as being gay or lesbian are easy targets. Whether they are gay, lesbian, bisexual, or questioning their sexual identity, even if they are accepted at home, the pervasive attacks, both emotional and physical, at school and in the community lead far too often to hopelessness and suicide. These realities mean that more than ever we need to create a welcoming and safe classroom environment and talk with students about LGBTQ issues, and "the most obvious entrée into discussions around gay and lesbian issues . . . is through literature" (Hermann-Wilmarth, 2007, p. 347).

However, talking about including LGBTQ children's stories in our classrooms is like tackling the proverbial elephant in the living room. Even with the growth of children's literature in the area of books including gay and lesbian characters, it is not unusual for teachers to meet with severe reactions about their inclusion in the classroom. Regardless of chilling statistics about LGBTQ bullying and suicide, many pre-service teachers say they would not include LGBTQ literature in their future classrooms as it is unfit for children (Schall & Kauffmann, 2003).

However, the quality and literary merit of the books, the relevance of the books to contemporary life, and perhaps the greatest collateral gift, the fact that they can demystify the fears that children have about a group of people often victimized in school communities, are reasons to include LGBTQ stories in school. Since fear is often the catalyst for aggressive bullying, alleviating children's fears with stories they can relate to is certainly a good argument for their inclusion in the classroom.

Quality Books You Might Consider Sharing in Your Classroom

The ability to tackle complex issues in upper elementary classrooms through the discussion of more challenging literature is evident in Schall and Kauffmann's (2003) work in Kauffmann's fourth- and fifth-grade classroom when they introduced children's literature with gay and lesbian characters. During the discussion, "children questioned why they weren't told about the reality of gays and lesbians" (p. 41), compared stories about name calling, and agreed they were old enough to read and talk about the books. Schall and Kauffmann discovered that "students wanted to understand all kinds of relationships" (p. 40).

I always include award-winning books in which there are gay or lesbian characters in my children's literature courses. Most students say they couldn't introduce these books into their classrooms, and some also suggest that the authors have an agenda when they include these characters. Some cite religious reasons for not even reading any of these books. My consistent response is "Then what are you going to do when you have a student who has same-sex parents, or self-identifies as gay or lesbian, or wants to share about a friend or relative who is gay or lesbian?" Many feel that that these events will never happen, not realizing how likely it is that they already have, and that their reluctance to accept them has likely silenced the students. And there the elephant sits.

Harbeck (cited in Graziano, 2003), attributes most practicing teachers' decision not to include LGBTQ literature in their classroom to (1) lack of training regarding the issues; (2) their feelings of homophobia, keeping them from handling the issues; and (3) the most common, fear that their colleagues might think they are gay or lesbian. As teachers, we have a responsibility to move toward greater preparation and understanding by informing ourselves and finding the tools that can create greater understanding about people whom we don't know. What better tool can we provide than a good story inviting the reader to see from another's experience and perspectives?

Jacqueline Woodson is an incredible storyteller, and her books often include gay or lesbian characters who are authentic to the story, for example Staggerlee, who questions her sexual orientation in *The House You Pass on the Way* (1997), and Melanin, an African American adolescent in *From the Notebooks of Melanin Sun* (1995), who learns that his mother is in a relationship with another woman—

further complicated by the fact that she's white. Woodson writes stories in the real world, with real characters like people who surround us in our lives. I believe that if there is an "agenda," it is to silence characters like Woodson's and, in effect, silence the day-to-day lives of children who don't see their families, their friends, or themselves in literature and begin to believe that they are all alone.

In 2008, 14-year-old Brandon McInerney was so intimidated, or frightened, or enraged, that he was driven to murder makeup- and-jewelry-wearing Larry King (allegedly because the 15-year-old openly gay boy sent him a valentine). I believe a well-chosen book could have initiated a conversation that could have staved off such a tragic event. Everyone in the class could have benefited from a conversation reassuring students that when a student self-identifies as gay, it does not threaten anyone else's sexual identity.

Alex Sanchez's book *So Hard to Say* (2004), about a boy beginning to self-identify as gay and working through his issues with his friends, or James Howe's story *Totally Joe* (2005), about a boy who comes out as gay and deals with the issues that arise in a school setting, could have brought enough of the fears, concerns, challenges, and ways to meet some of those challenges into the conversations of the classroom so that King, a victim of a gunshot wound to the head, and McInerney, a victim of his own anger, fear, and hate, might have found some new understanding to take with them into their real-world conflict.

Silencing the needs of LGBTQ students and their loneliness, along with relentless bullying in classrooms, corridors, and school bathrooms, contributes to a frightening increase in suicide among early adolescent teens today. These tragic events are so stunning that concerned individuals, from media personalities to the president of the United States, have taken to the airways to assure LGBTQ young people that they are cared about and that things will get better. Now, it is the job of all of us to make that happen. In fact, stories that offer greater understanding about children with same-sex parents or children who identify as gay or lesbian may be the only way to help alleviate the vicious bullying that has infested American schools.

The following books present a glimpse into the lives of children who are living with same-sex parents, display non-traditional gender role identity, or have a relative who is gay or lesbian. They are good books for all children and create opportunities for great conversations and deeper understandings.

Elementary

dePaola, T. (1979). *Oliver Button is a sissy*. San Diego, CA: Harcourt.
Parr, T. (2001). *It's okay to be different*. New York: Little, Brown.
Polacco, P. (2009). *In our mothers' house*. New York: Philomel Books.
Richardson, J., and Parnell, P. (2005). *And Tango makes three*. Illustrated by H. Cole. New York: Simon & Schuster.

Upper Elementary/Middle School

Coville, B. (2003). *The skull of truth*. New York: Simon & Schuster.
Garden, N. (2000). *Holly's secret*. New York: Farrar, Straus &Giroux.
Heron, A., & Maran, M. (1991). *How would you feel if your dad was gay?* Illustrated by K. Kovick. Boston, MA: Alyson Publications.
Woodson, J. (2008). *After Tupac and D. Foster*. New York: G. P. Putnam.

References

Austin, P. (2010). Opening the door to tolerance. *Book Links, 19*(2), 42–45.
Graziano, K. (2003). Differing sexualities in singular classrooms. *Multicultural Education, 11*(2), 2–9.
Hermann-Wilmarth, J. (2007). Full inclusion: Understanding the role of gay and lesbian texts and films in teaching education classrooms. *Language Arts, 84*(4), 347–356.
Schall, J. M., & Kauffmann, G. (2003). Exploring literature with gay and lesbian characters in the elementary school. *Journal of Children's Literature, 20*(1), 36–45.

Cited Children's and Adolescent Literature

Howe, J. (2005). *Totally Joe*. New York: Simon & Schuster.
Sanchez, A. (2004). *So hard to say*. New York: Simon & Schuster.
Woodson, J. (1995). *From the notebooks of Melanin Sun*. New York: Scholastic.
Woodson, J. (1997). *The house you pass on the way*. New York: Random House.

6

TEACHING STRATEGIES THAT REVALUE ELL READERS

Retrospective Miscue Analysis

Koomi Kim and Yetta M. Goodman

When we first met Jorge, a fourth grader, and Dae Youn, a third grader, they were convinced that they were poor readers of English, and they believed that reading in their first language was very different from reading in English. Both of them participated in retrospective miscue analysis (RMA) sessions at an after-school program at a university-based literacy center for an academic year. By the end of the year, Jorge and Dae Youn were able to reflect on their reading, talk about reading with us, and revalue themselves as English readers.

In this chapter we focus on our role as teachers as we support English language learner (ELL) readers who are already able to read in their first languages. We describe the kinds of dialogues that helped Jorge, who read in Spanish, and Dae Youn, who read in Korean, come to understand the reading process and themselves as readers in two languages. Our analysis of these dialogues reveals that RMA is a powerful way to reclaim teaching in the ELL reading instruction context.

Why Retrospective Miscue Analysis?

Retrospective miscue analysis (RMA) involves a series of sessions beginning with students reading aloud an authentic text into a recorder. Next, individually or in small groups, the students listen to the recorded reading with a teacher to dialogue about their miscues and to talk about what they were thinking during the reading. RMA "illuminates the voice of the reader" (Goodman, 1998, p. 311), and therefore makes the reader's thinking accessible to the teacher.

RMA is humanistic and reflective teaching that contains dialogic and student-generated learning contexts (Goodman, 2003; Moore & Gilles, 2005). RMA sessions are collaborative and instructional means to help readers *revalue* their own reading process (Goodman, 1982; Goodman & Marek, 1996), thereby helping teachers reclaim teaching as they learn about the strengths and needs of their students (Moore & Seeger, 2009; Wurr, Theurer, & Kim, 2008/2009). Our focus in this chapter is on the way in which teachers can facilitate students' problem posing and problem solving through RMA discussions about their reading experiences.

Vygotskian (1978) and Freirian (1998) theories support such conversations. Vygotsky (1978) states that the intellectual elements learners acquire are directly related to how they interact with others in problem-solving contexts. Similarly, Freire (1998) suggests that opportunities for learners and teachers to work together to identify learning "problems" are crucial to learning because the concepts addressed are relevant to the learners and the learners play an active role in the learning process. The talk that takes place during RMA sessions, which we also refer to as conversations, is part of an interactive and dialogic inquiry process. Engaging in reflective teaching in this way is a means of reclaiming teaching as relational and informed by teacher knowledge, rather than deferring to a scripted or prescribed program.

We found RMA useful to document the growth of ELL students, including their attitudes, perspectives, and development as readers. In this chapter we focus on two elementary school-aged ELL readers. We discuss five major teaching strategies that help teachers reclaim teaching through critical dialogue with ELL readers. We examine opportunities for: (1) gathering information about the students' views of themselves as readers; (2) demystifying readers' perception that second-language (L2) reading is different from first-language (L1) reading; (3) helping readers find and select resources to support their reading; (4) exploring new language forms and vocabulary; and (5) teaching ELL readers to talk about reading.

Gathering Information about the Students' View of Themselves as Readers

We began our dialogues with Jorge and Dae Youn by interviewing them with an adapted Burke Reading Interview (Goodman, Watson, & Burke, 2005) for ELL readers. We modified the reading interview for ELL students by adding questions about their reading in languages in addition to English (Figure 6.1). The adapted Reading Interview provided us with insights into the students' views of themselves as biliterate readers, their views about the reading process and their thoughts about reading instruction. These questions provided us with ways to discover and understand the ELL students' perceptions of reading in their first language(s) and English. Too often, teachers focus so much on students' learning of English that they don't get to know about and make use of their knowledge and abilities in their first language. It is helpful for teachers to discover as much as they can about the language use of their students in their homes and communities. The Burke Reading Interview questions for linguistically diverse children illuminate students' literacy backgrounds and learning processes as resources for their reading in

---

Reading Interview for Linguistically Diverse Readers

- When you are reading in your first language (L1 – name language) and you come to something that gives you trouble, what do you do? Do you ever do anything else?

- When you are reading in English and you come to something that gives you trouble, what do you do? Do you ever do anything else?

- Who is a good reader that you know in (L1– specify language)?

- If you knew that someone was having difficulty reading in your L1 (specify language), how would you help that person?

- If you knew that someone was having difficulty reading in English, how would you help that person?

- How did you learn to read in your L1 (specify language)?

- How did you learn to read English?

- What would you like to do better as a reader reading in your L1 (specify language)?

- What would you like to do better as a reader reading English?

- Would you like to read a story in your L1 (specify language) in class and share your experience with the book with everybody in class? What story would that be?

- Which kinds of things do you like to read in your L1 (specify Language)?

- What languages do members of your family read and write?

FIGURE 6.1 Reading Interview for Linguistically Diverse Readers

English. We encourage teachers to add questions to gain insights into literacy uses in the communities of students with whom they work.

Through the interviews and our follow-up conversations, we learned about Jorge's and Dae Youn's personal interests, their schooling backgrounds, their literacy histories, their reading habits, their attitudes to biliteracy, and their preferences in reading in their first language. During the initial reading interview, Jorge, a fourth grader who had immigrated to the United States two years previously from Mexico, told us, "Spanish is easy but English is not easy." Dae Youn, a third grader who had immigrated to the United States a year and a half previously from South Korea, told us, "English is very difficult to see and read. Korean, I don't have see carefully." He was referring to the distinct orthographies he used to read: Korean, which is a syllabic writing system called Hangul, and English, which is an alphabetic writing system. Both Jorge and Dae Youn knew that English was different from their first languages, and they believed that it was more difficult than their mother tongues. We know such attitudes about languages influence learning to read. The reading interview allowed us to understand Jorge's and Dae Youn's self-perceptions of their challenges as readers in English. Although many ELL readers are proficient and confident in reading in their first languages, they often have preconceived notions of themselves as limited readers in English. Their lack of confidence often deters them from reading a range of genres for varied purposes as they do in their first languages.

In response to the questions *How did you learn to read in your L1?* and *What would you like to do better as a reader reading in your L1?* Jorge said, "I read in Spanish well and my mom reads to me all the time in Spanish. I can read it fast. I am a good Spanish reader." Literacy is valued in Jorge's family. His parents read to him in Spanish, and family literacy plays an important role for him. On the other hand, when we asked, *What would you like to do better as a reader reading English?* Jorge said, "I can't read fast, I want to read fast and I want to better. I can't read big words well. I can read well in Spanish but not English. I want to sound out better."

Jorge helps us understand what we have learned from a majority of ELL students. Although they focus on comprehension to make sense in their first language by using appropriate reading strategies and by using their cultural and background knowledge as they read, they view reading in English as a decoding and word identification process. Chin's study (1996) of ELL adult Korean students corroborates our findings. She provides documentation similar to ours regarding her ELL students' self-perceptions. One of her participants described reading in L1 and reading an English text:

> Korean is my first language . . . so what do you expect? I just read on . . . whatever I read in Korean, it flows naturally, and I hardly get stuck. In case I do, I can clarify it based on the context most of the time. If I can't, I don't care and keep going because I know that the meaning will be eventually made clear somehow.

The reader compared her "natural" Korean reading to reading in English:

> I learned that I should identify a subject and a predicate in each sentence to make reading easy . . . even now I stick to that approach. Whatever I read, especially when I am stuck on a complicated sentence, first of all I divide it into a subject and a predicate and I also tend to parenthesize adverbial phrases and put a dash before a relative clause . . . then I can fix it up most of the time. [Translated from Korean into English]
>
> *(Chin, 1996, pp. 75–76)*

In our conversations with a range of ELL students, the more we were able to help them see the ways in which they make sense while reading in their first language, the more they were willing to use their proficient L1 reading strategies when they read in English (Kim, Chin, & Goodman, 2004).

After the interview, we conducted a Reading Miscue Inventory (RMI) (Goodman et al., 2005). Each reader was audiotaped while orally reading an entire article or chapter in English they had never read before, without any help from the listener. We selected materials that we knew were of interest to each reader. The transcript of the tape recording was marked for the reader's miscues (or unexpected responses). The analysis of the miscues provided information about the reader's comprehension processes and strategies used while reading the text; the miscues were used as the basis for our subsequent RMA conversations.

Demystifying the Perception that L2 Reading Is *Different* from L1 Reading

Dae Youn believed that "English is very difficult." Each week, as we discussed with Dae Youn (in English) the importance of taking into consideration his successful reading in Korean and adapting his reading stance as he read English, he became more reflective about his reading in both languages.

Our conversations initially focused on the high-quality miscues the students made during their reading. High-quality miscues usually are syntactically (grammatically) acceptable and semantically (meaningfully) acceptable within the sentence (Goodman et al., 2005). Discussing high-quality miscues shows readers the intuitive knowledge they have about language cues and reading strategies. Readers also come to see how active they are in making sense of what they read as they read. At other times, we selected miscues in sentences that were not fully acceptable, not high-quality, particularly when these miscues revealed the strategies readers used to make sense, such as in the case of self-correction. Conversations about corrected miscues made visible for the readers why they decided to self-correct certain miscues and not others.

Here is a high-quality miscue from Dae Youn's analysis (see Note on p. 59):

easy

0606 "Now, I want to clean something else."

(James, 1972, p. 6)

Dae Youn told us that this was the first time he had ever heard himself read. The reading had been audiotaped during the previous RMA session. At first his reaction was negative. He said, "Oh, that is bad." However, when Koomi asked Dae Youn whether his substitution of "easy" for "else" made sense, he began to explore the meaning of what he was reading:

Koomi: Does the miscue make sense?
Dae Youn: That is not right.
Koomi: Does that make sense?
Dae Youn: Umm . . .

Koomi: Does it sound like language?

Dae Youn: Yes, I think so. I was thinking that he [Harry] was looking for something easy to clean. . . .

Next, Koomi and Dae Youn discussed another high-quality substitution miscue, "here" for "there":

> **Here**
> 2801 There is Grandpa.
> 2802 He is making
> 2803 a model ship

(James, 1972, p. 29)

Koomi: Does this make sense in the sentence?

Dae Youn: Yes, it is OK.

Dae Youn initially focused on his performance by saying, "This is not right." However, when we looked at his use of the semantic and syntactic cueing systems (meaning and grammar), we moved the conversation beyond the graphophonic cueing system (print). Many students don't realize that it is acceptable to make substitutions that don't change the meaning of a sentence, and that in those cases there is no need to self-correct. We discussed with Dae Youn the concept that predicting appropriate words in specific English language slots (such as *here* for *there*) showed his control over English grammar because it indicated that he substituted one part of speech for a similar part of speech. We assured him that these are the kinds of miscues that proficient English readers, like ourselves, often make.

RMA sessions provide teachers and ELL readers with opportunities to discuss how they integrate reading strategies with what they know about the language cueing systems, thereby showing them they know more about English than they think they do (Kim et al., 2004). The process of analyzing their high-quality miscues empowers them to shift away from their negative self-perceptions as ELL readers "who don't know" to a more positive view that focuses on the knowledge that they have and are able to bring to their reading in English.

During our RMA sessions, Dae Youn and Jorge were constantly encouraged to pose questions while talking about their reading processes. As we often shared with them the kinds of miscues we make as readers, the students gradually took control of the RMA sessions and initiated discussions about their own miscues. In other words, RMA is an excellent example of how reclaiming teaching involves allowing and encouraging students to *own* aspects of their own learning. In the following example, Jorge initiated the conversation. He became aware that he integrated multiple language cueing systems when he talked about his miscues. In this example, Jorge accepted his miscues and focused on the meaning of the sentence:

$ vived imaginación
0308 Come on, Katy! It's your vivid imagination.

(Non-word substitution miscues are unexpected responses that are not real words in the language; they are marked on the transcript with a $—a dollar sign.)

Jorge: I said it [imagination] in Spanish. It is the same thing! But I don't know the other word, *vi-vi-d* [reading the word *vivid* very slowly].

Our discussion about substituting *imaginación* for *imagination* included exploring with Jorge what he had to know in order to produce such a high-quality miscue in that specific context. We talked about how he used knowledge of his first language to make an understandable and acceptable substitution that he was able to translate from English into Spanish, and how that had helped him make sense of his reading. This example also illustrates how RMA positions learners as collaborators in the assessment process. Jorge's expertise in Spanish informed us about his ability in translation and we taught him why the substitution of *imaginación* for *imagination* was appropriate.

Helping ELL Readers Find Resources to Support Their Reading

Through conversations with students in our RMA sessions, we debunked the myth that instructional and leveled reading materials are more effective than reading authentic texts for improving students' reading. By using authentic texts, we showed readers how to connect their background and experiences with concepts they were exploring in the text and, at the same time, ways the text provided a rich venue in which to discuss language components such as vocabulary and grammar (Freeman & Freeman, 2006, 2008). For our RMA sessions we emphasized the importance of our students reading a variety of materials beyond their school textbooks by taking their interests and needs into consideration. Although we helped them with their textbooks when necessary, we spent more time helping them find materials that connected to their daily experiences and expanded their understanding of issues in the United States. We discussed the kinds of books they read in their native languages, and helped them consider multiple ways to select interesting material and find related texts in English. We helped the students find and read folk stories, comics, chapter books, picture books, and magazine articles. They also searched websites for readings on issues they already cared about and wanted to study. We used these materials in our instruction. We encouraged family members and teachers to involve the students in discussions of socioculturally relevant and engaging materials. With many opportunities to engage students with rich texts, our ELL students connected what they read to their backgrounds and built connections to their growing understanding of American culture. The students learned that what made reading hard was their lack of prior knowledge to make sense of what they read.

Using varied texts from diverse genres helps ELL readers realize their capabilities and limitations, which are not simply their "English-related problems." Transcending their limitations by moving beyond instructional textbooks and adventuring into more complex but interesting reading material is central to the processes of inquiry, problem posing, and problem solving. There are lists of magazines and books for children and adolescents available on the Internet. When students are involved in finding such lists, they learn to search and read the Internet at the same time that they are learning to read English print. As our RMA sessions progressed, Dae Youn described the importance of reading interesting material.

> I like animal books or comics. I like Pokémon, Picachu talks to me when I read Pokémon. Picachu is not really animal but he is half animal and monster. I want to read and know more about him. And, I like the half monster and half cheese man [referring to the book *The Stinky Cheese Man and Other Fairly Stupid Tales*, by Jon Scieszka (1992)].

It is imperative to teach students how to look for and select resources so that they are able to explore reading in depth and move beyond their perception that they are only capable of reading a narrow range of prescribed materials. The greater the variety of materials they read in English, the better they get in their reading of English. As they become more confident in themselves as biliterate, they are able to use each of their languages as resources for the other. Reclaiming teaching means teachers reclaiming their decision making and reading material selection process for all students.

Exploring New Language Orthography and Vocabulary

Because many Asian languages have very different orthographies, or writing systems, there is a common assumption that the reading processes are also very different. RMA helps readers see the universal elements, common to reading in all languages, in constructing meaning. Jorge and Dae Youn, like many ELL readers, initially held perceptions and attitudes that their L1 was quite different from English, and these concerns affected how they approached their readings of English texts. They learned they could understand unfamiliar language and complex grammatical structures when they had knowledge about the subject they were reading and used the context of what they were reading, just as they did while reading in their first language. Making connections helped to ease their "border-crossing" (borrowing Giroux's term, 1993) between their first language and ELL contexts. The more connections they made from one language to the other, the more they were able to contextualize their new linguistic and socio-cultural knowledge.

Discussion questions such as "What does that mean to you?" or "Have you read anything similar in Korean (L1) or Spanish (L1)?" helped our conversations by focusing the readers' construction of meaning on making connections with their own experiences and revaluing the resources and support they could access from their first language. In our dialogues regarding the reading process, a number of critical learning moments occurred (Goodman, 2003) that were opportunities to teach strategies for learning new vocabulary. One valuable type of dialogue was about non-word-substitution miscues. We wanted to help Jorge and Dae Youn recognize how they were using their knowledge of language in a specific context to make sense of the text. Dae Youn explored one of his non-word miscues in the following sentences:

$ *vasim*
0502 It is fun to vacuum!

$ *vasim*
0503 "Whirrr" goes the vacuum.

Here is our RMA discussion after Dae Youn listened to his own reading of the passage above. (Remember that he had previously read the complete story without any help from us.)

Dae Youn: That [referring to the word *vacuum*] is a hard word to say.
Koomi: Can you predict the meaning?
Dae Youn: I know the meaning but I can't say the word.
Koomi: Do you want to say it in Korean?
Dae Youn: Chongso ki ro chongso ha da [cleaning with a vacuum cleaner].
Koomi: You made a very good prediction. How did you make the prediction?
Dae Youn: I understand the story, and also there is a picture of *chongso ki* [vacuum cleaner]. There are many hints.

An RMA discussion with Jorge focused on the following non-word substitution, mentioned briefly earlier:

$ *vived imaginación*
0308 Come on, Katy! It's your vivid imagination.

Jorge: I don't know that word, *vi-vi-d*.
Koomi: What do you think is the meaning? Do you want to make a prediction?
Jorge: It is something about imagination.
Koomi: You are making a very good prediction. What kind of imagination is it?
Jorge: Good imagination? A lot of imaginations?
Koomi: How did you make the prediction?

Jorge: Katy was making a lot of good imaginations.

Koomi: Yes, Katy was making very lively imagination. How do you say it in Spanish?

Jorge: Muy viva, la imaginación muy viva . . .

In these and other RMA sessions, Dae Youn and Jorge predicted the meaning of unfamiliar words by considering the context and relating it to concepts in their first language. We wanted them to become more consciously aware that they were doing this. The examples show that they went beyond the word and sentence levels by integrating (often intuitively) information they had about vocabulary and orthography from the language cueing systems with their comprehension of the text. Dae Youn and Jorge took risks to predict the meaning of unfamiliar words, and their predictions usually made sense since they were taking into consideration the context of the entire story rather than merely trying to sound out and pronounce isolated and/or unfamiliar words.

Teaching ELL Readers to Talk about Reading

As their time with us progressed, Jorge and Dae Youn gained more English with which to talk about their reading processes. Some of the terms they used with understanding included "miscue," "cueing systems," "prediction," "meaning," "making sense," "making connections," "context," and "text." They also used grammatical terms that related to parts of speech, such as "verb," "pronoun," "noun," and "adjective." In our final RMA session we asked, "Do you think you are a different reader today than before we started our RMA sessions?" Here are the responses from Dae Youn and Jorge:

Jorge: Predictions . . . we talk about make predictions and I make connections. I think I know why I like some books and I don't like some books.

Dae Youn: I read more now, I talk books and my miscues. Miscues, I make smart miscues. Also, you ask many questions if reading make sense. I think about that . . . I think both Korean and English.

We take advantage of opportunities to talk with our students in their L1 when possible, because reclaiming teaching involves bringing our students into the learning–teaching equation as often as possible. When we are not able to use their first language, we have students who speak the same language meet in small groups to discuss the reading process with each other in their first language. We then come back together and discuss their developing concepts in English.

The use of specific language (terms or vocabulary) in the context of dialogue and in more than one language whenever possible helps the students develop concepts about reading. Our dialogues are engaging and constructive in terms of demystifying and revaluing students' contradictions about how they perceive themselves as readers in any language. With time, ELL readers become aware that reading in their first language is similar to reading in English. In this way, they support and enhance their conceptual understandings of the language we use in reading in English.

Jorge and Dae Youn enjoyed our conversations about reading. They were always eager to talk with us. As a result, we learned that it is critical for our students to know that we respect and value their perspectives as part of the process of becoming literate in English and developing biliteracy.

Summary

Dialogues with ELL students provide assessment data that inform teachers about how to develop ELL literacy instruction. We learned that ELL readers initially tend to focus on the syntactic and/or the graphophonic cueing systems, rather than integrating the cueing systems simultaneously with the focus on meaning making, as they know how to do in their first language. This is probably due to a focus on reductionist instruction based on the surface features of language skills, vocabulary, and grammar.

World knowledge, cultural literacy, content knowledge, and critical literacy have been underrated for ELL students, especially elementary-aged students. Eventually, as we talked with them about how they read in their first, second, or third languages, Jorge and Dae Youn came to see that the priority in reading in any language is making sense.

Through our RMA sessions, ELL readers came to perceive their reading in English as an integrative meaning-construction process. Exploring their strengths in reading in their L1 became a resource for reading in English (Ruiz, 1988). They no longer viewed literacy in English as an intimidating experience. Reading in English lost its mystery and the students revalued themselves as biliterate and bilingual language users.

References

Chin, C. (1996). Korean ESL readers' perceptions about themselves as readers and about reading in English. Unpublished doctoral dissertation. The University of Arizona, Tucson.

Freeman, D., & Freeman, Y. (2006). *Teaching reading and writing in Spanish and English in bilingual and dual language classrooms* (2nd ed.). Portsmouth, NH: Heinemann.

Freeman, D., & Freeman, Y. (2008). *Academic language for English language learners and struggling readers*. Portsmouth, NH: Heinemann.

Freire, P. (1998). *Learning to question: A pedagogy of liberation*. In A. Freire & D. Macedo (Eds.), *The Paulo Freire reader* (pp. 186–230). New York: Continuum.

Giroux, H. (1993). *Border crossing: Cultural workers and the politics of education*. New York: Routledge.

Goodman, K. S. (1982). Revaluing readers and reading. *Topics in Learning and Learning Disabilities, 1*(4), 87–95.

Goodman, Y. M. (1998). Retrospective miscue analysis: Illuminating the voice of the reader in reflections and connections. In A. Marek & C. Edelsky (Eds.), *Essays in honor of Kenneth Goodman* (pp. 311–331). Cresskill, NJ: Hampton Press.

Goodman, Y. M. (2003). *Valuing language study: Inquiry into language for elementary and middle schools*. Urbana, IL: National Council of Teachers of English.

Goodman, Y. M., & Marek, A. (1996). *Retrospective miscue analysis: Revaluing readers and reading*. Katonah, NY: Richard C. Owen.

Goodman, Y. M., Watson, D., & Burke, C. (2005). *Reading miscue inventory: From evaluation to instruction* (2nd ed.). Katonah, NY: Richard C. Owen.

James, T. (1972). *Harry helps out!* Mahwah, NJ: Troll Associates.

Kim, K., Chin, C., & Goodman, Y. M. (2004). Revaluing the reading process of adult ESL/EFL learners through critical dialogues. *Colombian Applied Linguistics Journal: Issues on Literacy Processes, 6*, 42–57.

Moore, R., & Gilles, C. (2005). *Reading conversations: Retrospective miscue analysis with struggling readers, grades 4–12*. Portsmouth, NH: Heinemann.

Moore, R., & Seeger, V. (2009). *Building classroom reading communities: Retrospective Miscue Analysis and Socratic circles*. Thousand Oaks, CA: Corwin Press.

Ruiz, R. (1988). Orientations in language planning. In S. McKay & S. Wong (Eds.), *Language diversity: Problem or resource?* (pp. 3–25). New York: Newbury House.

Scieszka, J. (1992). *The stinky cheese man and other fairly stupid tales*. New York: Viking Children's Books.

Vygotsky, L. (1978). *Mind in society*. Cambridge, MA: Harvard University Press.

Wurr, A., Theurer, J., & Kim, K. (2008/2009). Retrospective miscue analysis with proficient adult ESL readers. *Journal of Adolescent and Adult Literacy, 51*(4), 224–233.

CHAPTER 6 EXTENSION

Scaffolding Young Children to Value Themselves as Readers

Carol Lauritzen

Tobe, a 9-year-old third grader, started his tutoring session with me with an announcement: "My mom found me in the family room and I was reading by myself."

While Tobe sounded quite matter-of-fact, I'm sure my voice revealed my joy. "Wow," I said, "that's exciting news! Tell me about it."

"Well, I was bored and I wanted something to do, so I thought, 'I can read a book' and so I got *Henry and Mudge* (Rylant, 1987) and read a story."

On this momentous day, Tobe took a tremendous step forward as a reader. Six months earlier, when we started working together, Tobe only read leveled readers, the little books that have a couple lines of text on each page. He was "glued to print" and addressed every unknown word in a left-to-right, sound-it-out fashion. While he was adept at using picture cues, he did not use a placeholder strategy or a "what makes sense" strategy or even a "skip it and come back to it" strategy. Reading was a chore he did because the adults in his life made him do it. When we started our times together, reading would have been his last choice of activities. At that time, he explained, "I'm not good at reading." As our work progressed, Tobe read voluntarily for the first time in his life. I believe that through our weekly tutoring sessions, in which I scaffolded his use of meaning-making strategies and demonstrated reading as a pleasurable activity, he not only started acquiring the strategies that good readers use but also began to value himself as a reader.

Just as Jorge and Dae Youn used retrospective miscue analysis (RMA) with Kim and Goodman as a means to revalue themselves as readers, young children can benefit from viewing their reading through the lens of miscue analysis and through discussions about their reading. The process for younger readers, however, may require more teacher feedback and support. Rather than using a taped procedure such as RMA, I generally provide information about miscues verbally during one-on-one reading conferences with young readers. A typical conference begins with the child bringing a book he or she is currently reading. I ask for a brief summary that allows the reader and me to enter into the story together. I typically say something like, "Tell me what has happened so far so I'll understand what you are going to read to me." After that, I ask the child to read aloud for several pages while I take note of his or her miscues. When we come to a logical stopping point, we have a conversation about the events, characters, or other aspects of the text. Then I select a few miscues that provide instructional talking points and direct the child's attention to them. Most often, these are meaning change miscues. Here is an example with Tobe reading the Magic Tree House book titled *Dinosaurs before Dark* (Osborne, 1992).

The text: *Jack reached into his backpack and pulled out a pencil and a notebook.*

Tobe: Jack (pause) into his . . . Jack reached into his backpack and pulled out a
p . . . (looks at the picture) notebook and a notebook . . . and pulled out a pen
and a notebook.

Tobe stopped before going on to the next sentence and after a brief pause he reread the entire sentence, self-correcting all the miscues.

After Tobe had finished reading the entire page and we had talked about why Jack was taking notes, I turned back to the sentence and said, "I noticed that when you came to this word [*reached*] you skipped it and then you self-corrected. What were you thinking?"

Tobe said, "I didn't know that word but when I saw *backpack*, I just thought what would make sense."

I asked about the second part of the sentence. Tobe said, "I looked at the picture and saw that he was writing in a notebook but then I knew that wasn't right because the word started with a 'p' and there was *notebook* at the end of the sentence so then I thought *pen* but *pen* doesn't have 'c-i-l' so then I knew it was *pencil*." I responded, "You are doing what good readers do. You are making sense and you are using the letters to help you figure out a word that would make sense." When asked six months earlier what he did when he came to something he didn't know, Tobe answered, "sound it out." Now he had a repertoire of strategies including "skip it and get clues," "correct it if it doesn't sound right or it doesn't look right" and "think to see if it makes sense."

In a very short time, when young children are coached about miscues in terms of "sounding right," "looking right," and "making sense," they can gain explicit knowledge about their reading process and learn helpful strategies to make meaning with text.

Teachable moments also occur when a child does not self-correct and meaning is lost, which is when it is appropriate to self-correct. The teacher might say, "I noticed that you read *blue* here. Why do you think you did that? Did that make sense?" This is a reminder to the child that meaning is at the heart of reading and it also gives the child a chance to think about his or her reading process and to self-correct; it gives the child a sense of control over his or her reading.

The conclusion of an RMA conference is particularly important. The reader should leave the conference with a positive sense of him- or herself as a reader. The teacher accomplishes this by identifying for the reader what makes him or her a good reader. Teachers of young children need to explicitly tell students the strategies good readers use and to specifically point out when the young reader has made use of one of these strategies. In this way, we provide the language of what good readers do so that children can take ownership of both the strategies and the language that describes them. This is particularly important for children who are struggling to become competent in reading. Like ELL students, young children often are focused on graphophonics. Guiding them to also use syntax and semantics as important language cues helps them see reading as a process of making sense. When teachers scaffold young readers through reflection on miscues, they learn to think about their own reading and gain control of their use of strategies. Each child needs to know and be able to state the traits he or she shares with good readers.

While it has been assumed that young children do not have the mental sophistication to be metacognitive, children like Tobe prove that assumption to be wrong. The language of reading made available through RMA enables a shift in the locus of responsibility that is critical to reclaiming the teaching of reading—from the teacher explaining the miscue to the reader, to the teacher asking the child about the miscue, to the child identifying and explaining the miscue for him- or herself. And, in the end, children use this self-knowledge to value themselves as readers, and teachers use it as a vehicle for reclaiming the teaching and learning of reading.

Note

For more information about children's reflections on miscues, see Davenport, M. R. & Lauritzen, C. (2002). Inviting reflection on reading through over the shoulder miscue analysis. *Language Arts, 80,* 109–118.

References

Osborne, M. P. (1992). *Dinosaurs before dark.* New York: Scholastic.

Rylant, C. (1987). *Henry and Mudge: The first book of their adventures.* Boston: Houghton Mifflin.

7

THE REALITIES OF CONFERRING WITH YOUNG ADOLESCENT READERS

Jennifer L. Wilson and Kristen Gillaspy

> The more we listen to students, the better our advice and help will be.
> *(Seventh-grade teacher)*

When we began observing teachers who regularly used reading conferences in their middle school classrooms, we noticed a surprising similarity. When students entered the classroom before the bell even rang, many surrounded the teacher, saying, "Are you going to conference with me today?," "When will it be my turn to conference?," or "Add me to your conference list! I have to tell you about my new book!" Whether or not the students could articulate why they looked forward to conferring, we saw that these reader–to–reader discussions created a more compassionate and respectful assessment and teaching experience for both the student and the teacher, and one which both parties anticipated.

We decided to study middle-level teachers, Jennifer as a teacher educator and Kris as a literacy coach, to gain insights into how to humanize literacy assessment processes. We viewed reading conferences as a critical assessment and as a teaching practice for involving learners in their own evaluation. Reading conferences reclaim reading by providing literacy support that is specific to students' needs and informed by their strengths and perspectives, particularly for struggling readers. The instruction is not set prior to knowing the students; rather, teaching is reclaimed because it is informed by teachers' understanding of the reading process matched to the students with whom they meet.

Harvey and Goudvis (2000) argue that reading conferences create spaces for students to "share their thinking with us," and offer a more accurate method for assessing students' abilities to make meaning from the texts they are reading (p. 189). Reading conferences are a vehicle to identify concerns and to build upon students' strengths by making informed instructional decisions (Gill, 2000).

Bennett (2007) explains, "We fail the learners in our classroom when we assume what students know and what they need. We need to talk to them to know for sure" (p. 124).

In our effort to encourage use of reading conferences in middle school classrooms, we needed a greater understanding of how teachers currently use conferences. Through observations of middle-level English/language arts teachers in South Carolina, we identified the most frequent kinds of conferences conducted and how those conferences reflected teachers' theories on reading and influenced students' reading identities.

Conferring with Young Adolescents

Conferring is a component of a "reading workshop" (Allen & Gonzalez, 1998; Atwell, 1998; Robb, 2000), in which students' independent reading of a wide variety of books is the crux of instruction. During independent reading time, as students engage in individual reading, the teacher holds individual reading conferences. Luke and Freebody (1997) argue that reading is a collaborative act that results in growth in the students' "meaning making capabilities through talk" (pp. 189–190). The teacher holds reading conferences with a few students each day, which enables a constantly changing and current understanding of the readers in the classroom (Flint, 2008; Gill, 2000).

Many scholars support reading conferences with adolescent readers. Atwell (1998) primarily focuses on comprehension discussions with students. She relates the talk she has with students about texts to the type of literary discussions she has around her dining room table with friends. Atwell's purpose is to give her students space to share their reading in talk that is "filled with jokes, arguments, stories, exchanges of bits of information, descriptions of what we love and hate and why" (p. 32). Her approach to reading conferences is informed by Rosenblatt's (1978) reader response theory. According to Rosenblatt, transaction is "an active process lived through during the relationship between a reader and a text" (p. 21). Atwell does not look for one right answer from her students during the conferences, but instead wants to know how they transacted with the text and what ideas and thoughts were created from that interaction. Teachers reclaim reading when they rely upon students' construction of text as a foundation for teaching, rather than seeking predetermined answers to predetermined questions.

Conferring is reclaiming the teaching of reading because it puts the learner and a particular text at the center of instruction. Reading conferences offer teachers of young adolescents a pedagogy that is developmentally appropriate. For example, middle-level teachers need to focus on the different literacy needs that come with reading a larger variety of genres and working with more complex texts. Santman (2005) explains that in her classroom, students read self-selected books while she meets with individual students for conferences. She suggests using a conference to "assess the student and determine something" to "teach him or her as a reader that day" (p. 8). Often she finds that she must design instruction at the site of the student's reading to help students with challenging text.

Teachers of young adolescents also must be sensitive to the emotional needs of older readers. Moore and Hinchman (2003), in response to "renewed attention to upper-grade reading and writing" (p. 2), argue that reading conferences are one of the most effective ways to work with struggling adolescent readers because they "protect students' privacy and self-esteem" (p. 160). Though respecting all students is important, young adolescents are especially vulnerable to criticism and negative self-images (Bomer, 1999). Robb (2000) understands that reading instruction should support students "who search for their adult identity and yearn for independence and control over their lives" (p. 13). In reading conferences with this age group, teachers protect space for students' voices to be heard and documented.

The Nature of Middle School Reading Conferences

In our work we found that conferences were not a frequently used tool in the classrooms of teachers who work with young adolescents in South Carolina. Many teachers we spoke with cited lack of time and/or lack of knowledge about what to say or do in a conference. We wondered whether conferring was equally important in the older grades (as we believed) and how it was different than or similar to conferences in the primary grades. We audiotaped conferences and discussed them with teachers who used conferences frequently in their classrooms. We observed conferences with students in various homogeneously grouped classes, including but not limited to advanced, proficient, and basic, according to the schools' structures. We also observed conferences that were conducted with students who represented a range of cultural and socioeconomic backgrounds. As we observed and spoke with these teachers, we saw the complexity of how conferences in the middle grades can be used, how they mirror teachers' theories of reading, and what their impact is on both learning and identity.

We identified three types of reading conferences teachers use with young adolescents: comprehension, strategy, and progress. We describe each of these and provide examples that illustrate them.

Comprehension Conferences

> They [reading conferences] tend to be informal "chats" between students and me about what they are reading.
>
> *(Sixth- to eighth-grade teacher)*

The most common type of conference teachers reported implementing and that we observed were comprehension discussions. In comprehension discussions the teacher focused on the student's meaning making with the text by having the students provide evidence of their text comprehension. These conferences reflected varied perspectives on text comprehension. Some teachers assessed students' literal comprehension through their retellings of the text. Other teachers focused more on analytical comprehension, or literary interpretations, asking for analysis of characters, conflict, or author's purpose. And some teachers moved to more critical components of student comprehension by exploring the theme of a text or through connections to world issues. Atwell (1998) explains that in these types of discussions the talk often moves "beyond the teacher's manual to new issues—reading process, analyses of authors' styles and techniques, relationships between reading and writing, between one text or author and others, between literature and our lives" (p. 34).

   In the following excerpt, a seventh-grade student and teacher engage in a comprehension discussion. Prior to the excerpt, Jessie, the student, led the discussion by retelling the first portion of the story and sharing her connections. (Underlined words represent overlap in the speakers' turns.)

T: This might be tough because I know you're only halfway finished, but because you're making such strong connections, I think you are also hinting around at making a claim about the theme of the book. What do you think the theme of the book will be? Who's the author?

J: Um (looks at book) Audrey Shafer.

T: OK, what do you think she was trying to say by writing this story? You know, like the big picture? What are we left with?

J: It could change, I guess, 'cause I'm not done, you know.

T: Right, but at this point. Just think like a reader. What might the overall point be?

J: Um, well like someone helping him, whoever it is. I guess that's the point. But also I guess like he's a little kid, you know, and now he's all alone with no parents or anything. So maybe it's something about that?

T: OK, keep talking about that. What would be the point of a story about a little kid living alone and dealing with all that tragedy?

J: He has to be tough and he has courage. But I guess he was kind of scared too. That's why he didn't want to tell about his uncle 'cause he didn't want to have to go live with somebody else.

T: So the theme could <u>be</u>

J: <u>Um</u>, something about how you have to like keep going even when things are so bad like they are for him. It's just really sad but you have to be strong and keep going.

T: What makes you think that?

J: Well, if he'd just given up and told someone, he would have to live somewhere else and that's just not what he wanted. Plus, once he's being taken care of, he just has to keep going and be brave even though he's all by himself.

T: Oh, OK, I <u>see</u>

J: <u>Like if it</u> was me, I'd freak out. Like, I don't know if I could've done all that and like not told. I'd just be scared to be alone all the time. But I'd feel the same way, too, you know 'cause I wouldn't want to go live with another person. He already wasn't with his mom and dad so . . . you know . . .

This conference was a comprehension conference focused on the theme of the book Jessie was reading, *The Mailbox* (Shafer, 2006). *The Mailbox* tells the story of a young boy who finds a new adoptive parent when his guardian dies. Since Jessie was already beginning to make connections with the text in the conference, the teacher suggested she think about the theme. Jessie initially hesitated, saying, "It could change, I guess, 'cause I'm not done, you know," but eventually offered her thinking about bigger issues in the text. She said, "Um, something about how you have to like keep going even when things are so bad like they are for him. It's just really sad but you have to be strong and keep going." The teacher's question, "What makes you think that?" led Jessie to go a step further with her thinking about the theme, and Jessie returned to the initial connections she made in order to explain how she began to determine what the theme might be.

Most teachers we observed, though attempting to create a student-centered atmosphere in the conference, were still working on the assumption that the meaning students were expressing was based on a specific, often singular, under-standing of the text. Most of the reading conferences we saw in this category focused on retellings, summaries, connections, and specific questions about figura-tive language, author's craft, and story elements. In comprehension conferences the teacher primarily gathered data about the student's understanding and connections to the text meaning and did not directly address or teach a specific comprehension strategy or analyze text features.

Strategy Conferences

> I feel like my conferences were unproductive, and I didn't really know what strategies to focus on.
>
> *(Sixth-grade teacher)*

Teachers also used reading conferences to focus on reading strategy instruction, particularly with adolescents who were experiencing difficulties with reading in school. In these conferences, teachers often chose protocols such as over the shoulder miscue analysis (OTS, Davenport, 2002) and retrospective miscue analysis (RMA, Goodman & Marek, 1996; Moore & Gilles, 2005) (see Martens & Doyle, Watson, and Kim & Goodman and their extensions in this volume). Both processes, founded in miscue analysis, focus on the strategies students successfully employ to make meaning from text. Davenport (2002) explains that miscue analy-sis "is a tool that allows us to explore why students make unexpected responses when they read" (p. 32).

In this type of conference, teachers provided students with instruction focused on a reading skill or strategy, addressed miscues, analyzed words, provided direct vocabulary instruction, or highlighted specific reading strategies such as predicting, inferring, etc. during conferences. In strategy conferences, the goal seemed to be that students gained perspective for how they apply "their knowledge of language to construct meaning while they read" (Moore & Gilles, 2005, p. 3).

The following example is an illustration of a student and teacher engaged in a strategy conference. Prior to the excerpt below, the student read a section of his current independent reading text aloud and provided a retelling. The teacher then focused the discussion toward helping the student, Jeremiah, gain a new strategy for determining an unknown word.

T: All right, um, that's pretty good. I want to ask you about one word. That word (points at *gravely*, which Jeremiah skipped during his reading and now pronounces as a nonsense word).

J: Gravvely? (said with a short [a] sound)

T: What does that mean? Look at the whole sentence like we do with *Watsons* [*The Watsons Go to Birmingham*, Curtis (1997)].

J: (Reads) *His parents froze like statues and looked at each other gravvely.* (Stops reading.) Weirdly? Like in shock, I think?

T: OK, like maybe in shock. It's actually pronounced *gravely*.

J: Gravely?

T: Mmhmm. And the way you know that, what part of that word do you recognize?

J: The -ly.

T: OK, you see the -ly. What about the <u>rest of it?</u>

J: <u>Oh, grave</u>.

T: Grave. What is a grave?

J: What is a grave? (laughs)

T: A grave, yeah.

J: What you're put into when you die.

T: OK, so it's where you're buried, right? So when you add an -ly to it . . .

J: Mmhmm

T: Think about the meaning of a grave; you know it's where you are put when you're buried. What else do you know about the word *grave*? If it has to do with where you're buried, what kind of feeling does it probably have?

J: Sad.

T: It's probably sad or really serious?

J: Mmhmm.

T: Yeah, 'cause like when . . . you know death, that's pretty serious. So if we say that we look at each other gravely, what does that probably mean?

J: Serious -ly.

In this conference, Jeremiah read aloud from a section of a fantasy book, *Heir to Fire* (Worley & Dubisch, 2006), which is the story of Ryan Morales, a boy living in Arizona who is tested when a portal to a lost city opens in the desert. The teacher had Jeremiah read a portion of the text aloud, made notes on the miscues he made in the moment, and then worked with him to think through one particular miscue where Jeremiah produced a non-word substitution. In the above excerpt, the teacher directed Jeremiah to the substitution *gravely*. The teacher first asked him, "What does that mean?" Then she led Jeremiah through the process of using context clues, when she said, "Look at the whole sentence." Jeremiah produced a meaningful prediction, "in shock," but it had a slightly different meaning than "gravely."

At this point, Jeremiah's teacher changed her tactic and led him to break the word apart in order to look for familiar words, saying, "What part of that word do you recognize?" The teacher demonstrated for Jeremiah the thought process for considering the connotations of the word *grave* that might apply to the character's parents in the story. For example, she said, "If it has to do with where you're buried, what kind of feeling does it probably have?" as well as, "OK, so if his parents, *his parents froze like statues and looked at each other gravely.* What else in that sentence tells you that they looked at each other seriously?" During the conference, Jeremiah answered the teacher's questions, often in one- or two-word responses.

While the teacher attempted to provide strategy instruction, we feel that the importance of a strategy lesson is to help readers see their own effective strategies and use them more consistently. Here, the teacher focused on meaning making, but appeared uncomfortable with allowing Jeremiah to construct meaning that didn't match her interpretation. This was similar to some of the comprehension conferences we saw in which teachers were looking for one specific interpretation of the text. In strategy conferences, teachers prioritize the student's awareness of strategies that are helpful in meaning construction rather than that the student's meaning match the teacher's.

We saw that teachers generally used strategy conferences when they perceived students as struggling in an effort to help them with meaning construction, while they used comprehension conferences with students they saw as proficient. However, as we see from the quotation that introduced this section, many teachers felt unsure as to what strategies they should teach during a conference. Interestingly, only one teacher told us she used a formal protocol, running record, to assess reading strategies during the reading conferences. Though we saw teachers take notes of students' miscues, they did not have a strong foundation in OTS or RMA, and the strategy lessons we observed reflected a skills and accuracy perspective about reading. It became clear that the majority of teachers in this study viewed miscues through a deficit lens, and subsequently focused on certain skills they felt the student should be able to demonstrate.

Progress Conferences

> [Reading conferences] tend to be informal "chats" between students and me about what they are reading.
>
> *(Eighth-grade teacher)*

The majority of the conferences that we saw were ones in which the teacher checked on reading progress. In progress conferences, teachers talked to students about the number of books they had read, whether they had completed their reading journal, their score on a comprehension test, etc. In other words, these conferences focused on the procedures of managing reading rather than the processes of reading. While these were not always the only method used during a conference, we found that teachers often started with progress comments like "What book are you reading?," "Do you like it?," "What page are you on?," and "How many books have you read this week?" but then quickly moved to other types of discussions. Atwell (1998) suggests using this type of monitoring for progress. She also looks for patterns in students' reading behaviors such as their ability to determine whether they can successfully commit to a book, as well as what emerges for each reader in terms of interests in topics, authors, and genres.

In progress discussions the teacher sets the tone of the conference, attempts to put the student at ease, and holds students accountable for their reading. The following excerpt provides an example of a teacher engaging in a progress conference with Ryan:

T: OK, Ryan, that looks like a new book since last time. What's the title?
R: *The Thief Lord* [Funke & Latsch, 2002].
T: When did you start reading this?
R: Um, about three days ago.
T: All right, and so how far are you?
R: Um, like 20 or so pages.

The teacher recognized that Ryan had a new text and checked on his progress. After getting a sense of how his reading was going with the new text, she continued the conference with a comprehension discussion to get a feel for his thinking about the text.

A second example of a progress conference, between a teacher and Hannah, illustrates how progress conferences often led into strategy or comprehension conferences:

T: OK, tell me how it's going so far.
H: I don't know.
T: How far are you?
H: Page 42.

T: OK. Let's see what you're thinking about it so far. Tell me how the book is set up, because I think this book is set up <u>differently.</u>

H: <u>From</u> two point of views.

G: Yeah, so how does it work when you read?

With Hannah, who is reading *Flipped* (Van Draanen, 2001), the teacher checked for progress but immediately saw that Hannah might be having difficulty when she said, "I don't know." The teacher shifted her focus to help Hannah think about text structure in the book.

In the last two examples, the teachers began the conferences with progress-type questions for the dual purpose of keeping record of the students' progress in their reading, as well as of setting the stage for the remainder of the conference. One teacher reported that reading conferences "hold [students] accountable and show them that I am interested in their reading." The examples above came from extended conferences and illustrate that progress conferences often transformed into another type of conference. However, many of the teachers we spoke with reported only using this type of conference, seeing the conference as strictly a monitoring tool to make sure students are "really reading."

Thinking More Deeply about Reading Conferences

Reading conferences in the middle school classrooms we observed revealed the influence of the teachers' purposes, reflected the teachers' theoretical understandings of literacy, and indicated how students' reading identities were positioned by the teachers, the students, and the contexts. Each of these elements affected the others. We now consider the complex relationships of purpose, theoretical understandings, and positioning that are central to reclaiming the teaching of reading.

The Teacher's Purpose

In the excerpts in the previous section, we saw that the teachers' purpose influenced the nature of conferences they conducted. Therefore, a shift in purpose will support teachers' efforts to reclaim their teaching. For example, in contrast to a strict accountability view of reading conferences, some teachers viewed conferences as a way to help students evaluate and monitor their own reading, discuss and extend the meaning of texts, identify effective strategies they use, and so on. When this occurred, the conference dynamics, regardless of the initial type of conference, changed. The students were given ownership over their reading process. This ownership influenced the students' identities. McCarthey and Moje (2002) suggest that "identity . . . shapes or is an aspect of how humans make sense of the world and their experiences in it, including their experiences with texts" (p. 228). It is therefore essential for students to have increased awareness of themselves as readers. We see this as a potential result of reclaiming reading conferences in which

teachers create meaningful, authentic discussions about the text, rather than impos-
ing particular strategies, interpretations, or views of the text on the reader. We
urge teachers to consider *what* they believe about reading (see Goodman and
Goodman, this volume), *why* they are choosing to conference with students, and
what their goal is for the conference, because answering these questions will guide
how they conference with students.

Theoretical Understandings

What teachers *believe* about reading is the stuff from which reading conferences
grow. Goodman and Marek (1996) suggest that during RMA, "teachers relinquish
control over the reader" in order to "help readers assume responsibility for their
own decisions concerning which strategies are most helpful at any particular point
in their reading" (p. 40). When strategy lessons focus on word attack skills or accuracy in reading, the readers are likely to continue to mistrust their own meaning-
making strategies and focus on "getting words" rather than constructing meaning.

Reading conferences have a strong teaching component, and decisions are
made based on in-the-moment information gathered. When teachers make these
in-the-moment decisions without a strong understanding of the reading process
or experiences in systematic reading observations, instruction tends to focus on
skills rather than meaning-making strategies. Recall the sixth-grade teacher who
said, "I feel like my conferences were unproductive, and I didn't really know what
strategies to focus on." Experience with miscue analysis provides teachers with a
systematic observation of readers as well as an understanding of reading strategies.
Teachers' perspectives on what *counts* as reading often change when they gain
experience with miscue analysis. Teachers become able to recognize a wealth of
successful reading behaviors demonstrated by their students. Thus, it is important
that teachers learn to use protocols like RMA and OTS to open opportunities
for students to revalue what they know and do as meaning makers. Teachers
can then make pedagogical decisions on that knowledge, rather than focusing on
skills, and use reading conferences to provide individually appropriate reading
instruction.

Positioning

We observed that conferences differed depending on whether the teacher perceived the student to be a proficient reader or a struggling reader. One sixth- to
eighth-grade teacher told us, "I conferenced with every student at the beginning
of the year, but they all seemed to have no problem comprehending information
or reading text, so I've stopped." We observed that when the teacher viewed the
student as a proficient reader, the student was asked fewer questions, given more
time to talk, and invited to guide the discussion. In contrast, when the teacher
perceived the reader as struggling, the teacher took on the role of expert, had an

agenda for teaching a specific strategy or skill, and offered little space for the student to negotiate the conference through his or her own talk.

In each type of conference, teachers can shape authentic dialogue by recognizing the positions taken up by the teacher and student and actively working to disrupt the traditional roles. One seventh-grade teacher explained this disruption best when she said, "I like talking about books with [the students] where they are the authority or an equal. Because they have read it on their own outside of class." Another teacher, sixth- to eight-grade, told us:

> I have a friendly conversation with the kids. We discuss books or how they feel about a book. I do not have any particular structure. I get a feel for the student. Then I get them to tell me more about what they want to read or have read. If they ask me questions, I answer.

When students are positioned as colleagues in a "friendly conversation," teachers engage in dialogue with students, "chatty, engaged, reflective, and opinionated" (Atwell, 1998, p. 270).

Recall Jessie's conference, in which the teacher made comments like "What makes you think that?" and "Oh, I see." This is very different than Jeremiah's conference, in which the teacher's turns were longer and more focused on having Jeremiah produce a "right" answer. When teachers engage in "reader-to-reader" dialogue with students, they move fluidly between teaching and assessing without dominating the discussion, all the while providing space for students to engage in the conference as a fellow reader. In this way the conference becomes a vehicle for holding up a mirror to the other, sharing their strategies, and highlighting what works, what doesn't, and what could be possible.

Conferences that Reclaim Teaching

To reclaim teaching, we can look at how students are positioned in reading conferences in order to ultimately create a space that fosters positive reading identities for students. As teachers become cognizant of the purpose they set for their reading conferences and their own beliefs about the reading process, they can better reflect on how their talk may be used to position students as readers. Such sensitivity and awareness mean that teachers are better able to gauge the tone of the conference, balance discussions, and create more authentic dialogue.

We offer the following questions for teachers to reflect on the purposes and ways in which they conduct reading conferences:

- What is my purpose for the reading conference? What do I hope to accomplish?
- Did my talk reflect my purpose?
- What do I believe about reading and how is this reflected in my talk during reading conferences?

- What do my students believe about the reading process?
- How can I work to disrupt students' views of reading as a task or a set of skills and promote a view of reading as a co-construction of meaning between the text and themselves?
- Who is the expert and who is the learner?
- How does my talk show the reader that I value his or her transaction with the text?
- In what ways does my talk affect the way students view themselves as readers and as valued members in the literacy community?
- How can I use the reading conference as an opportunity to foster positive reading identities among my students and disrupt traditional teacher–student roles?

References

Allen, J., & Gonzalez, K. (1998). *There's room for me here: Literacy workshop in the middle school.* York, ME: Stenhouse.

Atwell, N. (1998). *In the middle: New understandings about writing, reading, and learning.* Portsmouth, NH: Heinemann.

Bennett, S. (2007). *That workshop book: New systems and structures for classrooms that read, write, and think.* Portsmouth, NH: Heinemann.

Bomer, R. (1999). Conferring with struggling readers: The text of our craft, courage, and hope. *The New Advocate, 12*(1), 21–38.

Davenport, M. R. (2002). *Miscues not mistakes: Reading assessment in the classroom.* Portsmouth, NH: Heinemann.

Flint, A. S. (2008). *Literate lives: Teaching reading and writing in elementary classrooms.* Danvers, MA: John Wiley.

Gill, S. R. (2000). Reading with Amy: Teaching and learning through reading conferences. *The Reading Teacher, 53*(6), 500–509.

Goodman, Y. M., & Marek, A. M. (1996). *Retrospective miscue analysis: Revaluing readers and reading.* Katonah, NY: Richard C. Owen.

Harvey, S., & Goudvis, A. (2000). *Strategies that work: Teaching comprehension to enhance understanding.* Portland, ME: Stenhouse.

Luke, A., & Freebody, P. (1997). Shaping the social practices of reading. In S. Muspratt, A. Luke, & P. Freebody (Eds.), *Constructing critical literacies* (pp. 185–225). Cresskill, NJ: Hampton Press.

McCarthey, S. J., & Moje, E. B. (2002). Identity matters. *Reading Research Quarterly, 37*(2), 228–238.

Moore, D. W., & Hinchman, K. A. (2003). *Starting out: A guide to teaching adolescents who struggle with reading.* Boston: Allyn & Bacon.

Moore, R. A., & Gilles, C. (2005). *Reading conversations: Retrospective miscue analysis with struggling readers, grades 4–12.* Portsmouth, NH: Heinemann.

Robb, L. (2000). *Teaching reading in middle school: A strategic approach to teaching reading that improves comprehension and thinking.* New York: Scholastic.

Rosenblatt, L. (1978). *The reader, the text, the poem: The transactional theory of the literary work.* Carbondale, IL: Southern Illinois University Press.

Santman, D. (2005). *Shades of meaning: Comprehension and interpretation in middle school.* Portsmouth, NH: Heinemann.

Young Adult Novels

Curtis, C. P. (1997). *The Watsons go to Birmingham.* New York: Laurel Leaf.
Funke, C., & Latsch, O. (2002). *The thief lord.* Frome, UK: Chicken House.
Shafer, A. (2006). *The mailbox.* New York: Delacorte Books for Young Readers.
Van Draanen, W. (2001). *Flipped.* New York: Knopf Books.
Worley, R. M., & Dubisch, M. (2006). *Heir to fire.* Chandler, AZ: Actionopolis.

CHAPTER 7 EXTENSION

Conferring with Elementary Readers

Allen Koshewa

As Wilson and Gillaspy illustrate, reading conferences encompass a broad spectrum of practices. With my primary (kindergarten and first-grade) and elementary (fourth- and fifth-grade) students, I have also used a variety of other forums for discussing texts, including one-on-one book discussions, guided reading groups, literature circles, reading response journals, and peer response to readers' theater. The variety of conferences promoted more in-depth reading; addressed accountability; ensured that students wanted to read, and read for a variety of purposes; spurred conversations about text that engaged their intellect; promoted their sense of inquiry; and helped them critically examine predictions and inferences.

Reading and Writing Discussions

Ongoing discussions of the students' reading and writing experiences showed them that examining the relationships between texts and interpretations is essential to being a reader and writer. Increasingly, I found that more students were willing to have classmates analyze their reading and writing; eventually, even the most challenged readers and writers felt comfortable reading their writing in front of others as content was analyzed. Thus, the focus was on text and meaning making, and not a specific individual.

Readers gained great insight when they reflected on their own reading processes. I asked my students authentic questions about why they held certain beliefs or made certain assumptions as they read. Take the following dialogue with a fourth grader as an example:

Allen: So why did you think the father was a carpenter?
Kaitlyn: It said he was building something.

Allen: Let's look at the text. (AK and Kaitlyn reread the passage.) Oh, I think that was a reference to work he was doing on some home project, not to his profession. Did you find any other evidence that building was part of his job?

Kaitlyn: No.

Allen: So do you still think he was a carpenter?

Kaitlyn: Maybe not.

Allen: As we read, let's see if his occupation will be important in the story.

I sought to clarify what I felt was an unfounded assumption on the part of the student. By this time, however, rereading a passage for a closer look was embedded in our discussions and was not seen as a way to see who was right or wrong. This sort of dialogue honestly probed student thinking, reinforced the important view of reading as a transaction between reader and text, and assumed that predictions may or may not closely correspond with author intentions. I created a "culture of miscue" (Davenport, 2002) in which miscues were catalysts for insights concerning reading and thinking. When students said, "That's a miscue!" because they viewed all miscues as interesting, rather than because they wanted to catch another student making an error, reader-to-reader dialogue was facilitated and the playing field that can create an uneven distribution of power between proficient and struggling readers was somewhat leveled.

When I taught kindergarten, miscue discussions often stemmed from (1) conversations about miscues that I, my student teacher, or my teaching assistant made when reading transcribed student words; and (2) conversations about miscues that fourth-grade reading buddies had with my kindergarten students as the fourth graders applied what they learned about having miscue conversations.

Within conversations about miscues, I encouraged broader conversations about the social implications of text. For example, a discussion of a kindergarten student's story based on the prompt "the new president" showed how reflections on a story led to broader reflections:

Allen: Kevin, in your story you say that the White House is a castle. What are some differences between the White House and a castle?

Andrés: A castle is made of stone.

Lucas: A castle is from the old days.

Kevin: A king lives in a castle.

Michael: Kings wear crowns.

Estéfany: I like crowns.

Allen: What's similar about the position of a king and a president?

Michael: Kings rule and presidents rule.

Allen: Yes. Kings have power because their families had power. Obama, who will live in the White House, will be president because he was elected.

On the basis of this conversation, I was inspired to develop a curricular moment in which the students would have the opportunity to vote for or against something. Then we returned to Kevin's story to continue our exploration about the differences between kings and presidents.

Individual Book Discussions

Book discussions helped me monitor home reading assignments in both my primary and my intermediate classrooms and allowed my students and me to reflect upon a text. Having students retell a passage they read in a self-selected book and talk about their view of the passage allowed me to promote broader reflections while at the same time assessing comprehension and gauging student engagement. Furthermore, if students waiting for a conference listened in when I conducted the conferences, as Routman (2004) recommends, they too benefited from the conversation. When they participated, the learning was even more collaborative.

Discussions among the children about the selection of a book for home reading contributed to their choosing books that they could understand and appreciate. For example, discussions took place over who would borrow popular patterned books, which could be read independently at home. Other students discussed which non-fiction book to borrow for the evening, basing their talk on content and interest. Such conversations about books between children contributed to the success of subsequent book discussions.

Guided Reading and Literature Circles

Guided reading groups and literature circles provided spaces for student voices about text and provided me with rich data on student reading. I used guided reading groups and literature circles to promote better understanding of good reading practices, just as I did during individual conferences. Guided reading groups and literature circles provided the perfect opportunity for students to raise questions about a text. When my fifth graders pondered the implications of events in *The Girls* (Koss, 2000) or my kindergartners wondered why the bulls in *The Story of Ferdinand* (Leaf, 1936) all wanted to be in a bullfight, student questions generated discussions of power that transcended literal comprehension.

Reading Response Journals

Reading response journals also expanded student thinking about self-selected reading and served as a springboard for reading conferences. In my elementary classes, students wrote a response to home reading, each night choosing a different question, from either the fiction or the non-fiction lists that I provided. I borrowed some of the questions from previous sources, some I wrote myself, and students added others. One night a week, I responded to the week's entries and the next day conferenced with every student, commenting on the responses in terms of question choice and the quality of the response, and trying to point out a success and something to work on. As students chose from the repertoire of questions, developed their writing skills, and tried to apply my suggestions for improvement, they gradually strengthened their abilities to analyze and interpret text.

Peer Responses to Readers' Theater

Informal and student-to-student conferring during readers' theater also honed my students' analytical and interpretive skills. When peers in my kindergarten class questioned why a given student actor was not conveying the "no friends" sentiment of a character in *Yo! Yes?* (Raschka, 1993), I was thrilled that they understood that written words were meant to convey a life experience. Likewise, I was pleased the next year when my fifth graders, while reflecting on a readers' theater rehearsal of Donald Graves's poetry (Graves, 1996), noted that there are many ways to interpret a poem.

References

Davenport, M. R. (2002). *Miscues not mistakes: Reading assessment in the classroom.* Portsmouth, NH: Heinemann.

Graves, D. (1996). *Baseball, snakes, and summer squash: Poems about growing up.* Honesdale, PA: Boyds Mills Press.

Koss, A. G. (2000). *The girls.* New York: Penguin Books.

Leaf, M. (1936). *The story of Ferdinand.* New York: Penguin Books.

Raschka, C. (1993). *Yo! Yes?* New York: Orchard Books.

Routman, R. (2004). *Writing essentials: Raising expectations and results while simplifying teaching.* Portsmouth, NH: Heinemann.

PILLAR III

Reclaiming Curriculum

8

WHEN AN OLD TECHNOLOGY (STORYTELLING) MEETS A NEW ONE (DIGITAL PHOTOGRAPHY)

Changing the Face of Local Literacy Practices

Jane Baskwill

From my experiences as a teacher and principal and in my current work in family literacy as a teacher educator and researcher, I have learned that many parents and family members, not unlike the teachers I work with, lack confidence in their abilities to write well. They likely experienced writing instruction in school that emphasized product, not process, and often viewed spelling accuracy and correct grammar as the main indicators of writing well. Many recalled the days of writing assignments returned with red marks riddled throughout as evidence of their writing ineptitude. As a result, many did not see themselves as writers, nor were they confident supporting their children with writing in the current climate of an outcomes-based, one-size-fits-all writing curriculum. Teachers, like parents, saw writing as highly restricted and formalized.

Above all, parents didn't recognize the relationship between reading and writing. They were often marginalized by the curriculum, as invitations to become involved as parents relegated them to quizzing their children on lists of spelling words or listening to their children practice reading from a plastic bag of one or two leveled books. Parents were pushed further to the margins of a literacy curriculum that focused on demonstrable learning outcomes and one-size-fits-all pedagogy. Parent involvement was thus less about partnership and more about meeting standards, despite what research indicates are the benefits of expanding such involvement (Edwards, 2004; Epstein, 1995; Henderson & Mapp, 2002; Sheldon & Epstein, 2004).

We must find authentic ways in which to engage families with the literacy curriculum so parents can support children's literacy learning. When teachers create spaces for home–school contexts in which parents and children are active participants who use multiple literacies for collaborative meaning making, they reclaim the reading curriculum. In order to reclaim the reading curriculum so that it actively includes parents, teachers need to tap into the personal knowledge and experiences families have and to draw from an intimate knowledge of their interests, thus bridging the gap that currently exists between home and school literacies. We can attach new learning like print and digital book making to what families already know how to do, such as telling personal stories and interacting around children's picture books.

This chapter describes how the familiar act of telling family and community stories, first in words and then in digital images, provided a framework for engaging parents, children, and community members in writing, self-publishing, and using stories to enhance students' motivation to read and write, thereby increasing family participation in children's literacy learning. I draw from three action research projects that took place in rural Nova Scotia to describe how book making provided an authentic space for reclaiming reading curriculum. Teachers who worked with these family literacy projects found ways to incorporate important aspects of them into the literacy curriculum in order to create more authentic literacy engagements for children. The adage "It takes a whole village to raise a child" was demonstrated in the important role these family literacy projects played in the reclaiming of an authentic literacy curriculum.

Project 1, "Publish It!," asked families to create books out of personal stories in the publishing center in their local school. Project 2, "Picture It! Publish It! Read It!," brought together single mothers and their children in a workshop setting to learn about supporting their children's literacy while improving their own. Project 3, "Picture It, Dads!," was designed to change the assumed picture of dads' and male caregivers' minimal involvement in their preschool children's literacy development. In each setting, personal storytelling was a jumping off point for making and publishing books. From this beginning, process and product found their way seamlessly into everyday classroom practices.

Moving from the Known to the Unknown

Literacy learning is most effective in meaningful, social contexts (Brock, Boyd, & Moore, 2003). Writers who enjoy writing are motivated to write more (Guthrie, 2001), and writing is easier and more enjoyable when it occurs in a community of writers who share ideas and respond thoughtfully (Harwayne, 2001). When writers are given some choice of topic and audience and value the writing purpose, they are more likely to gain proficiency (Ball & Farr, 2003). Further, the immense amount of reading that occurs during the composing process as drafts are written, read, reread, revised, and read again supports the reclaiming of essential reading as central to the writing curriculum.

Vygotsky's (1962) notion of the zone of proximal development, which is so powerfully applied to children's learning, also inspires scaffolding in family literacy programming, enabling facilitators to move families from their existing levels of knowledge toward higher levels of understanding and expertise (Baskwill & Harkins, 2009). Personal storytelling is a bridge that helps families move from the familiar to the new, but also helps teachers to create an authentic literacy engagement for their students (Church, Baskwill, & Swain, 2007).

For the purpose of this chapter, I define personal storytelling as an oral narrative of the small moments or big ideas and events of everyday life. Personal stories often embody systems of belief or guiding principles of behavior that hold the key to traditions, rituals, and social ways of being. Personal storytelling is an interactive forum in which bonds are created, communication is fostered, and questions about daily lives are answered. Every life is a tapestry of stories woven partly from the stories of others and partly from those of our own making. The first threads of that tapestry come from the stories we are told by parents, grandparents, and siblings, coloring how we receive other stories and binding generations and siblings together. Each time a parent listens to their child tell a personal story, or a child listens to a story told by a parent, grandparent, or sibling, a bond is woven between them. Over time, their threads intertwine and become a family tapestry.

Personal storytelling, in a supportive environment, is a powerful way for children to find their voices, share their experiences, and establish themselves as creators of their own literature (Paley, 1990) which they will relish reading again and again. As part of home–school literacy programs, personal storytelling is a vehicle through which families and children co-construct everyday knowledge and experiences and "connect themselves to one another through their stories" (Paley, 2001, p. 14). Personal storytelling is also a portal through which to build literacy competence and confidence among families. When connected to publishing and reading stories, parental involvement and home–school communication increase, literacy development improves, and student enthusiasm for reading and writing grows (Albee & Drew, 2001; Sides, 1994; Tassopoulos, 1995).

Project 1: "Publish It!"

Having a set of books that my children and families have written has been awesome. I use them in class for mini-lessons and as mentor texts for writing. I send them home for sharing or as a springboard to a new writing activity. . . . These books are much more motivating than the leveled book collections I used to use exclusively. They also help raise awareness and build understanding among my families. They have helped me to get to know the needs and interests of my families better than ever before. Throughout this process, as a community of learners, both in school and at home, my children's literacy skills have grown because they now use and create *real* books to be used in meaningful ways across the curriculum.

(Angie, teacher, "Publish It!")

The "Publish It!" project involved parents or guardians and children in writing, self-publishing, and reading non-fiction picture books. The writing occurred in the computer labs of three schools in rural Nova Scotia. Families and children collaborated on writing, learned how to illustrate with digital photography, and published their books. Selected books were then available on a website for classroom and home use, along with links to other information for families and teachers on related topics.

The success of "Publish It!" was the result of partnering among the Valley Community Literacy Association (VCLA), a local adult literacy group, the adult education branch of the Nova Scotia Department of Education, the school staffs and local communities, and Mount Saint Vincent University. With some modest funding for two part-time coordinators, and lots of in-kind support in the form of advisory expertise, the use of the school's computer lab, and volunteers to help with the sessions, the project was able to sustain itself and gather momentum.

The first big task was to help families discover their stories. We used mentor texts (Dorfman & Cappelli, 2007) as models for their content and language as well as format and presentation. The mentor texts provided benchmarks toward which families strove and springboards from which families launched their own ideas. It was important to provide models that were within the reach of participants. Families needed to look at the books and think, "We can do this!" The mentor texts needed to be family oriented—books in which families could see themselves. They needed to be a manageable length, non-fiction, to highlight personal experiences, and to use digital photography for illustrations. It was important that families be able to use whatever language they needed to tell their stories without worrying about limiting or controlling vocabulary. This was no small mandate.

A collection of leveled books, designed to represent First Nations children and published in British Columbia by Eaglecrest Books (www.eaglecrestbooks.com/home.htm), was just the perfect set of mentor texts. We ordered several sets at multiple levels and made them available in the classrooms and the publishing center. This was just the impetus families needed to begin their own lists of topics for personal storytelling. Once there were an ample number of locally created books, they became the mentor texts, replacing the Eaglecrest Books for this purpose.

Once families were over the hurdle of what to write about, they became eager to learn how to take their oral story and put it into a written format. Families were invited to work with the coordinators on their story ideas in a workshop format. Families created storyboards to organize their words and digital photographs. Some families already had photographs they wanted to use, and we loaned digital cameras to other families. Families learned to use the scanner and we designed a publishing template so content could be smoothly transferred from the storyboard to a publishable format.

Technology help came from the coordinators and other parents and, of course, the children and school staff. We used programs parents might have had some experience with, such as Microsoft Word (2003), and we used PowerPoint (2003) for our first digital versions for the website. Later we used e-book/flipbook software to create books. (There are several sources of inexpensive software that can be found online, or see Condon & McGuffee, 2001.)

When the first published books came out of the printer and made their way onto the website, they inspired more families to accomplish what the published families had done. Word spread quickly and participation increased beyond expectations. As families talked about their publishing experience with others in the wider community, inquiries about the program came from neighboring schools and communities.

But merely publishing books was not enough. Artifacts made at school can easily become bits of memorabilia locked away in family time capsules or put in "safe" places for future generations. Families need to also be provided with ways to make these books part of their everyday reading habits. In "Publish It!," teachers used the books in multiple ways. They became umbrella or anchor texts for additional writing on related topics in classroom writing workshops. Sets of the books were placed in classroom and school libraries, where they were signed out and taken home. They provided the impetus for a continuing list of "Books We Need to Write." New publications were announced in classroom newsletters and became the subject of student podcasts, bulletin boards, and recess conversations. They were read by teachers, parents, community members, and students, and were promoted by local radio hosts. They were distributed beyond the schools to collections in the public library, doctors' offices, and community centers. All of these venues legitimized and normalized their use. Parents and children recognized friends and neighbors, made connections to the experiences of others, and saw demonstrations-in-use of how reading and writing go hand in hand.

The motivation to read these texts was observable by their popularity. Struggling and proficient readers alike were eager to read these books. Exciting conversations about writing were ongoing in classrooms throughout the day, and in homes and community centers after school hours. Comments such as "Didn't you write the book . . .?" and "I just read the book you wrote about . . ." were heard. Other schools borrowed the books and used the website for their own literacy programs, and they turned to the parents in "Publish It!" for advice about how to establish their own publishing centers. Families found their voices and gained greater confidence in themselves as they gradually took control of the project.

Project 2: "Picture It! Publish It! Read It!": Engaging Parents as Leaders in Family Literacy Activities

Parents and children keep telling me how much fun writing is. We have all learned how motivating the use of photos can be to spark new ideas or to recall an event. This takes away the fear and makes the experience more enjoyable. My children can't get enough of these little books. They want to read them to anyone who comes into our classroom. And they are always thinking about the next book they will write and the photos they want to take.

(Chris, teacher, "Picture It! Publish It! Read It!")

"Picture It! Publish It! Read It!" was a collaborative, community-based learning project designed to be a pilot study about how family groups might work together on literacy undertakings. My colleague Mary Jane Harkins and I represented Mount Saint Vincent University. Our community partners were the local rural school board and a non-profit community-based organization that provides programs for parents and children in Nova Scotia. Our focus was improving the literacy skills of single mothers so that they could support their young children's literacy development. In this project, all participants happened to be single mothers with male children between the ages 4 and 6. The moms and their children created books using photos they took of subjects of local interest. The workshops took place on Saturdays and were five hours long with lunch and snacks provided. In addition to Mary Jane and me, a teacher and teaching assistant from the school participated as facilitators.

Although participation was voluntary, this did not mean that the participants were confident, particularly when it came to writing. The mothers told us they had never considered writing with their children. In fact, they didn't know where they would begin. They also felt that their boys would not be able to sit still long enough to accomplish any writing task with them. They felt this was an area best left for the school to teach.

Once again, storytelling proved to be an essential component of the project. This time, we used a more visual approach to storytelling, and incorporated photography with language experience. We hoped these decisions would provide the mothers with a way to initiate storytelling from personal experiences and actively involve their young sons in the process. Photographs of the children, their families, and areas in their community were a wonderful springboard for inspiring mothers and children to write their own stories. They also served as a record of the activity.

We gave each family a disposable camera and took the group on a walk around the school yard and community. Parents and children took pictures of subjects that interested them. Upon our return, each family co-created a book using the photos as a visual storytelling tool, first to recall the trip and then to talk about the significance of each photo and its placement in the story. The mothers' and boys' readings of their worlds were expressed in writing and photos that were to be read by others again and again.

The mothers were surprised by their boys' interest in and enthusiasm for the task. They had little or no difficulty getting them to engage, and conversation was filled with rich language. Photography has "an important role to play in facilitating children's literacy experiences" (Labbo, Eakle, & Montero, 2002, p. 6). Sharing photos together as a family is a common experience in many households, and very non-threatening. It is something most parents and children have little difficulty engaging with and it is not looked upon as an activity requiring special knowledge or expertise. The photos in this project, as well as being enjoyable, were a visual reminder of their experiences. They sparked connections to other events in the playground, memories of growing up in the area, and times when the children were younger. They played an important role in helping the children to later produce an account of their time with their mothers. By the end of the session the mothers realized they were storytellers and that they could use photography to help connect their children to the stories they might tell.

Teachers saw that involving parents in the process of sharing photos taken together with their children had tremendous potential for the classroom writing curriculum. Teachers made storytelling an integral and natural part of their day-to-day teaching by using the photos taken by children and families as visual triggers for stories they wanted to tell in the classroom. Children were encouraged to read their photos as memory prompts throughout the curriculum: when sharing an experience, when talking about a book they intended to write, when recalling science observations, or when contributing to a social studies unit. Reading the photos by using them for storytelling was a bridge to supporting children's writing and reading, both at home and at school, in a positive and engaging way. The photos became a catalyst for conversation, vocabulary building, story building and confidence boosting, and provided an impetus for reading and writing in order to share knowledge and ideas among themselves and with others.

Project 3: "Picture It, Dads!"

> I learned that storytelling can be a powerful way to involve parents, especially fathers, in children's literacy learning. When Moira brought her book *and* her dad to school and they read the book together, there was such excitement and enthusiasm from the rest of the class. It sparked a flurry of writing and book-making at school and at home. In fact, Moira's dad offered to come to school to help make books with other parents.
>
> *(Shirley, teacher, "Picture It, Dads!")*

The "Picture It, Dads!" project (Baskwill, 2008) involved biological fathers, step-fathers, foster fathers, grandfathers, uncles, and male partners (hereafter referred to as "dads") in workshops that they helped design. The workshops provided participants with literacy materials and guided practice, which helped them develop knowledge about the importance of their involvement in children's literacy learning. The workshops also created a repertoire of dad-friendly strategies and raised participants' confidence in their abilities to engage in such activities on their own.

In "Picture It, Dads!," personal storytelling was a tool used during the dads' "Talk Time" portions of the sessions. Dads told stories of their own literacy experiences, and anecdotes about activities and experiences they had with their children. These personal storytelling opportunities helped the men build connections with each other and created a supportive safety net for asking questions and sharing new ideas or concerns. As the men's confidence grew, they desired to take a bigger role in their children's literacy development. They recognized the importance of what they were already doing and wanted others to realize it as well. As the title "Picture It, Dads!" suggests, the goal of this project was to affect the "picture" of male involvement in children's literacy development. One of the ways to do that was to insert dads into the books they made with their children in order to visually create that new picture.

Unlike the mothers in the "Picture It! Publish It! Read It!" project, from the very beginning the dads were comfortable with storytelling. In fact, they admitted that they hardly ever read a story straight through without making up their own versions. Even personal stories, when told to their children, took on a larger than life, action adventure quality. This was capitalized on during the bookmaking section of each workshop. The men and their children used word processing and digital photography to make a book, starring each adult and child pair, from a template inspired by a "touchstone" book (Baskwill, 2009). Thus, whenever dad and child read the book, they saw themselves as literacy participants. They made books patterned after favorite children's picture books: *The Gruffalo* (Donaldson, 1990), *Where's Spot?* (Hill, 1980), *The Mitten* (Brett, 1989), *If You Give a Mouse a Cookie* (Numeroff, 1985), and *Alphabet under Construction* (Fleming, 2002).

For each book, the accompanying photos were personalized so that somewhere in their version, under a flap or on a page, there would be a picture of the dad, or dad and child, as an integral part of the story (see Figure 8.1). There was also a page at the back of each book reserved for a photo of the authors—dad and child. The finished books were printed on a color printer as soon as the authors were finished, so each dad and child could take their personalized book home at the end of the workshop.

The combination of personal storytelling and making books using digital photography made an impact on the ways in which the men saw themselves as their children's literacy supporters and changed the way in which they were seen by their children and the school community. This was a powerful experience that had the potential to be retold each time the book was shared. Teachers not only used the books in their classroom literacy instruction but also found that storytelling was a way to activate knowledge fathers had about their children's interests, out-of-school activities, and family literacy knowledge and activities. This informed their curriculum planning and classroom practice. Teachers provided more opportunities for children to write more books that creatively starred family or friends. They found that the children were inspired to create their own books and learned how to insert their own photos. Teachers reported a lot of discussion

FIGURE 8.1 Dad and Child Read the Patterned Lift-the-Flap Book They Had Just Created

among their children about the appropriate photo needed for a page, placement and formatting issues, their own problem-solving techniques, and the application of these skills to other areas of the curriculum, including the ways in which they read books that they did not author.

Some Final Thoughts

Describing his experiences in the International School in Brussels, Belgium, Brewster (1997) demonstrates the power of teaching young children to make picture books. The reasons he provides hold true for supporting family literacy through the integration of personal storytelling and book making using digital photography. They direct efforts for reclaiming the writing and reading curriculum:

- *Integration:* Making books from personal stories, using digital photography, is a natural way for families to integrate two powerful modes of thought and expression: the linguistic and the visual. Through such a process, children write their way into reading.

- *Documentation:* Book making is a way for families to record meaningful experiences, while at the same time creating a lasting object (the published book) that can be reread and shared with others.
- *Validation:* Books provide families with tangible evidence of the experience, create a bond between the authors, and demonstrate that literacy experiences have value.
- *Communication:* Book making provides opportunities for families to create private expressions and to create opportunities for public sharing as they find multiple venues in which to have their works read.
- *Collaboration:* Making books with a partner, in these instances with a parent or family member (i.e., grandparent), enables participants to contribute to something larger than themselves, celebrating family efforts and underscoring the social nature of reading and writing.
- *Coordination:* Making picture books using technology provides families with the opportunity to use many skills, including problem solving and collaborative decision making—all essential components of reading.
- *Motivation:* Book making, and subsequent book reading, is highly motivating, particularly to families who struggle to find a place in their children's school experiences (adapted from Brewster, 1997, pp. 113–114).

In each family literacy project, personal storytelling provided the common ground, or point of connection, that helped families move out of their comfort zones and venture into new ways of interacting with and supporting their children during literacy-related tasks. The participants learned that they could tell personal stories both orally and visually and use these as springboards to making a more permanent record in the form of a picture book. They also learned that the act of co-authoring with their child was an enjoyable process and that they already possessed many skills that all family members could use and share in this setting. Parents and children gained confidence and, most importantly, they had fun, something many did not associate with literacy and, in particular, with writing.

In addition, teachers changed the face of their classroom literacy curriculum. They helped children and their families see themselves as writers, and saw themselves (and others they knew) in the books read in the classroom. Teachers validated children's out-of-school experiences and family knowledge, and used the books for collaboration, connection, and future writing and reading. The book making, and the books themselves, became a "third space" (Cook, 2005) that bridged home and school literacies through the creation and use of a new genre, the *family* or *community* photographic text. Regardless of whether teachers work independently to create bookmaking opportunities for their students and their families or whether they partner with community organizations or other teachers in their schools, these teachers find ways for parents and children to reclaim a reading and writing curriculum that is meaningful and more suited to their students' interests.

References

Albee, J., & Drew, M. (2001). Off to the write start: A parent–teacher–child story. *Reading Horizons, 41*(3), 129–141.

Ball, A. F., & Farr, M. (2003). Language varieties, culture, and teaching the English language arts. In J. Flood, D. Lapp, J. Squire, & J. Jenson (Eds.), *Handbook of research on teaching the English language arts* (pp. 435–445). Mahwah, NJ: Lawrence Erlbaum.

Baskwill, J. (2008). Picture It, Dads! Changing the picture of dads' and male caregivers' involvement in children's literacy development. *Canadian Children, 33*(2), 26–31.

Baskwill, J. (2009). *Getting dads on board: Fostering literacy partnerships for successful student learning.* Markham, ON: Pembroke.

Baskwill, J., & Harkins, M. J. (2009). Through a child's eyes: Using photography in a family literacy workshop setting. *Young Children, 64*(5), 28–33.

Brewster, J. C. (1997). Teaching young children to make picture books. *Early Childhood Education Journal, 25*(2), 113–117.

Brock, C. H., Boyd, F. B., & Moore, J. A. (2003). Variation in language and the use of language across contexts: Implications for literacy learning. In J. Flood, D. Lapp, J. R. Squire, & J. M. Jensen (Eds.), *Handbook of research on teaching the English language arts* (pp. 446–458). Mahwah, NJ: Lawrence Erlbaum.

Church, S., Baskwill, J., & Swain, M. (2007). *Yes, but . . . if they like it, they'll learn it!* Markham, ON: Pembroke.

Condon, M. W. F., & McGuffee, M. (2001). *Real epublishing, really publishing!* Portsmouth, NH: Heinemann.

Cook, M. (2005). "A place of their own": Creating a classroom "third space" to support a continuum of text construction between home and school. *Literacy, 39*(2), 85–90.

Dorfman, L. R. and Cappelli, R. (2007). *Mentor texts: Teaching writing through children's literature, K-6.* New York: Stenhouse.

Edwards, P. A. (2004). *Children's literacy development: Making it happen through school, family, and community involvement.* Boston: Pearson.

Epstein, J. L. (1995). School/family/community partnerships: Caring for the children we share. *Phi Delta Kappan, 76*(9), 705–707.

Guthrie, J. T. (2001). Contexts for engagement and motivation in reading. *Reading Online.* Retrieved August 11, 2004, from www.readingonline.org/articles/handbook/guthrie/index.html

Harwayne, S. (2001). *Writing through childhood: Rethinking process and product.* Portsmouth, NH: Heinemann.

Henderson, A. T., & Mapp, K. L. (2002). *A new wave of evidence: The impact of school, family, and community connections on student achievement.* Austin, TX: Southwest Educational Development Laboratory.

Labbo, L. D., Eakle, A. J., & Montero, M. K. (2002). Digital language experience approach: Using digital photographs and software as a language experience approach innovation. Retrieved from: www.readingonline.org/electronic/labbo2/

Paley, V. G. (1990). *The boy who would be a helicopter: The uses of storytelling in the classroom.* Cambridge, MA: Harvard University Press.

Paley, V. G. (2001). *In Mrs. Tully's room: A childcare portrait.* Cambridge, MA: Harvard University Press.

Sheldon, S. B., & Epstein, J. L. (2004). School programs of family and community involvement to support children's reading and literacy development across the grades.

In J. Flood & P. Anders (Eds.), *The literacy development in students in urban schools: Research and policy*. Newark, DE: International Reading Association.

Sides, D. T. (1994). Designing a home writing program to study the effects of increased parental involvement on second graders' writing skills. Unpublished Master's thesis. Nova Southeastern University, Fort Lauderdale-Davie, FL.

Tassopoulos, R. (1995). Write share: When parents become co-authors. *Teaching Pre K-8, 26*(1), 72–74.

Vygotsky, L. S. (1962). *Thought and language*. Cambridge, MA: MIT Press.

Children's Books Cited

Brett, J. (1989). *The mitten*. New York: G. P. Putnam.

Donaldson, J. (1990). *The Gruffalo*. New York: Macmillan.

Fleming, D. (2002). *Alphabet under construction*. New York: Henry Holt.

Hill, E. (1980). *Where's Spot?* New York: HarperCollins.

Numeroff, L. (1985). *If you give a mouse a cookie*. New York: HarperCollins.

CHAPTER 8 EXTENSION

Redefining What Counts as Literacy to Include Family and Community Resources

Corey Drake and Lori Norton-Meier

I really liked the math walk. I thought it was so cool to have the students out in their playground looking for math. I think it is such a great idea to have students look at their everyday lives for math. It comes out in the most unexpected places. What I really enjoyed was the way we connected it to literacy by having the students use the photos to write their own [story] problems. Using literacy along with math I think really made their learning meaningful.

(Pre-service teacher reflection)

As I participated more heavily in combining math and literacy education as a means to be successful in the world, I noticed more . . . "funds of knowledge" that could be used in the classroom. Community parks, restaurants, grocery stores, and libraries are great places to show students how the things they learn in school can be applied in real life.

(Pre-service teacher reflection)

These two pre-service teachers participated in learning and teaching experiences in an elementary school, where, along with teachers, parents, children, and teacher educators, they created spaces to focus on family and community funds of knowledge as curricular resources. Baskwill's chapter encourages teachers to use photography as a language, a way of making and expressing meaning, to engage families in self-publishing projects. These experiences provided opportunities for teachers to learn more about the language practices of the participating families and to include those practices in broadened definitions of school-based language. In our work, children's and pre-service teachers' photographs from home are used to expand teachers' understandings and definitions of language to include mathematics and the mathematical practices of families and children. We build on Foote's (2010) work, in which children's and parents' photographs from home are used to expand teachers' understandings and definitions of mathematics and of the mathematical practices of families and children. Reclaiming the reading curriculum is about redefining what counts as language and including arts (photography), mathematics, and community and family-based literacies in that broadened definition. The reclaiming and redefining process in turn encourages teachers to build curriculum that is based on students, as opposed to (or in addition to) standards and standardized tests.

We supported pre-service and in-service teachers in reclaiming the literacy and mathematics curriculum in similar ways by discovering and then building on children's family and community-based funds of knowledge (González, Moll, & Amanti, 2005) in literacy and mathematics. Four cohorts of elementary pre-service teachers participated in a partnership between our teacher education program and a local elementary school. The partnership was designed to help the pre-service teachers learn about incorporating family and community resources into literacy and mathematics instruction.

Pre-service teachers spent time at a local elementary school that served a significant number of English language learners. Eventually, the time they spent in the school increased to two full days per week. Pre-service teachers participated in a number of activities designed to support their learning about family and community as instructional resources, including community literacy and mathematics ethnographies and community resource projects. At the same time, the pre-service teachers worked with small groups of students on literacy and mathematics interviews, assessments, and tutoring, paying particular attention to accessing and understanding family and community resources and using them to plan instruction for their students. Each semester, the practicum experience culminated with a Family Math and Literacy Night, designed and led by the pre-service teachers. The local elementary school provided an interesting context for this work because, at the time of the study, significant demographic transitions were occurring that increased rates of immigration and poverty.

Math, Literacy, and Image as Language Experiences

We observed transformations when we urged teachers to expand their definitions of language with this question: "What are the literacy and mathematics practices of the community that can be connected to school-based literacy and mathematics?" Our goal was to help the teachers imagine how they could broaden the language curriculum and bridge it to the world outside of the classroom. Three engagements particularly affected teachers' future curriculum development: a community walk, parent–child book groups, and family math and literacy night.

Community Walk

In one elementary classroom the pre-service teachers went on a community walk with children to gather photographs of mathematics and literacy in the world around them. The children returned with cameras full of images they turned into mathematical adventures for their friends. The pre-service and cooperating teachers looked in amazement at the variety of ways literacy and mathematics came to life in the community, noticing, as one pre-service teacher commented, how they took these practices "for granted because they are so embedded in the fabric of our daily lives."

Parent–Child Book Groups

Another transformation occurred when two teachers created opportunities for families and children to engage around the current texts they were reading. One such experience asked each family member to describe in writing and in pictures a personal connection with *When I was Young in the Mountains* (Rylant, 1993), which was being read in class. The wall outside the classroom was soon covered with parent responses to the prompt "What I like about being big" paired with their child's response to the prompt "What I like about being little." The children shared the responses from their parents and compared them with their own perspectives as well as what they discovered about the characters as they read the book.

Family Math and Literacy Night

The pre-service teachers hosted a Family Math and Literacy Night for the school. They worked in collaboration with their cooperating teachers to plan engaging family literacy and mathematics experiences that would challenge young children as well as older siblings. The practicing teachers mentored the pre-service teachers and thought deeply about providing experiences that would reveal funds of knowledge. When the evening arrived, the teachers engaged directly with families since the pre-service teachers managed the activities. In one moment we observed a teacher engaging with a parent over an apple taste test. The parent shared with her that in his home an apple was a delicacy. When the teacher shared this story, she said she was amazed at what she had learned by interacting with parents in a "non-formal way learning together side by side over something as simple as an apple."

The tie that binds these examples with one another and with Baskwill's work with families is the opportunity each of these activities provided for teachers to redefine math and image as language to reclaim the curriculum. When parents, families, and communities create and share artifacts (photographs, drawings, literature responses, family night activities), school-based knowledge and out-of-school knowledge merge in meaningful ways. Through such experiences, teachers, including pre-service teachers, incorporate family and community-based literacy and mathematics practices into broadened understandings of what it means to use reading, writing, and mathematics.

References

Foote, M. Q. (2010). The power of one: Teachers examine their mathematics teaching practice by studying a single child. In M.Q. Foote (Ed.), *Mathematics teaching and learning in K–12: Equity and professional development* (pp. 41–58). New York: Palgrave Macmillan.

González, N., Moll, L. C., & Amanti, C. (Eds.). (2005). *Funds of knowledge: Theorizing practices in households, communities, and classrooms*. Mahwah, NJ: Lawrence Erlbaum.

Rylant, C. (1993). *When I was young in the mountains*. New York: Puffin Books.

9

DEVELOPING INTERCULTURAL UNDERSTANDINGS THROUGH GLOBAL CHILDREN'S LITERATURE

Kathy G. Short and Lisa Thomas

While we live within a world that is increasingly connected through mass media and globalization, North American culture continues to be characterized by ethnocentricism, isolation, and a lack of understanding about world cultures (Case, 1991). Many children obtain their world knowledge through television, with its focus on catastrophe, terrorism, and war, and so their understandings remain superficial, often grounded in fear and stereotypes. Although the development of intercultural understandings and global perspectives can be accomplished through a range of strategies, we are reclaiming the reading curriculum by engaging students in inquiries around global literature to highlight multiple voices and avenues for action. Global literature provides an opportunity for children to go beyond a tourist perspective of gaining surface information about another country. Through immersing themselves in story worlds, children gain insights into how people feel, live, and think in global cultures, both recognizing their common humanity and valuing cultural differences.

Integrating global literature into the curriculum, however, is not an easy matter. One issue is the limited (although growing) availability of culturally authentic literature set in other countries, along with educators' lack of familiarity with the books that are available (Freeman & Lehman, 2001). Once educators access the books, the problem remains of how to engage children thoughtfully with this literature when the books often focus on ways of living that seem far removed from children's immediate experiences and contain unfamiliar stylistic features and unusual names and terms (Tomlinson & Lynch-Brown, 1989). Children may view this literature as "exotic," failing to connect in significant ways and forming superficial understandings about people around the world.

We are engaged in a school–wide project to integrate global literature into the curriculum. Through action research, we reclaim an intercultural curriculum in which children and teachers engage in meaningful conversations and learning experiences around literature within a global context. This chapter focuses on the pedagogical issues involved in integrating global literature into the curriculum in order to reclaim reading.

Situating Our Inquiry within Theory

Because we define curriculum as *putting a system of beliefs into action* (Short & Burke, 1991), we spent time as a group exploring our beliefs about responses to literature and intercultural understandings. Harris and Willis (2003) note that the different definitions of multiculturalism are connected by a focus on the struggle against social injustice. They found that, despite current literacy wars, researchers continue to examine the school contexts that support children's responses to multicultural literature and the changes that teachers make in moving toward the inclusion of this literature in their classrooms (Brooks, 2006; Martínez-Roldán, 2003). Debates about cultural authenticity and the complex issues of power relations in society continue to dominate the field of multicultural literature. Fox and Short (2003) conducted a comprehensive review of research on cultural authenticity and indicate the pressing need for investigations that go beyond critical content analyses of books to focus on the ways in which children and teachers respond to authentic literature and on the effectiveness of social practices around the use of these books with children.

Scholarly discussions about global children's literature have focused on the value of this literature, its availability and authenticity, translation and publication issues, selection and evaluation, global trends, and use with children (Freeman & Lehman, 2001). Ideas on possible uses of these books are shared, rather than actual classroom examples of the integration of this literature into the curriculum and of children's responses to global texts. An increasing number of articles exist on the books themselves, but not on children's responses or on how this literature influences intercultural understanding. Our view of reclaiming the reading curriculum through global children's literature has included looking at what we do, how we do it, and the effects of the engagements.

Interculturalism as a movement grew out of the aftermath of World War II and is based in the work of European researchers and theorists. Although interculturalism and multiculturalism share similar theoretical constructs and goals, they have parallel scholarly traditions. Interculturalists see multiculturalism as focusing on the relationships between ethnic groups within a country and interculturalism as focusing on relationships between cultural groups across the boundaries of countries. The two fields share the belief that internationalism and multiculturalism are perspectives or orientations on life, not a special unit or book. Key scholars in intercultural education (Fennes & Hapgood, 1997; Hofstede, 1991; Hoopes, 1979) and global education (Begler, 1996; Case, 1991; Collins, Czarra, & Smith, 1998) inform our definition of intercultural understandings as an orientation toward curriculum in which learners:

- explore their cultural identities and develop conceptual understandings of culture;
- develop an awareness and respect for different cultural perspectives as well as the commonality of human experience;
- examine issues that have personal, local and global relevance and significance;
- value the diversity of cultures and perspectives within the world;
- demonstrate a responsibility and commitment to making a difference to, and in, the world;
- develop an inquiring, knowledgeable, and caring perspective on taking action to create a better and more just world.

Case (1991) argues that an intercultural, or global, perspective has both substantive and perceptual dimensions. The substantive dimension refers to the knowledge of various features of the world and how they work, including knowledge of cultural values and practices, global interconnections, present concerns and conditions, historic origins and past patterns, and alternative and future directions. The perceptual dimension consists in the orientations, values, and attitudes that establish the lens through which students perceive the world. This lens includes open-mindedness, anticipation of complexity, resistance to stereotyping, inclination to empathize, and non-chauvinism. These attitudes of mind are viewed as fundamental to a global perspective and are integral to the beliefs we brought to reclaiming the reading curriculum.

Situating Our Inquiry within the School Context

Our engagement in action research has allowed us to pursue action (change) and research (understanding) at the same time. Action research involves a cyclical process that alternates between action and critical reflection through planning, action, and data gathering about the results of actions. Those affected by the change are involved as collaborators who engage in a reflective process of progressive problem solving with the aim of improving their strategies, practices, and knowledge of the contexts in which they function (Cochran-Smith & Lytle, 1993).

The context for our work is a small K–5 public school within a large urban district in the southwest United States with a culturally and linguistically diverse population, serving a middle-class and working-class community. Lisa, the curriculum coordinator, established a Learning Lab as an alternative approach to professional development at the school. Lisa and the teachers decided on a school-wide focus, and teachers who wanted to be part of this focus brought their children to the lab for an hour once a week. Instruction in the lab grew out of intense teacher study and collaboration that was facilitated by teachers' involvement in a study group. The study group met after school twice a month. The ideas discussed within the study group were pursued within the Learning Lab, providing teachers with an opportunity to observe in the lab sessions and then critique the instruction and evaluate student work in study group sessions. Teachers also committed to exploring these ideas in their classrooms, but the ways in which they did so were individually determined, based on their own goals. Participation in the lab and study group was voluntary, but went across all grade levels in the school.

Within the context of the Learning Lab, study group, and classroom work, we gathered teaching journals, field notes, audiotapes and videotapes, and transcripts of study group and lab sessions. Teachers were also invited to write classroom vignettes about critical incidents through participation in a summer writing group. These vignettes were published in an online journal, *WOW Stories* (www.wowlit. org), over a three-year period.

This chapter focuses on our exploration of the pedagogical issues involved in creating a curricular context that encouraged the development of intercultural perspectives through interactions with global children's literature. Kathy's field notes of the study group sessions and the debriefing/planning discussions with Lisa were analyzed along with field notes on the lab sessions one day a week.

A Curriculum Framework for Intercultural Learning

We used a particular curriculum framework (Short, 2009) to enact our theoretical beliefs and organize instruction. This framework highlighted the use of global children's literature to support children's critical perspectives in explorations of (1) personal cultural identities, (2) cross-cultural studies, (3) cross-curricular international materials, and (4) sociopolitical global issues (see Figure 9.1). These ways of organizing this literature were integrated into engagements such as reading aloud, independent reading, literature discussions, writing workshop, and inquiry studies within the lab and in the classrooms as determined by each teacher.

Our focus on personal cultural identities highlighted the need of all children to explore their own cultural identities in order to understand why culture is significant in the lives of other children. We engaged in specific inquiries into children's identities and wove connections to children's life experiences into all of our units of inquiry. This focus on personal identity was complemented by cross-cultural studies in which students engage in inquiries into a particular culture to examine the complexity and diversity of that culture and to recognize that their personal perspective was only one way to view the world. The juxtaposition of these two types of engagements created conceptual understandings of culture.

In addition to occasional in-depth studies of specific cultures, intercultural perspectives needed to be woven into every unit of study so that the focus on culture was integral to the entire curriculum. This integration of the stories, languages, and ways of learning from many cultures highlighted the significance of multiple perspectives and developed interculturalism as an orientation. Inquiries around specific global issues focused on difficult social, political, and environmental topics, such as human rights or hunger, and considered the local and global

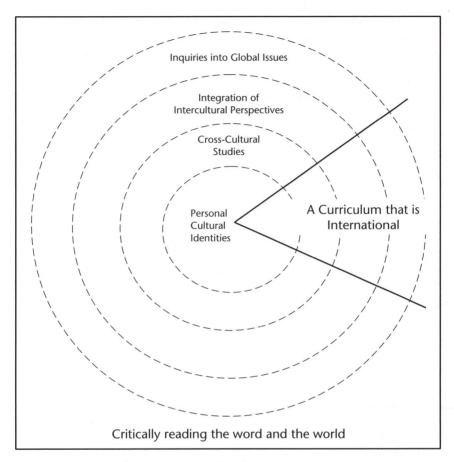

Inquiries into Global Issues

Integration of
Intercultural Perspectives

Cross-Cultural
Studies

Personal
Cultural
Identities

A Curriculum that is
International

Critically reading the word and the world

FIGURE 9.1 A Curriculum that is International

complexities of that issue. These inquiries encouraged students to go beyond talk to determine how to take action.

All of these components of a curriculum that is international were permeated with critically reading the word and the world (Freire, 1970). Without this focus on critically engaging with the ideas and texts, the four components could easily have become a superficial tour of culture in which students learned about internationalism as tourists who picked up isolated pieces of information but did not consider difficult issues of social justice and made no real change in their thinking about themselves or the world.

Tensions in Creating a Context for Intercultural Understandings

We struggled with a range of tensions to establish a curricular context that encouraged children to develop intercultural understandings and global perspectives through their interactions with global literature. Although we expected some of these issues, we did not anticipate the complexity of issues that we needed to consider in exploring an instructional context for intercultural thinking.

Inviting Engagement in Critical Dialogue

One of the first pedagogical issues was the significance of students being able and willing to think critically with each other about difficult issues. Our initial literature discussions indicated that most students did not talk about books from a critical stance. They took turns making a comment about the book instead of sharing new thoughts in response to peers' ideas. Students were not used to engaging with ideas and issues through dialogue around the books in order to challenge their assumptions by questioning "what is?" and asking "what if?" (Freire, 1970). We knew that without a critical stance, engagements around global literature could become a superficial tour of the world based on the beliefs that "if we just learn more about each other, we will like each other and solve the world's problems." We had well-behaved kids who raised their hands, took turns, and made comments rather than sharing with each other, let alone having dialogue with each other.

The pedagogical issues that were documented in our discussions about our struggle to encourage students to move toward critical dialogue included:

- encouraging personal connections and engaging with a book instead of just commenting on it;
- moving from sharing connections to using connections as a way to think about the story (e.g., "I have a dog" versus "They don't like him because he's Mexican. Some people don't like Mexicans. I know because I'm half-Mexican and that has happened to me");
- searching for the big ideas behind personal stories as children connected to the literature as well as focusing on issues they were wondering about;
- challenging students to not avoid difficult social and political issues, such as racism, through the use of clichés (e.g., "It doesn't matter what you look like on the outside, it's the inside that matters," an attitude of colorblindness);
- struggling to listen to and build from each other's thinking to explore an issue. Students were not used to thinking with others or needing someone to help them think through an issue;
- exploring the difference between ideas and issues as the basis for discussion and learning to dig deeply to identify and wrestle with issues.

This reclaiming work involved moving beyond the superficial and previously well-established habits of responding to deeper and more meaningful and critical dialogue.

Developing Conceptual Understandings of Culture

As we moved into discussions of books from many cultural perspectives, we realized the children needed an understanding of culture and why culture matters in order to challenge their view that cultures that differed from their own were strange or exotic. Children needed a conceptual understanding of culture as ways of living and thinking in the world. Our understanding of culture was based on Geertz (1973), who saw culture as the shared patterns that set the tone, character, and quality of people's lives.

We identified two types of inquiries in the study group discussions and the engagements with the students as essential to building a conceptual understanding of culture. One was inquiries that encouraged students to explore their own personal cultural identities—to realize they have a perspective and to value the role that culture plays in their own lives and worldviews in order to understand why culture matters to others. They came to see themselves as cultural beings through engagements such as neighborhood memory maps with a focus on memories as significant to who a person becomes, and cultural X-rays where students identified the attributes, behaviors, and values that influenced their cultural identities. Neighborhood memory maps invited students to sketch a map of their neighborhoods and to label these maps with stories of memories that influence their identities. Cultural X-rays (see Figure 9.2) involved creating visual

FIGURE 9.2 Fifth-Grade Cultural X-Rays

representations of each child's multiple cultural identities, identifying visible aspects such as age, language, and ethnicity on the outside of the body, and depicting the less visible cultural values as inside the heart. Students found it easier to identify cultural behaviors and characteristics that were apparent to others on the outside of their person than to identify their internal values, which they tended to see as what they liked rather than what they valued.

Another significant engagement involved students researching and constructing their own life journey maps (see Figure 9.3). Students were asked to create maps showing their life journeys. Some students chose sequential structures, such as time lines, highways, and game boards, while others used structures that represented events or people in their lives as part of a whole, like a puzzle or heart. One student used a graph format to merge the events and the emotions in his life journey.

Exploring their own cultural identities was helpful, but did not necessarily lead students to consider points of view beyond their own. The second type of inquiry involved in-depth cross-cultural studies to further develop children's conceptual understandings of culture and to help them realize that their cultural perspectives were only one of many ways to view and live in the world. Cross-cultural units are often poorly taught in schools because of an overemphasis on the "5Fs": fashion, folklore, festivals, foods, and famous people—what Hoopes (1979) represents with an image of an iceberg that shows the small surface tip of visible cultural characteristics above water and the much larger and deeper cultural values and beliefs beneath the surface.

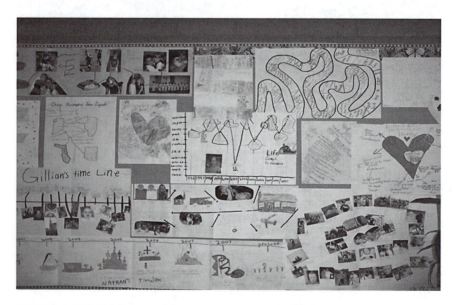

FIGURE 9.3 K–5 Life Journey Maps

The study group decided to move into a three-month study of Korean culture in the Learning Lab and used the iceberg model to evaluate the ways in which students thought about this culture in their artifacts and talk. These evaluations indicated that an in-depth study of a specific culture provided the opportunity to get at the complexity and diversity of that group in a way that integrating books from many different cultures does not. However, it also became clear that students easily got lost in facts once they began doing their own research, and so lost the broader conceptual focus on culture. We continuously encouraged students to consider conceptual understandings of culture during their inquiries through various reflection forms and class discussions.

Challenging the Assumption That One's Own Culture Is the Norm

Another pedagogical issue that emerged during the cross-cultural study was the awareness that students can understand culture conceptually and yet still view their own culture as the norm against which to judge other perspectives and cultures. For example, in an exploration of the Korean written language, students looking at various Asian languages made the comment that "Japanese books open back- wards." They were surprised when Kathy pointed out that it depended on a person's cultural perspective and that a Japanese person would see their books as backwards.

We also challenged this assumption by keeping a focus on connections as well as differences across cultures. The younger children were interested in everyday life in families and schools, and their comments and inquiries focused around cre- ating a sense of connection with Korean children. Therefore, we used some books in which the characters were engaged in everyday activities, such as taking care of a mischievous young brother or waiting for mother to arrive home, events to which children had many connections. The study group struggled with how to encourage connection across cultures without perpetuating the view of sameness as "We are all alike."

In addition to reading books that introduced the variety of ways in which "everyone is alike," we selected books that presented cultural uniqueness. Particular books from Korea became "anomalies" because they challenged the view that everyone is alike. Such books included a particular event or perspective that was anomalous from the children's cultural perspectives, such as a young boy and his sister traveling alone on the subway, leading to discussions about both the cultural connections and the differences between their culture and Korean culture.

Overcoming the Limitations of Available Materials

Another curricular and pedagogical issue was locating specific books to meet particular needs or issues that became evident through our evaluation of students' thinking about intercultural issues. We had many discussions about our search for and careful choice of particular books to support or challenge students' intercultural perspectives. Identifying and locating books was not a major difficulty once we identified the need, because of Kathy's expertise in global children's books and the principal's willingness to make funds available for purchasing new books. In other school contexts, however, the need to quickly identify and locate global books could become a major obstacle. Many of these needs could not be predicted ahead because they grew out of our careful analysis of student thinking in the study group.

One major issue was the lack of contemporary books about world cultures. The books we located about Korean culture, for example, were primarily historical fiction and traditional literature, with virtually no realistic fiction or poetry and only a few informational books. We located few books from other countries that focused on math and science topics or concepts. When we needed to access books in the native language, we needed the help of a native speaker who could read the website to order materials. Interestingly, the Internet search engines designed for children's use sent students to sites that focused on the surface features of culture, which greatly frustrated children during their Korean inquiries. It appeared to us that the adults creating those sites had limited perspectives on culture and on what children would be interested in exploring.

Exploring Cultural Identities through a Specific Culture's Languages

We believe that language is integral to identity, since the way people view and interpret their world is through language (Banks, 2001), and so we integrated a few books in Hangul (the alphabet of the Korean language) into our Korean collection. The children's interest in and excitement about the language led us to purchase and borrow over 40 picture books in Hangul and to engage in beginning language study with a native speaker. The children were highly engaged with trying to write and read Hangul, and their language explorations continued after our inquiry within the lab was completed.

These books played a number of key roles in the children's understandings about culture, in addition to language explorations. One was that these books were an important source of contemporary images of everyday life in Korea and showed the diversity of life in cities as well as rural areas. Given the lack of these images within books available in English, they were significant in preventing misconceptions about modern Korean life. The books had strong credibility for the children as cultural icons because they were published in Korea and read by Korean children. They were also the source of anomalies because they reflected everyday life naturally embedded within Korean culture and so supported children in seeing how their lives both were connected to and differed from those of Korean children. Despite the fact that no one in the school read or spoke Korean, the books played a critical role in inviting children to explore deeper aspects of cultural ways of living and thinking.

Developing an Expectation of Global Perspectives across the Curriculum

Our discussions in the study group led us to realize that our focus on personal cultural identity and cross-cultural studies resulted in students' considering inter-culturalism as a "special" study or unit instead of expecting global perspectives to be present in every study. Therefore, we knew global and intercultural perspectives needed to be woven into every classroom study across topics and subject areas. We began integrating literature, art, music, and experiences from a range of cultural perspectives across the curriculum and day. This integration was important to our reclaiming of curriculum, because more cultural perspectives were considered within all topics, so students came to expect that there are always diverse perspectives on an issue.

Moving from Topic-Based to Conceptually Based Inquiry Curriculum

The study group's decision to focus on the integration of intercultural perspectives across subject areas and units led us to plan experiences for the Learning Lab that were appropriate across all of the classrooms. Since each classroom had different science and social studies units, we searched for a broader focus that would cut across their units. After much discussion, the group chose *journey* as a conceptual frame for our work in the lab; we defined journey as a movement along physical, emotional, intellectual, social, or spiritual pathways that involve change.

Our work with this broad concept raised pedagogical and curricular issues. Teachers found that many of their units were ones they had done for years without questioning whether they were worth the time, and most involved a primary focus on gathering facts about the topic. Teachers' typical approach to units was challenged as they observed students developing a conceptual understanding of journeys and identifying significant issues within journeys, such as beginnings and endings, pain and healing, spiritual and emotional, dreams and wishes, people and relationships, growing and learning, and competition and movement.

Students initially struggled with conceptually and metaphorically defining "journey," wanting to rely on literal definitions. Their struggles made it evident that they were not used to thinking conceptually. Conceptual thinking includes, but goes beyond, topics and information to seek an explanation, to understand why in order to develop broad abstract mental constructs that serve as organizing ideas for a range of examples. Erickson (2002) argues that a conceptual lens supports metacognitive study, encourages thinking at an integrative level, and leads to deep and essential understanding.

Our discussions about the differences between topic-centered and conceptually centered teaching led to major debates about the mandated curriculum and why particular topics were significant in the larger scheme of students' lives. The discussion in the study group indicated a shift for teachers from planning projects around specific information (e.g., to learn about Egyptian and Roman civilization) to thinking about ways to engage students in exploring big ideas and conceptual frames (e.g., what is civilization and how is it established and destroyed?). Teachers noted that they no longer felt the need to cover a topic, but instead focused on the concepts and engaging students in a wide range of intercultural perspectives to develop conceptual understanding. Our discussions made it evident that it is difficult to integrate intercultural materials and perspectives into topic-centered studies and that a movement to conceptually focused teaching was essential to reclaiming curricular contexts for interculturalism.

Developing Tools to Challenge and Organize Our Thinking

One pedagogical issue that wove throughout the study in multiple ways was developing tools that students could use to think conceptually and to organize their thinking in order to more generatively engage with each other and with ideas and issues. We pulled from familiar tools like consensus boards, webs, and charts and developed new tools such as cultural X-rays and life journey maps. These tools kept the focus of inquiry open for children's wonderings and tensions and challenged them to think in more complex and conceptual ways. Our goal was to develop tools that challenged students to push their thinking but did not take away their participation in determining the issues and the direction of their inquiries. We spent a great deal of time talking about these tools and their purposes, and tried them out ourselves in the study group.

Later, when we recognized how tool development pushed our thinking in the study group, we realized that students needed to be involved in developing their own tools. At the end of their journey inquiries, students identified the issue of most interest to them. They spent time discussing that issue and developed a tool for sharing their thinking with others. The level of excitement in the room as they developed these tools was palpable and the students' talk and thinking changed dramatically. It was apparent that what a person knew depended on the tool that person used to think with—something researchers know when determining tools for analysis. For example, a group that explored the differing consequences of dreams and wishes developed a visual showing roads leading to a range of alternatives, such as road blocks, side trips, and new destinations (see Figure 9.4). Another group that focused on the changes that result from spiritual and emotional journeys, such as death and separation, shared their thinking on a tree, with the branches as the big ideas from their discussions to show change as a living, growing entity.

FIGURE 9.4 Fourth Graders Developing a Tool to Show Journeys of Dreams and Wishes

Living within an Interconnected World

Our action research focused on the intersection of intercultural understanding and global literature within critical inquiry as one means of reclaiming curriculum. The significance of our work was enhanced by the university–school collaboration and the rich learning context for teachers and children created within this school through the school-wide focus on global perspectives and the establishment of the Learning Lab and the study group. This context allowed us to examine instructional processes as well as to develop knowledge and understandings from those processes—both *how* we teach and learn (pedagogy) and *what* we teach and learn (curriculum) in building intercultural understandings and global perspectives. Teachers reclaimed their role in constructing curriculum through reflection and action research, and students (re)claimed their role as inquirers engaged in struggle and action upon the world. Our focus was on encouraging students to become critical thinkers who interrogated their lives and the world in order to work toward and imagine a better tomorrow.

Note

The research was funded by the Research Foundation of the National Council of Teachers of English.

References

Banks, J. (2001). *Cultural diversity and education.* Boston: Allyn & Bacon.

Begler, E. (1996). Global cultures: The first steps toward understanding. *Social Education, 62*(5), 272–276.

Brooks, W. (2006). Reading representations of themselves. *Reading Research Quarterly, 41*(3), 372–392.

Case, R. (1991). Key elements of a global perspective. *Social Education, 57*, 318–325.

Cochran-Smith, M., & Lytle, S. (1993). *Inside/outside: Teacher research and knowledge.* New York: Teachers College Press.

Collins, H. T., Czarra, F., & Smith, A. (1998). Guidelines for global and international studies education. *Social education, 62*(5), 311–317.

Erickson, H. L. (2002). *Concept-based curriculum and instruction.* Thousand Oaks, CA: Corwin.

Fennes, H., & Hapgood, K. (1997). *Intercultural learning in the classroom.* London: Cassell.

Fox, D., & Short, K. (Eds.). (2003). *Stories matter: The complexity of cultural authenticity in children's literature.* Urbana, IL: National Council of Teachers of English.

Freeman, E., & Lehman, B. (2001). *Global perspectives in children's literature.* Boston: Allyn & Bacon.

Freire, P. (1970). *Pedagogy of the oppressed.* New York: Continuum.

Geertz, C. (1973). *The interpretation of cultures.* New York: Basic Books.

Harris, V., & Willis, A. (2003). Multiculturalism, literature and curriculum issues. In J. Flood, D. Lapp, J. Squire, & J. Jensen (Eds.), *Handbook of research on teaching the English language arts* (pp. 825–834). Mahwah, NJ: Lawrence Erlbaum.

Hofstede, G. (1991). *Cultures and organizations.* London: Profile Books.

Hoopes, D. S. (1979). Intercultural communication concepts and the psychology of intercultural experience. In M. D. Pusch (Ed.), *Multicultural education* (pp. 9–38). Chicago: Intercultural Press.

Martínez-Roldán, C. (2003). Building worlds and identities: A case study of the role of narratives in bilingual literature discussion. *Research in the Teaching of English, 37*(4), 491[n]526.

Short, K. (2009). Critically reading the word and the world. *Bookbird: A Journal of International Children's Literature, 47*(2), 1–10.

Short, K., & Burke, C. (1991). *Creating curriculum.* Portsmouth, NH: Heinemann.

Tomlinson, C., & Lynch-Brown, C. (1989). Adventuring with international literature: One teacher's experience. *The New Advocate, 2*(3), 169–178.

CHAPTER 9 EXTENSION

Rethinking Cultural Authenticity in Global Literature: A Korean Example

Yoo Kyung Sung with Richard J. Meyer

The chapter by Short and Thomas brings back memories for Yoo Kyung of collecting global literature about Korea for a professional workshop, "Beyond Kimchi," in which teachers utilized children's literature to facilitate learning about Korean language and culture by non-Korean children. In order to reclaim curriculum as part of reclaiming reading, it is important to (1) reflect on building collections of global literature, and (2) rethink the concept of cultural authenticity in global literature so that cultural groups are accurately presented.

Considerations in Building a Collection

The collection included multiple genres and perspectives in order to represent diverse facets of Korean culture. In terms of genres, it included traditional literature (e.g., folktales, myths, and legends), historical fiction, realistic fiction, and non-fiction, as well as books published in South Korea (contemporary Korean literature) and in the United States (Korean diaspora literature). Contemporary Korean literature is written in the Korean language and shows glimpses of Korean children's lives and experiences in Korea. Korean diaspora literature refers to the books that are published in the United States and portray Korean populations who live outside of Korea: Korean immigrants and Korean Americans. Both types of literature depict contemporary Korean culture, but provide different perspectives, foci, and social contexts.

The majority of the Korean literature books were in the genres of traditional literature, historical fiction, and non-fiction; there were few contemporary realistic fiction pieces. Traditional literature is a useful tool to develop intercultural understandings of Korea because it conveys cultural values, ethos, beliefs, and customs.

However, a lack of contemporary realistic fiction is problematic because it may contribute to the creation of distorted images of Korea. The role of global children's literature cannot be overemphasized, since for many children Korean literature is "window" literature (Bishop, 1994) through which they develop perceptions about Korea and Koreans without direct experiences. "Literature has the power to help us see the world afresh, to broaden our experiences and change our perception" (Huck, 1998, p. 12). Lowery (2000) argues, "Literature plays an important role in shaping social reality, in that literature reflects society" (p. 8).

Our concern is that knowledge gained through literature may contribute to limited, inaccurate, even negative understandings of another culture if readers only get to read an unbalanced distribution of genres. Traditional literature alone cannot comprehensively and authentically portray Korean culture because this genre lacks a sense of contemporary life and experiences (Sung, 2009). Even non-fiction risks a lack of authenticity when the statistics, photos, and facts are not updated with trends, policies, and other changes. In addition, some contemporary realistic fiction cannot keep up with the realities of contemporary life. Images such as rice fields, thatched roofs, *hanbok* (a traditional outfit), rice paper doors, etc. in contemporary realistic fiction project a Korea of the past. When this sense of the contemporary is not authentically incorporated into global children's literature and traditional images of a country are overemphasized, the result may be a misrepresentation of modernity and a distorted, even romantic, impression of the country (Yenika-Agbaw, 2008; Sung, 2009).

Cultural Authenticity in Global Children's Literature

The issue of cultural authenticity is revealed in the following story of the native Nigerian novelist Chimamanda Ngozi Adichie. She recalls her experiences of writing novels in the United States:

> I had a professor who once told me that my novel was not "authentically African." Now I was quite willing to contend that there were number of things wrong with the novel [but] . . . I had not quite imagined that I had failed to achieve something called "African authenticity." In fact, I didn't know what African authenticity was. The professor said that my characters were too much like him. . . . My characters drove cars. They were not starving. Therefore they are not authentically African.
>
> *(TEDglobal, 2009)*

Adichie's global writing about Nigeria was criticized for violating the criteria of "African authenticity" that non-African readers have. Such images are likely to be outdated and inaccurate. The "imagined" notion of Africa is likely to include the natural environment, wild animals, decivilization, starvation, etc. Once misguided non-contemporary images of Africa grow familiar, audiences resist the authentic portrayal of contemporary Africa. Such distorted perceptions toward the "other" culture become settled and may be difficult to rectify.

Reflecting upon cultural authenticity emphasizes that the nature of culture is fluid, dynamic, and changing, and examines whether this dynamic nature is reflected in children's books. For instance, in *My Name Is Yoon* (Recorvits, 2003) the protagonist is an immigrant girl depicted through surreal paintings that make time and place ambiguous. Readers may assume that Yoon does not know any English words. An interpretation of Yoon as unable to understand English may not represent the current Korean elementary education system or Koreans' decades-long desire for English language education. Particularly since the 1980s, when economic and political conditions shifted toward a focus on globalization, many Korean children learn some English in their Korean elementary schools. Unless the book is identified as historical fiction, audiences may assume Yoon's story is contemporary. The portrayal of her experiences with the English language may underscore a stereotype of Korean people as having limited English skills. Many Korean immigrant children just beginning their understanding of English, like Yoon, face cultural and linguistic shock in their first experiences in US classrooms, which is also open to misinterpretation.

Being reflective about the ways in which cultures are depicted in the literature of Korea helped Yoo Kyung to rethink cultural authenticity in the field of global children's literature. Such reflection must always be a part of the discussion of cultural authenticity because authenticity is often reduced to accuracy. According to Mo and Shen (2003), "authenticity is not just accuracy or the avoidance of stereotyping but involves cultural values and issues/practices that are accepted as norms of the social group" (p. 200).

Reclaiming reading curriculum must involve discussions of cultural authenticity that honor culture as something that transforms, hybridizes, diminishes, and evolves. Deep reflection may support teachers and their students in creating curriculum in which they develop authentic intercultural understanding as well as critical perspectives on depictions of diverse ethnic groups. It may also lead them to seek sources that can interrogate, verify, or add to their emerging assumptions about a cultural group. Teachers could ask families of students at school, and other individuals from the country or group being studied, to read and discuss the books. Websites and book reviews (which should also be interrogated) may provide background information about countries and cultures. A culture has many faces, and one goal in reclaiming reading is to help readers to be aware of cultural authenticity as evolving and always contextualized in time and place. Teachers and students should consider how they will interrogate the validity of the present day within realistic fiction and across genres. They might ask why the collections of different genres available to them are unbalanced, consisting of larger collections of traditional stories and historical fiction compared to few contemporary books. Extending such thinking to books about other cultures is essential to reclaiming curriculum, reading, and schools as places in which we seek deeper understanding of our similarities, differences, and our responsibilities to make the world more safe, just, and caring.

References

Bishop, R. S. (Ed.) (1994). *Kaleidoscope: A multicultural booklist for grades K-8*. Urbana, IL: National Council of Teachers of English Press.

Huck, C. S. (1998). The power of children's literature in the classroom. In K. G. Short & K. M. Pierce (Eds.). *Talking about books* (pp. 3–13). Portsmouth, NH: Heinemann.

Lowery, R. M. (2000). *Immigrants in children's literature*. New York: Peter Lang.

Mo, W., & Shen, W. (2003). Accuracy is not enough: The role of cultural values in the authenticity of picture books. In D. L. Fox & K. G. Short (Eds.), *Stories matter: The complexity of cultural authenticity in children's literature* (pp. 198–212). Urbana, IL: National Council of Teachers of English.

Recorvits, H. (2003). *My name is Yoon*. New York: Frances Foster Books.

Sung, Y. K. (2009). A post-colonial critique of the (mis)representation of Korean-Americans in children's picture books. Doctoral dissertation. The University of Arizona, Tucson, AZ.

TEDglobal. (2009, Oct.). Chimamanda Adichie: El peligro de una sola historia. Retrieved from www.ted.com/talks/lang/spa/chimamanda_adichie_the_danger_of_a_single_story. html

Yenika-Agbaw, V. (2008). *Representing Africa in children's literature: Old and new ways of seeing*. New York: Routledge.

10

INVITATIONS

Tools for Thought and Action

Katie Van Sluys and Tasha Tropp Laman

In life, we're invited to parties and special events; we're invited to be members of organizations, clubs, learning communities, face-to-face and online forums, as well as participants in civic life. How we take up these invitations and what happens during and as a result of our participation varies depending on the ways in which the event is framed, who participates, and available resources. In classrooms, curricular invitations can share properties and practices that are often associated with the invitations we take up in our everyday lives. Curricular invitations take on real-life conditions and offer students opportunities to pursue issues of interest. As formal pieces of curriculum, invitations bring together initial resources around a focal issue and then ask that learners pave their own paths of inquiry depending on their lived experiences and interests. Inviting students to engage in inquiries that have no easy answers or a single right path calls for a complex perspective on the world in which we live as well as an understanding of the ways in which decisions about classroom activity shape the kinds of people students become.

We frame this chapter by sharing our current thinking about curriculum, literacy, and learning, then go on to detail what curricular invitations are and aren't, move into classroom examples that animate what curricular invitations look like in action, and share analysis regarding how these invitations allow learners to strategically utilize technology, learn from and with print as well as visual images, and make use of language(s) in ways that best suit their talents, interests, and compelling inquiries. Such activity is at the heart of reclaiming reading curriculum that, once again, places the learner at the center, the teacher as one of many experts, and the world of real and intriguing issues as the source of lifelong learning.

What Do We Mean by Curriculum, Learning, and Literacy?

If we see curriculum as a package of lessons written for teachers to follow, we provide students with prescribed information and then look for "signs of learning" by asking kids to retell what they've been told or apply the information provided to particular scenarios. However, if we stop and ask ourselves questions such as what and whose knowledge is included or excluded in the package of lessons, and why the lessons are organized and taught in particular ways, our views of curriculum change. If, as teachers, we (re)claim what is meant by curriculum, we create new options for learning, literacy, and our students' lives.

We see curriculum as acts of organizing environments for learning (Nieto & Bode, 2008), and pay particular attention to the spaces in which kids are learning by looking at resources and practices utilized. We ask ourselves: Do learners use their first languages? Do they turn to the Internet for needed information? Do they draw upon each other's talents and experiences as they learn together? Furthermore, when curriculum is a decision-making process that focuses on learners, not just content, we take on the responsibility to engage children in problem posing, inquiry, and action related to issues that matter in their lives and the lives of others. In fact, we're called to create classrooms where learning means developing strategies for exploring issues and making decisions about how to communicate thinking and take action (Lewison, Leland, & Harste, 2008) and where children are on the "front line of knowledge construction" rather than the sidelines (Harste & Leland, 2007, p. 7).

When literacy is narrowly defined as *the ability to read and write*, teachers' work focuses on decoding and encoding texts in conventional forms, thereby limiting what learners come to know about the world and themselves (Harste, 2003). Reclaiming curriculum means understanding literacy as a complex set of social practices. It means creating classroom spaces where available tools and practices mirror twenty-first-century life, and students' strengths and resources are useful and valued (Harste, 2003; National Council of Teachers of English, 2010; Van Sluys, 2005).

Since we read more than printed books and newspapers, this stance means recognizing the diversity of textual encounters in people's real lives. Readers are bombarded with multiple, often simultaneous, streams of information including visual images via the Web, billboards, advertisements, art, and so on. Readers are responsible for constructing and critiquing understandings about our social world through textual, visual (see Albers, this volume), face-to-face, and virtual interactions with others who may or may not share our cultural experiences.

What Do We Mean by Invitations in Classrooms?

Curricular invitations offer one set of possibilities to move us from beliefs and understandings about learning and becoming literate in the twenty-first century to possible ways of facilitating classroom practices that embrace such beliefs. Curricular invitations are pieces of formal, written curriculum created to convene learners around a shared issue of interest. It is important to consider where issues and ideas for invitations come from, how they move from an idea to lived curriculum, and what practices support their use.

Invitations are anchored in students' lives, concerns, and wonderings. While some students may directly express wonder, such as asking what the differences are between orangutans and gorillas, other wonderings are embedded in students' everyday actions and require keen listening to yield possibilities for generative classroom curricular invitations. For example, when one teacher overheard a hallway conversation about how easy some people think it is to learn another language, she invited students to explore the complexities and challenges of learning languages (Van Sluys, 2005). The actual invitation was written on a piece of paper stapled to the outside of a folder containing a few multilingual books, a book of English idioms like *A Chocolate Moose for Dinner* (Gwynne, 2005), and an article on language learning. The invitation read:

> Questions have come up about how easy (or hard) it is to learn new languages. You're invited to explore the resources provided and other resources you can collect to further your thinking about this issue. As you work, you might think about:
>
> • What do you notice about English as you explore materials provided?
> • What do you think people need to know to understand and use English?
> • Can you make any connections between English and other languages?
> • What do you do to make sense of language you don't understand?

Invitations, which are different from centers, don't prescribe steps learners must take; they create conditions that gather learners around a shared interest, provide resources to initiate inquiry, and position learners as decision makers who determine how to, what next, and so what. Centers, on the other hand, are independent or small-group work stations with specific tasks for students to engage with or accomplish (Diller, 2003). In other words, with invitations, curriculum (i.e. activity) is rooted not in prescribed knowledge outcomes but in beliefs that the world is filled with questions and issues to explore—and what we know today may not be what we understand tomorrow. Notice how the *learning languages* invitation shared the genesis of the invitation, invited students to explore related issues, and provided possible questions. Students gathered at the invitation could then decide how they wanted to proceed.

Because oftentimes students are not experienced in making their own decisions or paving their own learning paths when in school, teaching through invitations should highlight engagement in productive decision making and suggest or model, but not mandate, possible actions regarding where the group might go next. We also help students see the benefits or challenges linked with their decisions. (See Van Sluys, 2005 for further information.)

Invitations, in life and in classrooms, are always social. In classrooms, learners use language(s), visual information such as drawings or sculptures, technological tools, and practices that involve taking in information, questioning, studying, and making decisions based on students' current understandings of the world (Van Sluys, 2005). For example, in the course of an inquiry, students might ask a classmate to provide an interpretation of a piece of art and a rationale for their opinion. They might consult websites, newspapers, blogs, or books to further inform their thinking. In addition to taking in information, students also produce texts and knowledge as they frame questions to pose to a company, critique advertisements, and construct texts to generate thought and conversation among members of their classroom communities at large (Lewison et al., 2008; Van Sluys, 2005). Learners not only are invited to *do* invitations but also take time to share their work by describing to classmates the paths their inquiries have taken and their intentions for next steps. For instance, in the *learning languages* invitation above, the group decided to share with classmates by highlighting the discovery of a connection between the meaning of an English word, *reign*, and the Spanish word for queen, *reina*. They also shared next steps, including their intentions to return to this invitation and use the Internet to see whether they could learn more about how other languages are related to English.

In this chapter, four invitations from one primary and one intermediate classroom illustrate the ways in which young people engaged with materials and one another. Their experiences make visible the ways (re)claiming curriculum in their classrooms created spaces for students to utilize multiple texts (both print and visual), technological tools, and their life resources to further personal and collective understandings of the world and each other.

Introducing Rooms 2 and 4

The examples shared in this chapter are drawn from two multiage and multilingual classrooms that we worked in extensively. Room 2 was a primary classroom, home to 24 first through third graders and their teacher of two years. Just up the stairs, Room 4 was home to 28 fourth through sixth graders and their experienced teacher. The young people in both classrooms brought with them a broad range of experiences including being in classrooms with their siblings and cousins, living transition-filled lives between houses, parents, and countries, and experiences living in and learning in nine languages beyond English (Russian, Hebrew, Spanish, Portuguese, Korean, Arabic, French, Berber, Vietnamese). Some were in their first year of school in the United States; others had spent their whole school career in this school. Some fourth graders were emergent readers, some second graders were experienced memoirists, and some newcomers were experienced readers and writers in their first language(s). In other words, Rooms 2 and 4, like all classrooms, were filled with students with diverse strengths, interests, and intentions. To help readers understand a little about the young people engaged in the upcoming examples, we've included parenthetical notes next to a particular student's name the first time their name is mentioned indicating their grade, followed by their first language. Each of the invitations featured opens with an introduction that details how and why the invitation was created, includes questions offered to launch activity, lists initial resources, and details what transpired as students began to create maps, interrogate ads, become researchers, and study images of Mexico.

My Maps

Readers need textual encounters that reach beyond fiction narratives and non-fiction books. With an intentional commitment to diversifying literacy practices via the sorts of texts students interact with, the teachers in Rooms 2 and 4 designed an invitation around Sara Fanelli's (1995) *My Map Book* to see where this book might take children. The book challenges conventional notions of maps using mixed media artwork to share two-page maps including "A Map of My Day" and "A Map of My Heart." The following invitation was typed and attached to a folder containing two copies of *My Map Book*.

My Maps

Cartographers make maps to provide information about the world(s) around them. You're invited to explore the maps created by Fanelli in *My Map Book*. Consider the following questions as you decide upon a direction for your work.

Does one of the maps appeal to you more than others? What do the maps tell you? What do they not tell you? What has Fanelli decided to include (exclude) from her maps? If you were to map parts of your world, what would you map? How? Why?

As you read, talk, and/or create, think about how elements of design shape the meaning readers make.

In Room 4, Ana Cristina (5th, Spanish) first took up this invitation with two classmates; she quietly sketched a map of her Mexico neighborhood—with a few seemingly fictitious elements as she inserted a new classmate's house not far from her *abuela*'s (grandma's) home. Classmates pored over the pages of Fanelli's maps, discussing details and the humor included in the author's maps—particularly in the illustration "Map of My Dog." Wrapping up their day's work, the students decided to share two ideas with classmates during sharing time and then added Ana Cristina's map to the folder. On another day, a different group of three boys began not with Fanelli's book but with the collection of classmates' maps tucked into the folder. Then they skimmed *My Map Book*, stopping at the "Map of My Family." At this point, group members sketched maps of their families—talking all the while. As Gino (4th, Spanish) used Fanelli's map to scaffold the labeling of his map in English, the three boys (4th to 6th, English) discussed the extended members of their families and where they lived, as well as actual and hoped-for relationships with various family members.

In Room 2, Grace (2nd, English) crafted a map animating her social relationships and the necessary steps for making social plans (asking permission for friends to visit, her mother's response and her friends' eager replies). Rachel, her sister, began with a Fanelli-like map of her house but then moved to creating a "Map of the Book I'm Reading," sharing happenings and predictions with regard to her reading of *Wringer* (Spinelli, 1997). Megan (3rd, English) also responded to a student-made "Map of My Boredom" that was tucked inside the invitation folder. Megan drew a picture and wrote a caption reflecting her own boredom in respect to recent standardized testing.

Mother's Day

Late in April, as students in Room 4 gained more experience of reading with a critical eye by considering multiple perspectives, questioning authors' intentions, and attending to voices heard and voices excluded from texts, students questioned the word choice in newspaper headlines and wondered about editorial choices when selecting certain pictures to accompany articles. With Mother's Day around the corner and print ads filling mailboxes and newspapers, their teacher created the following invitation:

Mother's Day

Lately class members have noticed newspaper ads as well as the fine print in book order leaflets. They have noted what ads include and exclude. You're invited to examine some of the recent ads related to Mother's Day that are included in this folder. You might choose to consider some of the following questions as you read and think with other invitation participants.

What do you notice? What questions come to mind?
What do you notice about gender?
What do the ads tell you about celebrating Mother's Day?
How does the organization of the ads contribute to meanings?
Who benefits from these messages?
What options do you have as a reader of these texts?
How might you respond?
Resources: Mother's Day ads from newspapers, magazines, store circulars.

As some of the first participants settled into their work, Nokomo (4th, Russian), a student learning English, declared, "These not moms, they models or university students" when referencing a discount store ad featuring four thin young white women. Searching through the collection of ads, the student found fuller-figured women and identified them as moms: "These moms"; to which her classmate responded, "Not mine." After a while the "Not mine" comment was expanded when Fernanda (5th, Spanish) noted that she wasn't thinking about age or body image; rather, she was pointing out that while the featured women were white, her mother was "not white." Her comment moved the group discussion to ways in which the ad could be rewritten, which led to their need to know "how much of America not white?"

They consulted census information using a Spanish-language mode of an Internet search engine, typing "How many Americans black and white?" in the text box. Nokomo suggested entering "black and white." When their search results yielded information linked to black-and-white photography, Fernanda switched to the Spanish version of the search engine and typed "población de los Estados Unidos" (population of the United States). Sitting alongside, observing the girls at work, Katie suggested using the limiting term *race* in conjunction with their previous search. Locating the needed census information, the girls recommended revisions to the ad. Weeks after the invitation had first been shared with the class, Ana Cristina (6th, Spanish), María (5th, Spanish, Ana Cristina's cousin), Nina (4th, Hebrew), and Amy (5th, English) paged through the ads in the Invitation folder and listed things their mothers really liked: long walks, time with kids, and time away from kids. They then wondered about the origins of the holiday and the differences between *el día de los madres* in Mexico and US notions of Mother's Day. Using a computer, they searched, read, and pasted findings into PowerPoint in order to organize the information.

Becoming a Researcher

The children in Room 2 expressed an interest in knowing more about what it means to be and become a researcher as they became more acquainted with Tasha, a university researcher. Tasha created an invitation for the first through third graders:

Becoming a Researcher

Some researchers study things (people and places) by watching, listening, and asking questions. Researchers use tools—audio recorders, cameras, clipboards, paper . . .

You're invited to use the tools provided to study people in your classroom. You may watch people doing invitations and write or draw what you see. You may ask them questions about what they are doing and record their responses. You could also interview people about school, things they like to do, or ask other questions that you want to know more about.

Write, draw, or talk about what you learn from your research by examining the photos you take, listening to your audio recordings, and rereading your notes.

The first three young people in Room 2 to engage with this invitation began by negotiating who would use the recorder. Lee (1st, English), who often struggled with writing, quickly figured out that he could take photos and write the students' class numbers that the teacher used for record keeping in order to keep track of the photos that he took. Allen (2nd, English) directed peers to "ask questions," to which Jackie (1st, English) asked, "What kind of questions do we ask them?" After constructing some initial definitions of work they thought researchers did, they decided to work as a team, one person taking pictures, one taking notes, and another audiotaping their peers. They moved around the room using these multiple tools to observe, interview peers, and record observations. When others spent time with this invitation, they took notes on their classmates' activity—acts not too far from what they saw Tasha and their teacher doing when they took field notes or kidwatching notes. They snapped pictures of their classmates' work (of which 90 percent included students engaged in invitation work vs. posed pictures). They pooled their notes, recordings, and photos to construct multimodal primary documents of invitations activity and commented on the variety of things classmates did with invitations.

Images of Mexico . . . Magic Windows

Can you tell whether a book is set in Mexico just from the illustrations? After a class debate about the setting of the picture book *Friends from the Other Side* (Anzaldúa, 1997), an invitation was created to explore the many faces of life in Mexico, including images of cosmopolitan city life, ancient cultures, and the biodiversity of the Mexican states. The original invitation read:

> Look at the books *Amigos del otro lado/Friends from the Other Side and Tomás and the Library Lady* (Mora, 2000). Where do they take place—the United States or Mexico? Why might some readers respond "Mexico" and others "the United States?" You're invited to explore images of Mexico, inquiring into the images you and others hold and why. As you look at these books as well as the other materials with this invitation, think about:
>
> What images come to mind when you think about Mexico? Where do these images come from? You're invited to think, read, talk, and explore images of Mexico. What do you notice? Do your ideas about Mexico match or challenge what you see? What surprises you? How might you explain your surprises?

Resources:

Poetry: *My Mexico/México mío,* by Tony Johnston, 1996.

Picture Books: *Amigos del otro lado/Friends from the Other Side,* by Gloria Anzaldúa, edited by Harriet Rohmer and David Schecter, 1997.

Tomás and the Library Lady, by Pat Mora illustrated by Raul Colón, 2000.

Magazines: *National Geographic* "Emerging Mexico," a special issue volume, August 1996.

Faces "Mexico," *Cobblestone,* December 2000.

Photographs and student artifacts.

While the original invitation contained the resources listed, students added materials as their inquiries took them down different paths. For example, when two students encountered Carmen Lomas Garza's (1999) *Magic Windows/Ventanas mágicas* elsewhere in their classroom, they added it to the folder. Opening the text, students discussed *papeles picados* (thin paper, typically about 12 × 18 inches, with many fine patterns cut into them, strung together) and how they connected with their conceptions of Mexican life and culture. Then they began creating. They became intrigued by the intricate designs and symbols contained within these banners often hung as part of Mexican festivals and celebrations. As they folded, designed, and cut their own *papeles picados,* student talk addressed the how-tos, the symbols they were attempting to embed in their tissue paper banners, and memories linked to Mexican *ferias* (fairs), Fourth of July picnics, and family reunions.

Collective Analysis: So What Does Student Activity Teach Us?

Stepping back and examining the curricular activity that unfolded across the four invitations, we saw trends that speak to the ways that invitations offered students new literate possibilities.

Technology as a Tool

Students turned to technology for numerous reasons throughout their inquiries. The Mother's Day participants used the Internet as a tool when they needed to access data immediately to follow up on a hunch. Their life experiences told them that America wasn't composed only of white moms, as the discount store ads illustrated, and in order to confirm and further their thinking they needed census data. When another group of students wondered about variations between US and Mexican traditions with regard to Mother's Day, PowerPoint was a tool for organizing research findings. Group members pasted information, searched, read, and revised slides, then shared a part of their PowerPoint with classmates. What they shared was far from a polished presentation; PowerPoint was an effective visual tool that supported their verbal sharing of emergent conclusions regarding their day's work.

In Becoming a Researcher, young researchers used technology to gather data as they observed and interviewed learners in their classroom. Their photos and audio recordings enabled them to capture often fleeting moments and later to return to episodes to discuss classroom activity. Using technological tools helped students step out of their usual engagement and take on a new stance that made the familiar strange.

The students' use of technology in these examples mirrored genuine life uses of these tools. Users often turn to the Internet for just-in-time information or cut-and-paste information across applications when investigating an issue or concern. We also use technology to compose, revise, and publish texts, but this function is far from the only way technology is used in the real world. Hence, young people need curricular opportunities that harness technology in moving inquiries forward, not just word-processing their final copy of a story, making PowerPoint presentations, or using a computer-packaged program. Students integrated these tools as part of their thinking and their learning. They engaged in mini-inquiries much like those we often find ourselves conducting: Googling unknown information, skimming multiple sources, integrating these findings into current understandings, and moving on. In other words, invitations aren't seeking "finished products"; rather, we use them to develop the practices needed for living in a world constantly generating and sharing new knowledge.

Multiple Languages: Multiple Insights

The featured invitations illustrate how curriculum in both mono- and multilingual classrooms can be created in ways that encourage learners to think about language use and invitation activity. Although they were not always in fluent, grammatically correct English, communication was central to all featured invitations. Students explored issues and constructed shared understandings through language. "These not moms" represented powerful thinking and launched meaningful group work as participants used their existing knowledge to question images, search for information that validated their experiences, and create a new text to help their peers interrogate the images they too were bombarded with as Mother's Day approached. Likewise, students chatted and noticed each other's work as they collaboratively created texts, made maps, or designed and cut *papeles picados*. The artifacts prompted thoughtful questions and furthered inquiry. Students' shared experiences facilitated ways to initiate, respond, and turn-take within conversation.

Within students' oral and written language experiences, the types of language in use varied across invitations and time, involved a variety of linguistic genres and registers, and expanded meaning potentials. Students debated social meanings of language as they shifted from "black and white" to "race" as search terms; and students learned ways to pose questions for interviews. They told stories and engaged in the language of inquiry by building from the known, posing questions, generating possible hypotheses, searching for and interpreting information, and reflecting on and sharing new and growing understandings. Students also used languages other than English to research the Web, read multilingual texts, and chat with friends who shared similar first languages. Invitations, and the conversations inside of them, opened possibilities to cast curriculum and learning in a new light. Our global context demands a new norm, one in which literate people possess wider ranges of abilities and multiple literacies and language practices. Reclaiming curriculum in the twenty-first century values these kinds of communicative actions wherein learners make meaning with, through, and from multiple resources and multiple people, and across multiple languages.

Beyond Words: Images as Meaning Making

We live in a world where meaning hinges on powerful visual images as well as printed or spoken words. The students working with the Mother's Day invitation illustrated this point when their inquiry began with an observation about the "mother models" portrayed in the discount store ad. When Nokomo declared, "These not moms!" (referring to four white women seemingly in their twenties), she and her classmates began to critically read images. When these same girls found US census data that confirmed their thinking and their experiences about the significant percentage of Americans who are not white, they printed their findings, cut out the ad, and pasted both onto a large sheet of paper that marked the beginning of a poster to communicate their learning with classmates.

The Mother's Day participants were not only consumers of other people's images and worldviews but also producers of images. Following Fanelli's lead in *My Map Book*, students added to the collection of maps—including maps of their bedrooms, families, hairstyles, books read, and their boredom. Megan moved from a visual image to written text inspired by her classmate's Map of My Boredom and composed a commentary on the boredom she experienced with testing.

Lastly, students' use of image offered opportunities for analysis, discussion of representation, and movement between different forms of representation. The student researchers analyzing the photos they'd taken and those creating their own *papeles picados* engaged in numerous debates over the visual meanings constructed. These invitation participants understood image as more than a textual feature that could help them decode print: they understood visual image as a tool and resource to communicate and unpack particular worldviews; they had a sense of what image could accomplish that words might not; and they had the classroom spaces to explore and experiment with images that extended their own, as well as their classmates', thinking. Curriculum grew from the students' knowledge, not some external other. Generating curriculum from lived experiences positions learners' lives as worthy of study, questioning, and exploring. Utilizing, designing, challenging, and creating images offered opportunities to convey meanings that students might not have conveyed in words.

It's All about Possibilities

The invitations shared in this chapter reveal sets of social practices that are possible when we position curriculum as an ongoing decision-making process aimed at involving active participants in our classrooms and beyond. The invitations animate our thinking about literacy as a complex, social activity in which students collaboratively consume, critique, and produce meanings. The students' actions provide images of what curriculum, literacy, and learning *can* be when we reclaim these concepts and construct spaces in which students are granted access to tools and practices that involve a variety of texts, position art as integral, and understand that using technology well means embracing new practices rather than replicating previous practices in new contexts.

As we contemplate integrating new practices into our classrooms, we need to keep our beliefs about children, curriculum, and the world close at hand. If we believe that cultural and linguistic resources matter, we must accept meaningful approximations. If we believe that our students and who they become are at the heart of curriculum, we must tune into their lives and craft invitations linked to experiences and wonderings. If we believe that learning happens in the company of others, then we must create spaces that foster dialogue and interaction. If we believe that being a participant in our social world involves texts that include more than books, then we need to offer opportunities to interact with an array of media (from art texts to digital and multilingual texts). If we believe that being literate means more than consuming messages from others, we must welcome and teach critique and action. And if we believe learning does not always end in creating a perfect final product, we must see curriculum as ongoing, tentative, and oftentimes unfinished, trusting that the learning processes and literacy practices that students engage in are not momentary or ever truly finished.

The students in Rooms 2 and 4 engaged in critical inquiries when the curriculum in their classrooms attended to how learners made decisions, pursued lines of inquiry in the company of others, and shared their thinking in ways that encouraged others to be active participants. Watching classroom life in other states and cities, we see students yearning to pursue important questions: Why is an African American's last name White? What are earthquakes? Why are houses in Haiti not strong? Given the issues on our minds and the kinds of people and practices our world needs, we now invite you to reclaim curriculum in your classroom by listening closely to the issues and interests on your students' minds and crafting an initial invitation or two to begin constructing curriculum together.

References

Anzaldúa, G. (1997). *Amigos del otro lado/Friends from the other side.* San Francisco: Children's Book Press.
Diller, D. (2003). *Literacy work stations: Making centers work.* Portland, ME: Stenhouse.
Fanelli, S. (1995). *My map book.* New York: HarperCollins.

Garza, C. L. (1999). *Magic windows/Ventanas mágicas*. San Francisco: Children's Book Press.

Gwynne, F. (2005). *A chocolate moose for dinner*. New York: Simon & Schuster.

Harste, J. C. (2003). What do we mean by literacy now? *Voices from the Middle, 10*(3), 8–12.

Harste, J. C., & Leland, C. (2007). On getting lost, finding one's direction, and teacher research. *Voices from the Middle, 14*(3), 7–11.

Johnston, T. (1996). *My Mexico/México mío*. New York: Penguin Books.

Lewison, M., Leland, C., & Harste, J. C. (2008). *Creating critical classrooms: K-8 reading and writing with an edge*. Mahwah, NJ: Lawrence Erlbaum.

Mora, P. (2000). *Tomás and the library lady*. New York: Dragonfly Books.

National Council of Teachers of English (2010, February 13). Retrieved from www.ncte. org/positions/statements/21stcentdefinition

National Geographic. (1996, August). "Emerging Mexico" A special issue volume.

Nieto, S., & Bode, P. (2008). *Affirming diversity: The sociopolitical context of multicultural education*. Boston: Pearson.

Spinelli, J. (1997). *Wringer*. New York: HarperCollins.

Van Sluys, K. (2005). *What if and why? Literacy invitations for multilingual classrooms*. Portsmouth, NH: Heinemann.

CHAPTER 10 EXTENSION

Reading the World through Moodles and Wordles and Digital Texts

Kathryn Mitchell Pierce and Edward Kastner

Middle school students are passionately curious about who they are and who they might become. Their peer relationships are keys to their worlds, values, and dreams. We invited a group of middle school students to reflect on their social experiences at school and to share their insights with others. We set up parameters that would ensure that all students engaged in reading, writing, photography, and development of a final display. In addition, we created learning engagements that highlighted the value of collaborating with others. We chose the question *What is the social and emotional climate of our school?* and the primary method of sharing (large display panels with photographs and text), but the content was shaped by the students.

The Photovoice process provided us with valuable ideas for helping students study their school and then share their perspectives with others (see www. photovoice.org). As Van Sluys and Laman explain in the main part of the chapter, "invitations bring together initial resources around a focal issue and then ask that learners pave their own paths of inquiry depending on their lived experiences and interests" (p. 167). The following look at Justin's experience showcases some of the strategies and resources we made available to students and how we supported them in taking a critical look at their school. Writing and using digital media helped students learn critical reading strategies and supported their reclaiming of reading.

Justin's Story: Shifting to a More Critical Lens

We asked our students to photograph students around our school and even after school. Many of these photographs captured students socializing in the cafeteria during lunch. Small groups were then asked to look closely at their photographs, to *describe* what they saw, and to write interpretations in the form of captions. This process helped them distinguish between observation and interpretation, and highlighted ways that experiences and assumptions affect interpretations. Initially, Justin's discussions about a cafeteria photograph focused only on the groups of students sitting talking and laughing together. After describing the photograph in detail, discussing it with others in his group, and writing informal reflections about it, Justin noticed that one student appeared to be sitting alone, looking at the others who were sitting and talking in groups. His descriptive caption read (translated into conventional spelling):

> In this picture there is a boy sitting completely alone. It appears that no one is even at this boy's table. All around the boy is social interaction. In the background to the right is a group of girls laughing. To the left is other girls laughing.

As the project developed, Justin and his classmates generated hypotheses or thesis statements about the social and emotional climate in our school, grounding these statements in the data they collected through their photographs. They used the photographs and conversations to "read" their school through a new lens.

Moodle Discussion

Students used online forums in a secure Moodle site to share descriptions and insights about their photographs (see www.moodle.org). By creating online opportunities for conversation, we were able to capture student discussions, which made their ideas visible and tangible. Using transcripts from these online discussions, students talked about what their own group had written and then looked at the writing from other groups. The transcripts allowed students to clarify what they had written, to revise their thinking in light of what others had said, and to see how their ideas compared to their classmates'. In small groups, students then crafted thesis statements to represent their views about our school and supported their ideas with references to particular photographs.

Reading Wordle Images

We felt that conversations about the photographs and the transcripts would help students recognize the power in the messages they were creating. Identifying themes or patterns in the writing was more difficult than we anticipated. Using the transcripts from the online discussions, we created a Wordle for each discussion forum to highlight themes. (Wordle is available at www.wordle.net.) Wordle images show frequently occurring words in a larger type size. Figure 10ext.1 shows the Wordle created from the online discussion of potential thesis statements in Justin's small group.

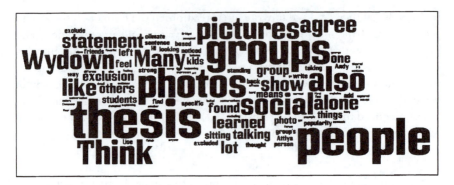

FIGURE 10ext.1 Wordle, Created at wordle.net

After having learned to look closely at photographs and to distinguish between observation and interpretation, students applied these skills as they read the written online discussions. They looked closely at the Wordle images and talked about what they saw in the graphic representations of their discussions. They made connections across the words that appeared in larger fonts and considered the significance of words in smaller fonts. The conversations led to revised and more focused thesis statements.

Revision as Re-seeing

Justin's group revised their thesis statement several times during the project. Initially, their thesis statement read: *There is a lot of social tension in our school.* As their inquiry evolved, they revised their thesis statement to: *There are many social groups at [our school] that exclude people based on popularity and social skills.* Justin then revised his caption so that it better reflected his group's thesis statement. His caption helped others see what he and his group had learned to see:

> In a middle school cafeteria a lot of social tension occurs. Some students sit alone. Some laugh and talk with friends. Sometimes students with less of a popularity status are not allowed into a conversation. They sit alone and glare at everyone else who is having a good time. As they stare they see an open seat, but fear they will not be accepted. So they remain in their seat, wondering why they and not anyone else is sitting here alone.

Justin's revised caption shows his insights into the angst associated with seating patterns in a middle school cafeteria. As a very popular student, Justin was always part of various social groups. His writing reflects his ability to now read the cafeteria through a new lens—to see differently; he reclaimed reading by reading his world.

In his reflection at the end of the Photovoice project, Justin wrote:

I have learned that a person sees a lot more exclusion when they are looking for it. For example, before I started this project I was just focused on talking and laughing with my friends. I didn't look around to see the exclusion that was happening behind my back . . .

In the lunch room it is a test of who's friends with who. Often students fail this test, but they try to hide it from their peers. They often sit with groups of students who they are not friends with or who do not like them. Even though they are sitting with the group, they are not engaged in any conversations. They are being verbally excluded. Sometimes they are even told deliberately they are not welcome at the table.

Justin explained that, in the past, he was so focused on conversations with his own friends that he didn't really see the students who were alone. Justin and his classmates now saw the cafeteria and their school differently. The culminating display provided them with an opportunity to show what they wanted to communicate to others about their inquiry, and their school.

Quite consistent with the learners in Van Sluys and Laman's main part of the chapter, Justin and his classmates developed new ways of seeing the social environment in their school, which then prepared them to act differently. Learning to recognize and look past assumptions is a difficult task. The students learned to do this with photographs—to look closely at the details (to read them aesthetically and emotionally) so that they could understand how their own experiences and biases influence what they see. They can now use these insights to help them "read" other texts—print texts, posters, videos, and commercials—with a critical eye.

PILLAR IV
Reclaiming Language

11

VISUAL DISCOURSE ANALYSIS

What's Critical about Pictures, Anyway?

Peggy Albers

> The use of visual languages is compelling for many reasons, not the least of which is that their graphical nature can act as an analogical representation of the actual domain in a way that is not possible with purely textual systems.
>
> *(Rob Kremer, 1998)*

The purpose of this chapter is to describe *outsider* literacy, which is the idea that visual texts are not considered (lie *outside* of) typical practices of reading and writing in classrooms. In my work as an artist and as a reading researcher, I interrupt commonplace notions of literacy as anchored in print to recognize the significance of visual texts for reclaiming reading. In this chapter I suggest that teachers and students can interrupt a historically casual dismissal of visual texts for deeper analysis and discussion. When reading teachers interrupt visual texts, they glean insights into learners' uses of art as an authentic language system. They also communicate to students that they have a right to engage in a curriculum in which a range of language forms is valued.

Reading the many languages of visual texts is part of being literate in this century. In this chapter I suggest that it is essential to study the visual texts that students create in literacy and English-language arts classes, especially when reading and writing print-based texts forefront accountability. According to Krauth (cited in Weeks, 2007), the current generation of students is visually oriented, or what Weeks (2007) refers to as the "eye generation." Krauth states that as much as 50 percent of the information students acquire today comes from visual texts rather than written texts. Students often passively consume and are more easily manipulated through images without lending a critical eye to reading the messages that are sent and received (Albers, Harste, Vander Zanden, & Felderman, 2008). With this in mind, positioning art as an important language system, in which meaning is constructed, interpreted, and read visually, is an essential facet of reclaiming reading.

Reclaiming language and literacy from a visual standpoint means attention must be paid to how and which texts are perceived as significant, and to what extent visual information is integrated into language arts and literacy curricula. Often, students are only offered opportunities to read and respond through written language; for some students, especially English language learners or learners who struggle with reading, this means disenfranchisement and marginalization from participating in classroom conversations and learning. Positioning art as a significant language system means literacy is opened up to a range of ways in which students can communicate, including illustrations created around a literary text, short video documentaries posted to YouTube, podcasts uploaded to websites, and more.

Our work as reading teachers is grounded in Halliday's (1985) notion that we learn language, learn about language, and learn through language. Students in the twenty-first century learn visual languages (digital, watercolor, clay, among many), learn through visual language (content, technique, concepts, etc.), and learn about visual language and how it works in texts (critical literacy, discourses). When curriculum is open to art as a language system, students learn to interrogate a variety of messages, including those posted on billboards, magazine advertisements, posters in their cafeterias, toys (see Wohlwend & Hubbard, this volume), and various digital texts. Engaging in such work, as a number of scholars suggest (Albers, 2007; Harste, Chung, & Grant, 2006), is the essence of creating critical literacy classrooms (Vasquez, Albers, & Harste, 2010).

In the United States and other countries there is a great deal of emphasis on standardized testing, and if the current legislative direction continues, teachers' merit pay will be based upon students' test scores. Students are asked to study the same curriculum and taught to respond with automaticity through assignments such as five-paragraph essays. I call limiting students to written texts like these an *insider* approach because their work relies upon expected, verbocentric practices and uses of written language. This *insider* approach suggests that the purpose of literacy is to perform well on tests, to operate on a mechanical level when using language, and to follow prescribed, scripted programs. Such insider approaches distance teachers and learners from the essence of literacy, which is (see Goodman & Goodman, this volume) an ability to read and interpret a range of messages and to communicate across a range of media. Understanding that various media are languages that belong in the language arts curriculum is important in our work to reclaim reading.

The term "outsider literacy" arises from my interest in outsider art, a term that defines art created by patients in mental institutions. In the late nineteenth century, over a 30-year history, psychiatrist and historian Hans Prinzhorn had amassed a collection of 5000 artworks created by patients diagnosed as insane. He analyzed them, and presented convincing evidence that the artworks demonstrated insights into the creative process, and were not simply detailed and ornamental images that were disturbing and startling. This *outsider* art was created by patients' self-taught knowledge of art, and they integrated what they learned through observation of the world and art into their artworks. Prinzhorn analyzed the pieces and presented convincing evidence that they demonstrated the art makers' insights into the creative process. In contrast to art critics who called these artworks "lower form[s] of expression than [those] by 'real' artists" (Maizels, 1996, p. 13), master artist Paul Klee compared these artworks to the visual markings of children—his own childhood art included. He suggested that outsider art was much more than "random scribbles or pathetic fantasies, or even interesting clinical evidence" (Maizels, 1996, p. 14). Rather, these artworks were raw, spontaneous, and original, much like Mose Tolliver's paintings (see Figure 11.1), and untouched by traditional and classic frameworks.

FIGURE 11.1 Mose Tolliver, *Turtle*, Outsider Artist

FIGURE 11.2 Albers' Representation of Water Buffalo in Two Compositions

A self-proclaimed outsider artist myself, I understand my own art as more than random, as marks that communicate intentional messages, which are flexibly read by those who view and handle my pieces; my art is informed by my ideologies and energy as an artist. Figure 11.2 presents two examples of my work; they are raw and spontaneous in that they arose not from years of study in art school, but from my own immediate interest in wild animals and my need for art to have a function, in this case as a canteen and a cup.

It is from this outsider perspective that I study students' visual texts. I see that their visual marks are self-taught, raw, spontaneous, and original; they integrate content knowledge, and arise out of the discourse communities with which they identify (Gee, 2005). I also understand that even though students spend a great deal of time creating their visual texts, they are often given little talk time in classes. They are likely considered decoration. They are glanced at and perhaps tacked onto the wall, but often sent home at the end of the day or week with congratulatory comments on effort or aesthetic appeal, and often deemed "perfect" by educators who view them. I argue that teachers must (visually) interrupt present thinking that art as a language system functions only as decoration. They should do close readings of visual texts from an outsider perspective to discover students' creative processes and to gain insight into their use of authentic visual language. In so doing, teachers will reclaim the reading of such texts.

Visual Discourse Analysis

Each visual text that is drawn, painted, constructed, or fashioned in classrooms proves the existence of the power and desire of learners to create. For the majority of children and adults, visual texts arise from both their experiences with art in their everyday worlds, and their self-taught knowledge. They create texts with form, technique, and messages quite often like those of outsider artists, which are "untutored, spontaneous, and sometimes irrational" (Rexler, 2005, p. 6). It is important for teachers to understand how to analyze visual texts, including their structural and graphic features, as well as the discourses that underpin the messages within them. In the next section I present visual discourse analysis (VDA), a theory and method that elucidate how language operates within visual texts.

Grounded in semiotic principles (Albers, 2007), VDA studies cueing systems within visual texts: *graphic* marks on paper or canvas, *syntax* or structures and conventions within visual texts, *semantics* or meaning conveyed in the text, *pragmatics* or the context out of which these texts arise, and *tactility*, or the sensory relationship between meaning and how this meaning is made through media. Inherently embedded in VDA is a critical perspective that acknowledges that no text is neutral and that language both produces and is produced by ideologies. That is, VDA allows viewers to identify how certain social activities and social identities get played out in the production of visual texts. Put another way, visual discourse analysis offers ways in which teachers can analyze the language within visual texts; the marks within visual texts; and the social, school, public, and community contexts in which art as a language is used.

Four language tenets underpin VDA. First, visual language is reflexive: it creates and reflects the context and reality in which it was created. Students often create visual texts that are intertextually related to support or extend their understanding of a written text. At the same time, these messages shape viewers' interpretations and responses, most often to the written text. In Figure 11.3, for example, Patrick designed and created a three-dimensional visual text based upon his reading of *Lord of the Flies* (Golding, 1959). His visual text conveyed his interest in and interpretation of the remote island setting of this novel. Viewing Patrick's text positioned his classmates to talk about the role that setting plays in the dissolution of civilized behavior, a theme in the novel.

Second, language allows for situated meanings to occur—that is, images or texts that are "assembled on the spot" (Gee, 2005, p. 94) in a given context and based upon previous experiences with art and/or with ways visual texts assess meaning. In this example, Patrick's three-dimensional text was literally and figuratively assembled "on the spot," and based upon his reading of Golding's novel. Students learn early on that visual texts are assessments; they must visually and clearly suggest intertextual relationships between the elements of the visual text to events in the literary texts.

Third, language is composed of many different social languages (Bakhtin, 1982). How students speak visually differs from how artists speak. Artists study art as a

FIGURE 11.3 Patrick's Visual Text in Response to *Lord of the Flies*

language and discipline, while students who have little training in art draw from personal experiences with art. In essence, students' visual texts are "hybridized" (Gee, 2005, p. 105); they contain clues or cues that indicate intuitive knowledge of art principles and elements. Patrick's visual text represented several social languages: those conducted around literary texts, those communicated through art, those around being a student, and those as a self-taught artist. Unique to art as a language system was Patrick's ability to have social agency, largely because there were few strict and confining principles around visual language assigned to him.

The fourth tenet of language suggests that the cue systems of visual texts are units of analysis: graphic, structural, semantic, pragmatic, and tactile. Patrick's text allowed viewers to construct meaning because it contains graphic and tactile elements (rocks, sticks, green paint); syntactic organization of elements that enable viewers to read this as an island; semantic presentation of a remote island as the setting of the novel; and pragmatically situated text produced in an English-language arts classroom.

Just as Prinzhorn did with outsider art, one of the first steps I took in reading and analyzing school-generated visual texts from an outsider perspective was to study a great number of them, appreciate them for what they were and how they were created, and then ask how the textmakers used materials and what effects they were trying to achieve. I considered such questions as the following:

- What type of art was this student doing (sculpture, painting, collage, etc.)?
- How were these materials used, and what effects did these materials create?
- What struck me about the art in the first place? Did the imagery appear to tell a story?

- Where did the student invest her or his energy? In line, color, geometry, surface, texture? In images, words, or graphic scrawl?
- What visual elements occurred and reoccurred, and in what relation to each other?
- Did the student draw upon other works of art to convey a message or imitate a style, technique, process, and so on?

These questions help reclaim languages by acknowledging that *language* is not a singular way of making meaning with words.

Analyzing Language in School-Generated Visual Texts

I saw eight distinct "urges" around which students, kindergarten through graduate, generated 1000 visual texts that I studied with VDA. I use Prinzhorn's term "urges" (cited in Maizels, 1996, p. 14) rather than "purposes" to describe the way in which students created and renovated ideas through visual means. Their urge to create visual texts was both artistic and pragmatic, in that they attempted to convey an aesthetically pleasing visual meaning, often associated with literary texts or original writings. Next, I discuss four of these urges: wordplay, flatlands, narrative originality, and repetition.

Wordplay, or the Urge to Play Artistically with Words

Artist Paul Klee once stated that writing and drawing are identical processes (Naubert-Riser, 1988). Students combined writing and drawing in some of the texts; they played with words and arranged them as art objects. Texts in Figure 11.4 are examples that define this category. Students seemed to see written language both as play and as a means to convey information. They arranged written language elements, such as their signature, cutout print, and typed print, in and on their texts. For these students, written text took on roles as abstract graphic elements, artistic play, and information, capable of expressing a symbolic message as well as literal meaning. In the top left-hand image in Figure 11.4, after studying Shakespeare's sonnets this high school student symbolized her understanding of Shakespeare's literary contributions to the English language by using a portrait of Shakespeare upon which written language was transposed. This student did not intend for viewers to read the written language, but written text served as a single symbol of Shakespeare's literary influence. Written text was artful symbolism, and became an abstract element in this visual text.

After being asked to create an original story based upon other short stories they read, a seventh-grade student played with and created her own font and artistic symbols to present the title of her picture story, "Serpentine Girl and Grocer's Boy" (see the top right-hand image in Figure 11.4). In so doing, she positioned and invited the viewer-reader into her story through stars, swirls, boxes, dots, and

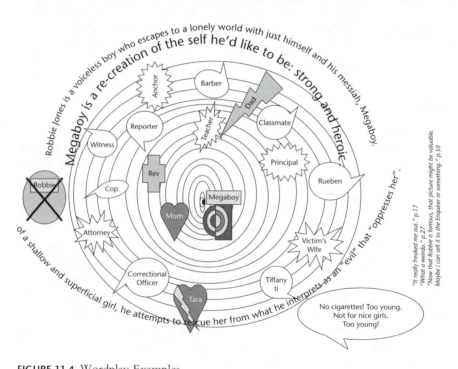

FIGURE 11.4 Wordplay Examples

exaggerated tails on the ends of alphabetic letters, all in a range of colors. In the bottom image in Figure 11.4, in response to a young adult novel, *Making Up Megaboy* (Walter, 1999), this graduate student played artistically with the structure of written text by disrupting the left-to-right, top-to-bottom conventions, and intended the viewer to read written text in a circular pattern. Written text was presented as semantically pleasing.

Across visual texts as wordplay, students invented creative ways to communicate information as well as aesthetic interest. They renovated, remixed, and invented new aspects of language, by combining what they knew about written language and what they knew about art. They designed, created, and/or assembled creative messages around literary texts that they had read or original stories they had written. Invention and play with language are at the heart of meaning making and reclaiming language as part of reclaiming teaching.

Flatlands, or the Urge to Represent Story and Symbol on Flat Surfaces

In visual texts I call "flatlands," students represented their learning or their expressions on paper, cardboard, or other flat surfaces. Written language almost always is conveyed in schools on notebook paper, lined paper, or computer paper, because these are inexpensive and neat media that can be easily tacked on a wall. That flatland images are promoted and supported as the single most important way to communicate visually speaks to a larger Discourse of what is art, which is likely to be objects that hang on walls in homes and in galleries. Learners are likely to move immediately to flat surfaces for creating messages, whether print- or art-based, and are positioned to think and create in two dimensions rather than three (Eisner, 2002).

Characteristics of flatland work in the artwork I studied included that symmetry was important, and that images ran along vertical or horizontal axes. There was also a need to connect elements more organically as in a visual story, or through a collage of cut-out isolated objects that had a one-to-one correspondence with events or objects in a literary text. Often, flatland work that was drawn or painted appeared as if it was created from the perspective of a child, and indicated the extent to which the student was self-taught in art. Although these flatland visual texts were two-dimensional, they often took on a complexity of thought through the organization and structure of the elements within the text.

In Figure 11.5 a multimedia collage made with photos, markers, and pencils is delineated along a vertical axis with the upside down bottle directly above the student herself. The artmaker, who was a graduate student, represented her busy life as a series of events she must juggle to maintain balance, as indicated by her use of symmetry. In the drawn elements, she demonstrated her self-taught knowledge of drawing bodies, but her body was childlike in its construction and in composition, without a sense of body proportions. She included in her text

FIGURE 11.5 Flatlands Example

what appeared to be disparate objects that she had cut out from magazines, but when placed alongside each other and within the same text, these objects collectively constructed a story of her busy life. These objects individually identified the discourses in which she saw herself as an active participant (vacations on tropical beaches, a recent marriage and love associated with it, teacher and student, college graduate). Interestingly, the student used art as a language to show her own smallness against the very objects that defined her. The volume of these objects takes up most of the space on this visual text. The student was artistically weighed down by these objects and pushed into the flatness of the paper, almost oppressed by the very various events and experiences that she valued.

The visual text in Figure 11.6 also represented the artmaker's urge to tell a story on a flat surface. Her picture ran along both a vertical and a horizontal symmetry. Vertically, this student divided her portrait into two seemingly similar sides, organically showing an implicit relationship between elements on the left side of her face and those on the right. However, read along the horizontal line of symmetry, this portrait takes on a childlike appearance, with the eyes, nose, and mouth all disproportionate in relation to each other, a common characteristic of a child's representation of the human head. The flatness of paper and green tempera paint brought this textmaker into her imagined world, elaborated through strong highlights of yellow and lowlights of black mixed with green. At once, these accents of color both graphically and symbolically represented the highlights and lowlights of her sense of self in this imagined world. Although we know that her skin is not green and eyes are not yellow, this textmaker had a "plasticity of visual experience" (Gombrich, 1994, p. 28) which enabled her to alter the reality of her self-portrait. She was recognizable, however, because of the various detailed elements in her image that pointed to her unique features (curly hair, and the assignment of creating a self-portrait). On an initial reading, this portrait appears somewhat happy. The mouth and left eyebrow have a slight upturn, as do both of the eyes; these curves suggest happiness and contentment (Bang, 1991). Further, the size and volume of the face seem to indicate self-confidence, and the color is rich, thick, and strong. However, when the elements are studied more closely, this textmaker's image is far from happy and content. The face takes up nearly the entire paper, and the eyes, nose, and mouth are disproportionately large, features that were in stark contrast to her actual petite body, small face and fine facial features, and a shy and quiet demeanor. Further, the yellow eyes look at and down on viewers; the left eye demands that viewers (Kress & van Leeuwen, 2006) challenge the artmaker's sense of resignation, while the right eye invites us to experience her resignation.

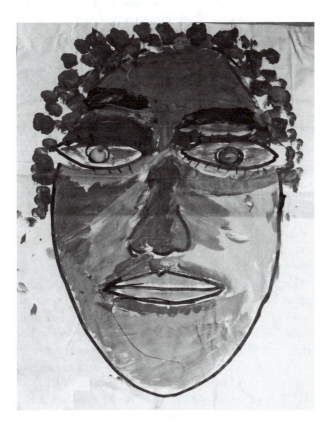

FIGURE 11.6 Flatlands Example

Across the range of flatland texts, students were allowed to invent and rein-terpret concepts about self, literature, and other interests in ways that lay outside traditional representations. Unlike what are commonly understood as two-dimensional and "flat" or uninteresting representations, students' urges to create flatland texts were full of complexity. Flatland texts made visible the contradiction between their real lives and their imagined and visual lives, thus positioning flat-lands as a way for students to convey complex messages about themselves and the world.

Narrative, or the Urge to Represent Originality

Across the collection of visual texts there was a significant urge to tell a story. In this category, visual narratives were never finished, but often only captured a moment or detail in a literary text such as a picture book, short story, or essay, or expressed a moment or detail in an original text the artmaker created. This moment or detail, represented visually through an object, was not static, but individual objects served to represent a sequence of events. In their narratives, students turned details into stories through imagination, spontaneous invitations to create, and their self-taught knowledge of art. When accompanied with written texts, visual narratives often told a different story than the written text.

The top image in Figure 11.7 is a visual narrative illustrated by Anya, age 5, about her aunt, who had recently graduated from college, accompanied by a written text transcribed by her mother: "I love you! Happy graduation! I hope it will be a nice day. I hope there will be flowers! You are a wonderful aunt! I love you!" As readers, we are often told that illustrations tell the written story; however, Anya's visual text and written words suggested that the story written is not always the story illustrated. On the surface, Anya's picture seemed to indicate a static moment: Anya and her aunt together under blue sky and shining sun. However, in this picture Anya used signs in complex ways to tell a more descriptive story. In visual narratives, objects serve as picture subjects, or what the picture is about. Size, volume, and color can be likened to "adjectives" and "adverbs" used to describe more vividly elements of a story. When viewed in this way, Anya's visual narrative has a subject, Anya and her aunt; their position in the center of the page indicates the centrality and significance of their relationship. The large size of Anya and her aunt as picture subject does not capture the concept of "graduation," but captures instead her "wonderful" feeling about her aunt. Together they float in midair, hovering between the green grass and blue sky, a magical element attrib-uted to the genre of fantasy, which allowed Anya to be with her aunt even though she was physically 600 miles away. Adding vivid description to her story was Anya's use of color to indicate setting, atmosphere, and mood. The bright blue sky and bold yellow sun with strong, straight rays give her story an atmosphere of happiness and joy. Interestingly, Anya's visual narrative contained only one detail in her written text ("nice day"), which indicated that her visual narrative stood

FIGURE 11.7 Narrative Examples

alone as its own original story, complete with the who, what, when, where, why, and how.

In the bottom image in Figure 11.7, LaShonda, age 7, created a multimedia text made primarily of clay and toothpicks to interpret Mem Fox's (1998) *Tough Boris*. Her visual narrative included Boris, the boat, the mast, and the undulating waves. This clay narrative indicated LaShonda's interest in retelling the story and interpreting the illustrations in Fox's book, while inventing her own signs through clay for water, Boris, and the ship. Although her clay piece seemingly indicated a static object, the undulation of the clay signified the motion of the water and the subsequent movement of the ship. Her oral story about this text was simple—"I liked Boris in the ship"—but it didn't capture the complexity of the visual story. Like illustrations, her clay story captured a moment in time in the story, but viewers understood that this moment was preceded by other events and would be succeeded by others. As visual texts in this category indicated, the urge to create narrative stories through art as a language allowed for original thinking and expression, and indicated a much more complex story than the one told or written.

Repetition, or the Urge to Emphasize and Explain

Students often used repetition in images or as elements of their artwork. Repetition became a mantra of sorts, in which students wished to reiterate a point again and again. These repetitive patterns and intricate details became an impenetrable field where picture objects, images, words and/or phrases, or elements clashed and collided. Such repetition might be considered "obsession," as students could not stop repeating or overlapping. Students' interest in one object suggested that they held onto an idea, repeated the symbol or object that represented the idea, and continued to mine the element until they could not say any more. Visual repetition was often simple in design, and elements related to each other conceptually and physically. In the top image in Figure 11.8, for example, in a context of studying patterns in math, a fourth-grade student studied the colors of the plastic handles of scissors and arranged and rearranged them, pinks to pinks, oranges to oranges, and so on, to connect the colors, and creatively express a multicolored three-dimensional sculpture of everyday objects used in their class. In the bottom image, a collaborative two-dimensional mixed-media text made with pencil, color, and magazines and entitled "Individual," two ninth-grade students expressed their interpretation of diversity as they understood it in a short story they had read. Although they saw each hand as individual, especially through use of color, their repetition of the hand image, and the overlapping of hands, meant that the text lost some of its conceptual and ideological impact, and read more as "sameness" rather than "individual." When shape and size are considered, all hands—traced around their own—were exactly the same with the exception of color—elements that lay in contradiction to their concept of diversity. Further, diversity for them was located solely in race, especially as race is viewed in terms of color. In Figure 11.8, repetition served as paradox: repetition of image object was reassuring but, at the same time, it conveyed mindless production and empty concepts, particularly in the case of school and diversity.

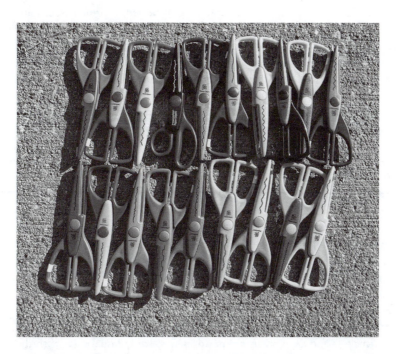

FIGURE 11.8 Repetition Examples

Visual Discourse Analysis in Reading Classrooms

To interrogate student-generated visual messages, viewers must know and learn the language of art—size, volume, color, position on the page, selection of objects, and so on—in order to respond intelligently to text. Just as critical literacy argues for careful and close readings of how people are positioned in print-based texts, who has control and who does not, the language they use, the clothes they wear, and so on, so too must we make careful and close readings of visual texts.

When visual discourse analysis is part of teachers' ongoing conversations with readers, or becomes part of regular reading assessment, teachers can find significance in how the texts are created, identify the urges that underpin these texts, and encourage viewers to notice visual elements from a different perspective. Statements like "That's a really nice piece" or "This picture is perfect" can be transformed into more substantive discussions in which students talk about parts of the message told visually and the discourses that underpin these messages. The categories of wordplay, flatlands, narrative originality, and repetition are fluid. Nonetheless, they enable educators to look at visual texts within their classrooms in a more systematic way.

Further, questions about the contents of visual messages are likely to elicit critical conversations rather than conversations that are limited to a literal one-to-one correspondence between elements in literary and visual texts ("This object represents so-and-so"), or those that are driven by an aesthetic stance ("That's a pretty picture"). For example, educators might invite the textmakers of the bottom image in Figure 11.8 to interrogate their own stance toward diversity by asking, "How is the repetition of the hands representative of 'individual'?" As a result, students as artmakers and art viewers are positioned to study visual texts with the complexity for which they were created.

Discussion

The presentation of how students use visual language in this chapter makes significant, and gives names to, the types of texts that students create in reading and language arts classrooms, and positions these texts as valuable information about students' literacy practices. By analyzing these texts as outsider art, I intend to elevate them to a status often afforded only to print-based texts. Brief but systematic analyses of marks on the page, study of objects remixed and repurposed to communicate very different messages, and identification and understanding of art principles (repetition, color, design, proportion, and so on) indicate that art is language.

Further, such analysis demonstrates the potential of art to carry particular meanings that gesture toward larger Discourses about concepts like "diversity" and "individualism" and what society suggests these concepts mean. In claiming the design, creation, production, and framing of visual texts as literacy, educators can reclaim the importance of authentic language in reading all texts, print and visual. Doing so supports the notions that language exists to make meaning, and language is a tool by which meaning is constructed. The "urge" that drives this chapter is to argue for systematic and significant treatment of visual texts as legitimate communication of what and how meaning is constructed. Treating them in this way encourages educators and researchers to take an active stance toward the reading and analysis of visual texts, to really look at them, elevate them to the position of insider literacy practices, and study them with the seriousness they deserve.

Reading and reclaiming the language of visual texts does not come without tension. When educators invite students to create meaning visually from personal interpretations of literary texts or creation of original texts, they must be prepared to discuss the issues that arise when knowledge about how to read visual language is facilitated. Just as picture books can position students to read critically, so too can visual texts and media position viewers to read messages from a critical stance. Vasquez (2010) argues that we must get beyond "I like the book." I argue in a similar vein for moving beyond "I like this picture" and into conversations that matter. In naming visual texts as insider literacy, and reading them, educators reclaim art as a language that breaks through the "ceiling"—a ceiling that values only reading and writing as insider practices—and positions visual communication as central, viable, and important to twenty-first-century literacy.

References

Albers, P. (2007). Visual discourse analysis: An introduction to the analysis of school-generated visual texts. In D. W. Rowe et al. (Eds.), *56th yearbook of the National Reading Conference* (pp. 81–95). Oak Creek, WI: NRC.

Albers, P., Harste, J. C., Vander Zanden, S., & Felderman, C. (2008). Using popular culture to promote critical literacy practices. In R. T. Jimenez et al. (Eds.), *57th yearbook of the National Reading Conference*. Oak Creek, WI: NRC.

Bakhtin, M. (1982). *The dialogic imagination*. Austin: University of Texas Press.

Bang, M. (1991). *Picture this: Perception and composition*. Boston: Bulfinch Press.

Eisner, E. W. (2002). *The arts and the creation of mind*. New Haven, CT: Yale University Press.

Fox, M. (1998). *Tough Boris*. New York: Voyager Books.

Gee, J. P. (2005). *An introduction to discourse analysis: Theory and method* (2nd ed.). London: Routledge.

Golding, W. P. (1959). *Lord of the flies*. New York: Perigee.

Gombrich, E. H. (1994). *The image and the eye: Further studies in the psychology of pictorial representation*. New York: Phaidon Press.

Halliday, M. A. K. (1985). *An introduction to functional grammar*. London: Arnold.

Harste, J. C., Chung, M., & Grant, S. (2006). Analyzing visual data: A functional approach to the development of a semiotic framework. Paper presented at the National Reading Conference, Los Angeles.

Kremer, R. (1998). Visual languages for knowledge representation. Paper presented at KAW'98: Eleventh Workshop on Knowledge Acquisition, Modeling and Management, Calgary, Alberta, April 18–23, 1998. Retrieved on October 7, 2007, from http://ksi.cpsc.ucalgary.ca/KAW/KAW98/kremer/

Kress, G., & van Leeuwen, T. (2006). *Reading images: The grammar of visual design* (2nd ed.). New York: Routledge.

Maizels, J. (1996). *Raw creation: Outsider art and beyond*. London: Phaidon Press.

Naubert-Riser, C. (1988). *Klee*. London: Bracken Books.

Rexler, L. (2005). *How to look at outsider art*. New York: Harry N. Abrams.

Vasquez, V. (2010). *Getting beyond "I like the book": Creating space for critical literacy in K-6 classrooms* (2nd ed.). Newark, DE: International Reading Association.

Vasquez, V., Albers, P., & Harste, J. C. (2010). From the personal to the Worldwide Web: Moving teachers into positions of critical interrogation. In B. Baker (Ed.), *The new literacies: Multiple perspectives on research and practice* (pp. 265–284). New York: Guilford Press.

Walter, V. (1999). *Making up Megaboy*. New York: Delacorte Books for Young Readers

Weeks, L. (2007, July 6). The eye generation prefers not to read all about it. *Washington Post*, p. C02. Retrieved August 16, 2007 from www.washingtonpost.com/wp-dyn/content/article/2007/07/05/AR2007070502055_2.html?referrer=emailarticle

CHAPTER 11 EXTENSION

Seamlessly Art

Jerome C. Harste

Peggy Albers' chapter shows us that the humanities represent humankind's ways of communicating with each other. In order to expand our communication potential, the arts—language, art, music, dance, drama—need to become a seamless part of the ongoing curriculum and central to our reclaiming of the many languages we use to make meaning. Because of an existing emphasis on written language, by third grade too many children say they can't sing. By fourth grade, too many children say they can't draw. Here are some examples of what I mean and why I think integrating the arts throughout the curriculum is so important.

Prisca and Ray Martens (2009) talked with second- and fourth-grade children about the elements of art in conjunction with reading. They focused on such concepts as color, line, shape, and how each of these affected meaning. Prisca and Ray studied the children's comprehension of the picture books and found that as children's understanding of art increased, so did the quality of their miscues and their understanding of the story. They also invited children to compare the original books to modified versions in the basal. The children's critiques of the changes that were made to the original text and how these changes affected meaning were caustic. Basal readers were no longer seen as innocent.

The seventh graders Phyllis Whitin (1996) was assigned to teach maintained they had read on average only one book up to this point in their lives. She introduced them to Sketch-to-Stretch, an instructional strategy that asks students to sketch what they think the story means to them using no words, or as few words as possible (Harste & Short with Burke, 1986). Over the course of the school year she varied Sketch-to-Stretch so that children found pieces of art that they thought represented the meaning of the story. At times she challenged them to represent what a story meant to them in clay and, in still other instances, in mathematics and music. By the end of the year, students had read as many as 38 books. The literature discussions Whitin audiotaped sounded more like English majors in a university setting discussing the book than typical seventh graders. Sometimes by approaching things from the side rather than hitting the nail on the head we invite children to revalue what they thought they initially disliked. In this case, Phyllis highlighted art rather than reading in the minds of her students, to the benefit of both literacy and learning.

Jean Anne Clyde and the teachers she works with developed what they call the Subtext Strategy (Clyde, Barber, Hogue, & Warz, 2006). They introduced the strategy to children by showing them Henri Matisse's "The Piano Lesson" (http://smarthistory.org/matisse-piano-lesson.html). In this piece of art a piano teacher is sitting behind a student as he plays the piano, while the father reads a book and waits for the lesson to be over. Jean Anne and her teachers gave each child six sticky notes. On three sticky notes (one per character), she asked them to think about what each character might be saying aloud or publicly. On the remaining three sticky notes (again, one per character) they wrote what each character might be thinking privately.

From this initial experience with art, Jean Anne and her teachers moved to books. After an initial reading, they identified the characters they wished to focus on and the number of Post-it notes needed. Children jotted down what they saw the characters as saying publicly as well as what the characters thought. Jean Anne and her teachers found this strategy supported children in thinking more deeply about a text as well as in identifying the systems of meaning that were operating implicitly in the story being told. To fully understand "The Piano Lesson," one needs to understand, for example, that not all parents can provide their children with piano lessons. Piano lessons represent a particular kind of lifestyle, one of privilege in some ways. Children involved in piano lessons often detest them, but are forced to participate because that is what all their friends are doing or their parents dictate. Piano lessons became a matter of "keeping up with the Joneses" and a status symbol not only of what can be afforded but of good middle- and upper-class parenting. As these teachers used the Subtext Strategy over time, children got better and better at unpacking underlying meanings. They also used this strategy to unpack the underlying meaning in newspaper articles, political cartoons, and content area materials. While this strategy didn't involve a physical production of art, it did involve envisioning the setting of a story in one's mind, and thinking through what might be happening on the surface level as well as at a deeper level relative to meaning making. Imagining is art, too. In fact, imagining-what-might-be is what art supports and what education should really be about.

Karen Smith (2000) used drama to help children overcome writer's block. One day when I visited her class, a student asked for help, saying she was stuck and didn't know where to go with her writing. Karen asked the student to pick out several of her sixth-grade classmates, acquaint them with the story, and have them enact the story up to the point where she was stuck. Within minutes the student's problem was solved. The stories produced in Karen's writers' workshop, of course, complete with illustrations, became favorite reading material in the classroom and were often checked out to go home. Sumara (2002), a leading Canadian language arts educator, argues that we need to help children "linger in texts." Given my experience, art as drama is an important way of lingering.

Almost 20 years ago a group of teachers in Indianapolis came together to create a public school option called the Center for Inquiry. The curriculum for this school featured inquiry-based learning (built curriculum from the inquiry questions of learners), multiple modalities, and critical literacy. While much of the curriculum was organized around focused studies (ones either the students or the staff as a whole selected) and invitations (see Van Sluys & Laman, this volume), the arts were integrated seamlessly throughout. In "Celebrating Indianapolis" (one of the school-wide themes), children picked an aspect of Indianapolis to study. An invitation asked them to think about what Indianapolis would look like in art and what Indianapolis would look like in music. We didn't try mathematics, although we should have. Without fail, everyone walked away revaluing Indianapolis anew.

I would love to see easels in every elementary classroom, kindergarten to Grade 6. At the Center for Inquiry, easels are a reality. I also wanted musical instruments in every classroom. I wanted children to think musically about what background music might go with a story, how a story they read might be told in music, and so on. What I found was that music can be very disruptive. While I haven't given up on music being an integral part of the language arts curriculum, I do now see the need for extra rooms where children can go to put their thoughts and work to song. If the children you teach do have access to musical instruments, ask them, sometime, to have a Written Conversation over a book they have read (Harste & Short with Burke, 1986) and then follow up by asking them to have a Musical Conversation over the same book. The results can be fascinating and insightful, and provoke a whole new round of conversation.

Graves (1983) once called the way we organize schools the cha-cha-cha curriculum. "Put away your reading books, it is now time for math. Put away your math books, it is now time for spelling." He envisioned a different curriculum, one that flowed. So do I. Rather than art being something special or relegated to Friday afternoon, I want teachers to be able to seamlessly move from art to language, from language to music, from music to mathematics, from mathematics to drama, all in the name of meaning making. I must admit—despite my intimate involvement with the Center for Inquiry for many years—that I have yet to see my ideal seamless curriculum fully come to life. But I keep hoping. Too often, I think, the cries for accountability and evaluation make us edit our dreams before we ever get to try them. But I keep dreaming. You might not be able to get it right either, but you can get us closer, and Peggy Albers' chapter gives some good advice. It isn't enough that we value the arts. We need to talk explicitly about the arts with the children we teach so that they, like us, can come to revalue literacy in all its glorious potentials.

References

Clyde, J. A., Barber, S., Hogue, S., & Warz, L. (2006). *Breakthrough to meaning: Helping your kids become better readers, writers, and thinkers.* Portsmouth, NH: Heinemann.

Graves, D. (1983). *Writing: Teachers and children at work.* Portsmouth, NH: Heinemann.

Harste, J. C., & Short, K. S., with Burke, C. L. (1986). *Creating classrooms for authors.* Portsmouth, NH: Heinemann.

Martens, P., & Martens, R. (2009). Learning to read the verbal and pictorial texts in picture books. Paper presented at the Annual Meeting of the National Reading Conference, Albuquerque, NM.

Smith, K. (2000). *Multiple ways of knowing* (Teleconference). Champaign, IL: Whole Language Umbrella/National Council of Teachers of English.

Sumara, D. (2002). *Why reading literature in school still matters: Imagination, interpretation, insight.* New York: Routledge.

Whitin, P. (1996). *Sketching stories, stretching minds: Responding visually to literature.* Portsmouth, NH: Heinemann.

12

VALUING HOME LANGUAGE TO SUPPORT YOUNG BILINGUAL CHILDREN'S TALK ABOUT BOOKS

Jeanne Gilliam Fain and Robin Horn

A critical facet of reclaiming reading is reclaiming the rich language transactions that occur in critical literacy classrooms when we open the floor to children's voices and experiences. Reclaiming language is further enriched when multiple languages are welcomed into the classroom (see the chapter by Freeman et al. and its extension, this volume).

In this chapter we present some ways for reclaiming language in critical literacy classrooms as part of reclaiming reading. We share what happened when young bilingual children attended to ideas about fairness and used their local knowledge of crossing the border between Mexico and the United States to mediate their understandings of words and ideas in relevant children's literature. We demonstrate ways in which talk supported children in making their identities public, and discuss what mattered to them in what they read. And we suggest ways teachers can circumvent English only and other restrictive mandates so children can have critical conversations about rich literature.

Critical literacy is a transformational part of reclaiming language in reading because in critical literacy classrooms, readers shift from being receivers of knowledge to being co-investigators and problem posers (Freire, 1970). Reading as problem posing encompasses authentic learning that positions learners to take critical roles within learning. In critical literacy classrooms, learners use language to examine their positioning in the world and learn to evaluate the "realities" of the world. Teachers and children learn how to learn alongside each other through exchanging rich language.

Lewison, Flint, and Van Sluys (2002) condense 30 years of research about critical literacy into four dimensions. *Disrupting the commonplace* challenges learners to look beyond the familiar and try on new ways of examining old ideas. *Interrogating multiple viewpoints* pushes us to explore the positions and perspectives of others.

Focusing on sociopolitical issues challenges us to discover the role of institutional systems and the power rooted within these systems. *Taking action and promoting social justice* involves moving from thinking and discussions to children and their teachers becoming agents for change.

In her preschool classroom, Vasquez (2004) embraced the four dimensions of critical literacy. Preschoolers learned to think outside of themselves and learned to empathize when a fellow classmate couldn't eat what was offered at a school barbecue. Children thought about the structures of school when preschoolers were not included in some of the school functions set aside for older students. Vasquez invited the children to use literacy for real purposes and they were challenged to negotiate their understandings from a critical perspective. Vasquez took on a facilitating role and showed young children that they had a voice and their voice mattered, especially when they were able to take a stand within the context of schooling. The four dimensions of critical literacy are integrated throughout the children's discussions of the border that we share in this chapter.

In critical literacy classrooms, children learn to consider multiple points of view, interrogate them, and compose their own perspectives after taking risks within dialogues. Foss (2002) describes such critical literacy practices as "peeling the onion." She challenges middle-class middle school students to explore their identities through writing and discussion. She facilitates discussions that move her students to look beyond the familiar in terms of race, age, social class, religion, background, family structure, and language(s) spoken. In the next section we present similar discussions with bilingual urban second graders.

Setting the Scene: Classroom and Talk about Immigration

Like Vasquez and Foss, we invited children to talk about sociopolitical issues, such as immigration, that we knew were important in their lives and local communities in the southwest of the United States. We have been a part of the school community for years and were familiar with many of the families and their children. We wanted the children to use their experiences with languages and their cultural knowledge to talk about these critical issues. We hoped the conversations would provide children with space to have their voices heard (Boran & Comber, 2001).

Robin (second-grade teacher) and Jeanne (university researcher) worked together to develop curriculum that built upon the bilingual voices of the learners in Robin's classroom (Fain & Horn, 2006). Robin was required to work within English Only laws, a Sheltered English Immersion model, and a specific reading program that was implemented district-wide. These mandates sharply opposed the theories we shared about language as social and fundamental to identity and learning. They meant Robin and the children could not read books in languages other than English in the classroom. As we thought about how to work within the existing political parameters and yet build space for critical learning, we chose to organize the curriculum with broad content themes that incorporated the various goals from the state, district, and school. We also created a process that involved families in literature circles so that children could have access to books in their native language(s) at home.

The themes around which we created curriculum included sense of place, fairness, milestones, and points of inspiration. They came from our understanding of young learners and questions that we believed the children would find relevant, and from our knowledge of the children's communities, their families, their languages and cultures. The themes led to literature studies that included personal and social knowing, knowledge systems, and sign systems (Short, 2007).

The literature discussions about immigration that we present here were part of the fairness theme. The students' questions and knowledge were accepted and woven into the study. They expressed particular interest in fairness as it spoke to equity issues that affected them on the playground and in the classroom. They wrote about fairness in their writing journals. Robin and the children made a web about their understandings of fairness. Children read independently and were read aloud many quality books about fairness (see the list of children's books at the end of the chapter). These activities and our reflection about them added depth to our discussions about the literature.

Drama enabled children to experience first-hand some essence of the difficult concepts and power struggles historical figures faced regarding fairness and set the stage for the literature we subsequently introduced. Although we realized that the activities provided the children with only a glimpse into the substantive equity issues in the children's literature, we wanted the children to physically move to increase their understanding. For example, prior to reading *White Socks Only* (Coleman, 1996), we had students get in line by shirt color. *White Socks Only* is a picture book that conveys the emotions of discrimination through telling how a girl's misreading of a sign that said "whites only" as "white socks only" led to resistance and change in her town. The children wearing red shirts, whom we privileged, were allowed to get drinks from the water fountain. The ensuing discussion about fairness was tempered by the children's first-hand experience, which was sufficiently relevant to the children that their talk was lively.

We conducted a similar role-play connected to *A Picture Book of Rosa Parks* (Adler, 1995), a biography for children that situates the well-known story of Rosa Parks' refusal to sit at the back of the bus in a broader historical context about the civil rights movement. Children were randomly assigned to go to the back of an imaginary bus in the classroom. Having the children move, physically, to the "back of the bus" may have helped some empathize with Rosa Parks and her contemporaries and helped prepare for discussion.

After both role-plays, children read and discussed the books. We related the historical experiences to issues of discrimination that many of the children grappled with in their own lives. Children discussed the challenges of standing up for the languages they speak and difficulties they faced translating for their parents in tough situations. They also discussed how they handled it when they felt others wanted to take "their language" away, and the majority of them said that they would not allow it. The children's resistance to policies of language appropriation reflected our resistance and our search for ways to include their home languages and cultures in activities within and beyond the classroom.

Responding to Literature at Home and at School

We took time to learn about the cultural and linguistic backgrounds of the children and we saw their language as a resource even though we were limited to instruction in English in the classroom. We purposely selected children's literature available in Spanish and English to complement and support the themes. To begin, throughout a two-week period Robin read aloud four books for literature discussions. The four books that we selected focused more specifically on the issue of crossing the border within the fairness theme. After hearing the read-alouds, the children chose one book to take home to read with their families. Many families encouraged their children to select a book in their native language. We sent home an open-ended invitation for families to respond to the literature, and a family response journal accompanied each book.

Over the next week, families read the book and responded in the journals with thinking, questions, and connections in writing and drawing. Families were encouraged to use their native languages, and adults and children responded enthusiastically in Spanish, English, or both.

Figure 12.1 is Susan's family's journal response to *Super Cilantro Girl* (Herrera, 2003), a fantasy about an 8-year-old girl who wants to help her mother when she is detained after a visit to Mexico and not allowed to return to the United States. Although the story ends ambiguously and readers don't know whether Susan dreamed her mother's return or it really happened, the issue of "legal" border crossing raises questions and encourages discussion. Susan and her mother responded to the story; Susan's mother wrote in Spanish. Susan was bilingual but wrote in English.

This family response was a combination of Susan and her mom relating Susan's response to the story. The Spanish portion in Figure 12.1 says:

> The children dream at times when someone wants something and children are able to dream it or the children dream that they can accomplish things like going to places to look for those that they want to know or dream of things that may cause them to have fear.

Susan's mom also wrote another response in which she indicated that this story demonstrated a reality for many families today. Her translated response was as follows:

> This in reality is a story that relates to the situation that we have today that many families are living with when they are separated and there are people

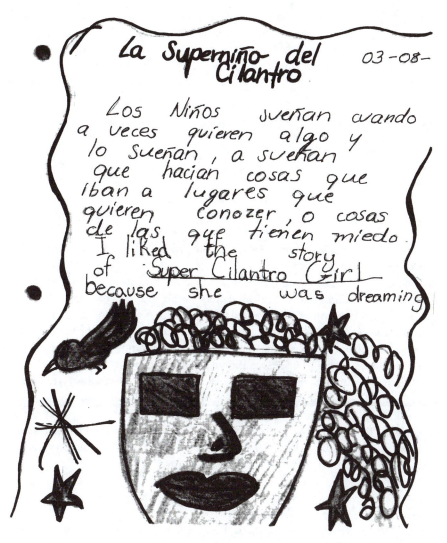

La Superniño del Cilantro   03-08-

Los Niños sueñan cuando a veces quieren algo y lo sueñan, a sueñan que hacían cosas que iban a lugares que quieren conozer, o cosas de las que tienen miedo. I liked the story of Super Cilantro Girl because she was dreaming

FIGURE 12.1 Family Response Journal Entry from *Super Cilantro Girl*

who have a green card and they have to risk their lives in the desert for the power to reunite with their loves ones. I would hope very soon there would be a solution to this problem and that we would come together with the Mexicans to work to give our families a better future. We need to unite to build reformed justice!

This mother's writing was representative of many entries in the family response journals.

Children brought their family response journals to literature circles in the classroom. Our discussions often began with children reading aloud journal entries and sharing what their families thought about the book. In this way, we challenged policies that excluded our students' families' voices and languages from the classroom.

Insights into Children's Perspectives on the Border

We identified border crossing as a prominent theme in the literature and in the children's real lives. Three literature discussions that focused on the topic included *Super Cilantro Girl/La Superniña del Cilantro* (2003), *Pablo and Pimienta* (1999) by Ruth Covault, and *Friends from the Other Side/Amigos del otro lado* (1993) by Gloria Anzaldúa. In *Super Cilantro Girl/La Superniña del Cilantro*, Esme's mom can't return to her daughter across the border until she gets her green card. *Pablo and Pimienta* tells the story of a young boy who is separated from his father as he crosses the border between the United States and Mexico. *Friends from the Other Side/Amigos del otro lado* describes a friendship between Joaquín, who recently arrived in the United States, and Prietita, a Mexican American girl, as they experience the challenges of discrimination in a US border town. Immigration themes in these books consisted of central characters displaying their border knowledge, the various roles of police and characters' positions in regard to authority, and the power of a green card. The setting of the border was also vividly illustrated.

Children brought their life experiences to the discussions. Most were born in the United States and visited Mexico regularly to see their grandparents. Their personal local knowledge of crossing the border mediated their understandings of the books. The discussions included their understandings of the challenges and dangers of crossing the border. One discussion started with the children figuring out why Super Cilantro Girl would cross the border:

Jeanne: OK, what do you think? Why is she crossing the border?
Reyna: To go get her.
Miguel: She was trying to do . . . she was trying to pick up her mommy.
Reyna: So she could go away.
Alejandro: To cross the border.

The children started with what they knew directly from the text: the main character in *Super Cilantro Girl* needed to pick up her mom. The discussion soon moved to their general knowledge of crossing the border. The children described what identification people must own in order to cross the border. They talked about how you have to have a "little card that has a picture" and after additional discussion we decided they were referring to passports. The children knew that identification is needed and "sometimes people, they don't have it." And in those cases, they added, people "just jump over" and "cross over the border."

Jeanne: What happens if you jump over the fence?
Reyna: The police!
Jeanne: You get caught?
Sandra: I don't know.

The children all talked at the same time in a flurry of ideas and strong opinions. They talked about how the "the police will kill you" or get you with an "electric gun, razor [taser] gun," and they mimicked shooting sounds. They agreed that the police will come and put you into jail and they will take you "if you jump over the fence" and that "you have to hide" and the police will "take your passport again and you can't have it anymore." "You have to stay in Mexico" and "you can cross the border but you have to jump over so you won't get caught."

The discussion became more passionate as the group moved to various perspectives about the ramifications of crossing the border. They thought it was a serious crime if you did not have "papers" and that the police were required to enforce the law. They saw the police as having authority to enforce the border. In terms of interrogating multiple viewpoints, one of the dimensions of critical literacy, they started to examine each other's perspectives. The children realized there were consequences for getting caught crossing the border illegally. They also saw the role of the police in enforcing the border if you don't have proper identification. There was great respect for each other as they shared their perspectives, and they were quick to agree with each other. They explored the sociopolitical as they realized police have the power to act and even kill.

We ended our conversation about *Super Cilantro Girl* by exploring some questions: What do you think about the border between Mexico and the United States? Why is there a border and gates? Why do you have to have a passport? Why can't you just go from place to place? The children agreed that they didn't really know why they couldn't "go from [Arizona] to Mexico." We didn't really get to taking a stand or promoting social justice completely, the fourth dimension of critical literacy; the children described immigration as "being messed up," but they were really not sure what to do about it in terms of action.

In another discussion group, Robin and the second graders discussed *Pablo and Pimienta* (Covault, 1999) and raised similar viewpoints regarding the border. When she asked what happened when the police came if you tried to cross the border; one student responded, "They take you to jail." Another student, Antonio, indicated that if the police come, you have to hide.

Reyna: It's where you have to take papers to go through.
Robin: You gotta have papers to go through? What papers do you have to have?
Reyna: You have to have the paper, or tickets, from who are you taking.
Antonio: If you are not born there, you can't go past.
Robin: It is, so what kind of papers do you need to have, what's on the papers?
Alex: Red, white, and blue.

Reyna: Like when you were born.
Robin: When you were born, like a birth certificate?
Alex: You know what? I was born in Mexico.

Maria jumped into the conversation to explain that her brother told her that Mexico used to be part of America, but that she forgot exactly what he told her. Robin asked, "What happens if you don't have any papers?"

Maria: You can't go back through. They take you back.
Reyna: They take you back.
Jesus: Sometimes if you don't listen to them, they take you to jail.
Robin: They take you to jail? And how long do you have to sit there?
Jesus: Like one thousand years old.
Robin: Really?
The students: Noooooo!
Jesus: If you are less than 20, you can get out if you pay $1000 in money.

The discussion then moved into a beginning definition of *la migra* (border patrol). Robin asked the students to reflect upon what a *migra* is, and the students immediately responded. Two students said that the *migra* took their moms away. Jesus indicated that "in Guadalajara, there's some really bad people that can steal you." The students then agree that you can count on the police but not the *migra* because "they're bad people." This group tried to explore the power the *migra* and police have over people crossing the border.

In a discussion of *Friends from the Other Side/Amigos del otro lado* (Anzaldúa, 1993), children discussed another word, this time the derogatory term "wetback." The discussion started with Ricardo's response journal that attended to when someone called the character Joaquín *"un mojadito"* (a little wetback). We explored the pages of the book together and read the part of the book that uses the term "wetback." Jeanne then asked the group to define the term.

Juan: Like somebody—somebody that is not nice to other people.
Jeanne: A wetback is someone who's not nice to other people?
Ricardo: No, it's that they're wet.
Jeanne: They're wet? Why would they be wet?

Jeanne asked, "Where did the word 'wetback' come from?" Although the children couldn't explain it, Irma, with some encouragement to speak up, said, "That he didn't have the same skin as them." Jeanne explained that the term "wetback" comes from the idea that some people have to cross a river to enter the United States. She asked, "So do you think that it's OK to call someone a wetback? Or a *mojado*?"

Beatriz: No! . . . Because they, they, um they use people put–downs.
Jeanne: How do you think they felt in the story when the kids were calling them
    a *mojadito*?
Juan: Bad.
Beatriz: Sad.
Jeanne: OK, so that was the part you connected with? Yeah? So have you ever had
    someone say something not nice to you like that?

Juan acknowledged in a sad voice that he had been called a wetback.

Learning from Children's Perspectives

Literature discussions conducted at home provided students with important opportunities to hear a story and discuss it in more than one language. They also had access
to family stories that related to the book they read, framing their conversations in
two languages. We read stories aloud in class in English because we were mandated
to do so, but families read the books in their native languages. Children had support
from their families during discussions in their homes. This linguistic and cultural
mediation assisted students as they discussed multiple perspectives of the literature
and achieved greater comprehension. They were motivated to read texts that connected directly to their lives because the books were the beginning of discussions in
which their families' cultural and linguistic capital mattered in the school setting.

Robin noticed that the students in literature discussions often revealed their
expertise on issues, perhaps reflective of conversations that took place at home,
and were able to take critical perspectives about the texts. They demonstrated
confidence in their knowledge of the books. The children's talk moved beyond
the text, a sharp contrast to their conversations around basal stories. The relevance
of the literature meant the children were able to make more connections and
discuss story elements at a more sophisticated level.

One implication of laws and mandates that created the English-only system is
that parents have fewer teacher-provided opportunities to partner with schools in
their children's learning. Government mandates regarding immigration create a
situation in which parents are often fearful to come to the schools or take part in
their children's classroom learning. We have to continue to build safe spaces that
honor the languages and cultural resources of children in our classrooms. There
may not have been freedom to use the child's first language in the classroom, but
as educators we supported the families' knowledge of language by sending home
resources such as quality children's literature in the children's native languages.

Robin sought to honor the fact that children came to the classroom with rich,
diverse linguistic backgrounds. She sought out ways to connect with them to
create meaningful literacy experiences and to use books with children in real
ways. Reclaiming the importance of language in reading instruction was a way
for Robin to respond to No Child Left Behind, English-language mandates, and

anti-immigration policies that created a wedge between school and the families she cared about. Literature discussions invited parents to participate in their child's learning, validated their home language and culture, and used their experiences as a resource in helping the children learn.

References

Boran, S., & Comber, B. (2001). *Critiquing whole language and classroom inquiry*. Urbana, IL: National Council of Teachers of English.

Covault, R. M. (1999). *Pablo and Pimienta/Pablo y Pimienta*. Flagstaff, AZ: Northland.

Fain, J. G., & Horn, R. (2006). Family talk about language diversity and culture. *Language Arts, 83*(4), 310–320.

Foss, A. (2002). Peeling the onion: Teaching critical literacy with students of privilege. *Language Arts, 79*(5), 393–403.

Freire, P. (1970). *Pedagogy of the oppressed*. New York: Seabury.

Herrera, J. F. (2003). *Super Cilantro Girl/La Superniña del cilantro*. San Francisco: Children's Book Press.

Lewison, M., Flint, A., & Van Sluys, K. (2002). Taking on critical literacy: The journey of newcomers and novices. *Language Arts, 79*(5), 382–392.

Short, K. G. (2007). Children between worlds: Creating intercultural connections through children's literature. *Arizona Reading Journal, 23*(2), 12–17.

Vasquez, V. (2004). *Negotiating critical literacies with young children*. Mahwah, NJ: Lawrence Erlbaum.

Bibliography of Books used in the Fairness Theme Study

Adler, D. (1995). *A picture book of Rosa Parks*. New York: Holiday House.

Anzaldúa, G. (1993). *Friends from the other side/Amigos del otro lado*. San Francisco: Children's Book Press. [Bilingual: Spanish/English]

Bradby, M. (1995). *More than anything else*. New York: Scholastic. [English]

Bunting, E. (1999). *Smoky night/Noche de humo*. Riverside, UT: Sandpiper. [Spanish and English]

Cohn, D. (2002). *¡Sí, se puede! Yes, we can! Janitor strike in L.A.* El Paso, TX: Cinquo Puntos Press. [Bilingual: Spanish/English]

Coleman, E. (1996). *White socks only*. Park Ridge, IL: Albert Whitman [English]

Coles, R. (1995). *The story of Ruby Bridges*. New York: Scholastic. [English]

Covault, R. M. (1999). *Pablo and Pimienta/Pablo y Pimienta*. Flagstaff, AZ: Northland Publishing. [Bilingual: Spanish/English]

Garcia, V. C. (1998). *The cactus wren and the cholla/El reyezuelo y la cholla*. Lyndhurst, NJ: Lectorum. [Bilingual: Spanish/ English]

Herrera, J. F. (2003). *Super Cilantro Girl/La Superniña del Cilantro*. San Francisco: Children's Book Press. [Bilingual: Spanish/English]

Krull, K. (2003). *Harvesting hope: The story of Cesar Chavez/Cosechando esperanza: La historia de César Chávez*. San Diego, CA: Harcourt Children's Books. [Spanish and English]

Lorbiecki, M. (2000). *Sister Anne's hands*. New York: Puffin Books. [English]

Woodson, J. (2001). *The other side*. New York: Putnam Juvenile. [English]

Yashima, T. (1976). *Crow Boy/Niño Cuervo*. New York: Puffin Books. [Spanish and English]

CHAPTER 12 EXTENSION

Reclaiming Language as a Community Text

Andrea García and Kathryn F. Whitmore

In classrooms with multilingual children, teachers and educators like Fain and Horn understand the power of using high-quality children's literature to invite all readers into literature conversations, regardless of their native language or their proficiency in the language of prestige in their academic setting. When language policies narrowed Horn's freedom to use her students' heritage language in the classroom, she invited her students to hold literature conversations at home. By providing books in Spanish and English, her students and their families discussed literature together at their leisure in both languages. In our separate and different contexts (Andrea in New York and Kathy in Iowa) we also worked with families to validate their cultural and linguistic resources by gathering around books in the community.

Andrea visited with Spanish-speaking families participating in book discussions that took place in the community space of the public library. As an extension of the project entitled "Together—Book Talk for Kids and Parents," the program was designed to bring children and parents together to have intergenerational dialogue around award-winning books that feature humanity-based themes, such as American identity, freedom, or courage. A children's librarian and a humanities scholar served as facilitators, guiding 9- to 11-year-old children and their parents. While "Together" had been in existence for four years with monolingual English-speaking families, the dual-language extension of the project was new. Literature read in "Dual Language Together" was available in English and Spanish, or as bilingual texts; families that spoke both languages were invited; and the facilitation team was bilingual. These conditions reinforced the goals of the program to reach linguistically diverse families so that they could make use of their heritage language in the interpretation, analysis, and discussion of selected books at home and with others at the library.

Kathy, along with classroom teachers Stacey Medd and Karla Brendler, co-facilitated a family literacy group called "Escuela Familia" (School Family). "Escuela Familia" invited bilingual families with 5- to 12-year-old children to their elementary school to respond to literature in Spanish and English. Like "Dual Language Together," this group evolved from successful, predominantly mono-lingual family literacy groups in the school and was inspired by growing numbers of Spanish-speaking immigrant families in the community. "Escuela Familia" occurred after school in one teacher's classroom, but it also included the facilitators' regular visits to the families' homes, and a summer day camp held in the children's neighborhood.

Examples from our experiences with "Dual Language Together" and "Escuela Familia" illustrate how we constructed spaces in communities for conversations about books to reclaim language as essential to reclaiming reading. They emphasize that inherent in the effort to reclaim language are the rights of language users to use language as a resource, to take risks to engage in critical conversations, and to reclaim libraries and other community sites for reading conversations.

Reclaiming the Right to Use Language as a Resource

At the beginning of the "Dual Language Together" project, some parents appeared to be uneasy about their children speaking Spanish in a public space. During one night discussion early in the program, while talking about the book *The Librarian of Basra* (Winter, 2004), one of the girls responded in Spanish to a question posed in Spanish by the librarian. Almost immediately, and with a subtle yet commanding voice, her mother directed her to speak in English, and the child quickly code-switched to English to continue her response. When this same concern was observed in another parent, the co-facilitator of the group reminded parents and children that any language was welcome during book discussions. The follow-up conversation focused on ensuring that children and parents alike felt comfortable to make linguistic choices to participate in the conversations.

Similarly, many of the parents in "Escuela Familia" lacked information about the critical importance of continuing their children's Spanish development at home while the children learned English at school. This perspective slowly shifted, owing to an array of experiences in the group, including reading aloud a children's book in Spanish to begin each meeting and direct verbal validation of Spanish during household visits conducted in Spanish. In one project, "Escuela" families composed and published family storybooks in Spanish, and made audiotapes that turned them into "books on tape." Spanish became a visible and more official language of the school when barcodes were added to the books and all children in the school could check them out as part of the legitimate school media center collection.

Reclaiming the Right to Use Language to Take Risks and to Engage in Critical Conversations

In our separate but similar work, community literature discussions created spaces in which both parents and children were positioned as proficient language users who were emergent bilinguals (García, Kleifgen, & Falchi, 2008). Parents used English as their second language to communicate ideas, and children took risks with Spanish as their heritage language. During a read-aloud of *In My Family/En mi familia* (Garza, 2000) an "Escuela Familia" mom named Carolina was propelled into talk by a description and painting of a party. Although Carolina's English was developing and her grammar was not conventional; the meaning of her message came through clearly:

> In my country is the dancing is in the street. Yeah, every family in the New Year and in the Christmas every people is in your neighborhood is in the night every the dancing and the musica is salsa. Every different music every people families outside. Or maybe in the one house every the neighbors and then my house they eat.

Carolina's enthusiastic description sparked other adults' willingness to speak a combination of beginning English and more developed Spanish to share memories of parties and holidays in their home countries.

Risk taking was also evident in terms of the children's participation and discussion of certain topics portrayed in the books. One night, after one of the "Dual Language Together" facilitators had read aloud *Smoky Night/Noche de humo* (Bunting, 1994), issues of discrimination became a topic of conversation in Spanish by the adults. Yet, when one of the boys, Jason, made a connection in English to how one of the characters in the story may feel about going into a place where people are different from you, other children jumped in to share their experiences with difference in their schools. Before long, Jason's mom connected to similar experiences that she felt Dominicans have in relation to other Hispanic ethnic groups in her country, and the conversation shifted from an adult-led discussion to a collaborative exploration of meaning.

Reading stories aloud at the beginning of each session in both groups created for the families an immediate shared experience. Literature conversations encouraged bilingual families to take risks with their language use as legitimate members of the community. In doing so, they made use of their linguistic and cultural funds of knowledge (González, Moll, & Amanti, 2005).

Reclaiming Libraries and Neighborhoods as Sites for Community Conversations for All Readers

Conducting literature conversations in public spaces such as libraries and neighborhoods creates welcoming spaces for intergenerational reading experiences.

Achieving welcoming conditions is even more important when educators reach out to linguistically diverse families who may not always feel comfortable in such events, especially in schools. The library recreated for culturally and linguistically diverse families the ideal of democratic participation and invited children and parents to entertain multiple perspectives as they engaged in dialogue with others who may have different worldviews than their own. The library was a public space where a reading community helped parents and children negotiate their complex lives and multiple identity affiliations, not just as "Latina/o" but as individuals who belonged to different generations actively constructing their cultural practices and traditions to extend beyond ethnicity and nationality.

Regular household visits and a summer day camp in the children's neighborhood established relationships between "Escuela Familia" families and teachers. During the day camp, children used water from the pond close to their trailer homes to water-paint, wrote poetry about the nature they saw and heard and read it to each other, and made sound maps of the spaces along their streets. Children, older siblings, and other extended family members, including parents, gathered under trees in the fresh air to read good books. Relationships grew that increased the families' comfort and they gradually became more involved in the mainstream family activities at their children's school.

Reclaiming language means not only that families are allowed to use their languages to engage in dialogue with one another, but that a historically marked language, Spanish, is repositioned to serve as a resource for children and parents to mediate their participation in critical conversations about issues that matter. Using literature to frame critical conversations about issues relevant to readers' lives allows them to use language as a community text. This means that linguistically diverse families can be active authors of the stories they compose and active readers in the stories they encounter because they are allowed to build their interpretations of texts from a familiar place and in a familiar language.

Note

The project described by García is sponsored by the New York Council for the Humanities supported by the "We the People" initiative of the National Endowment for the Humanities.

References

García, O., Kleifgen, J. A., & Falchi, L. (2008). From English language learners to emergent bilinguals. *Equity Matters*, Research Review 1. New York: Columbia University.

González, N., Moll, L. C., & Amanti, C. (2005). *Funds of knowledge: Theorizing practices in households, communities and classrooms*. Mahwah, NJ: Lawrence Erlbaum.

Children's Literature Cited

Bunting, E. (1994). *Smoky night/Noche de humo*. Illustrated by David Diaz. San Diego, CA: Voyager Books.

Garza, C. L. (2000). *In my family/En mi familia*. San Francisco: Children's Book Press.

Winter, J. (2004). *The librarian of Basra/La bibliotecaria de Basora*. New York: Harcourt.

13

BILINGUAL BOOKS

Bridges to Literacy for Emergent Bilinguals

Yvonne Freeman, David Freeman, and Ann Ebe

<table>
<tr><td>Hay tantísimas fronteras</td><td>There are so many borders</td></tr>
<tr><td>que dividen a la gente,</td><td>That divide people</td></tr>
<tr><td>pero, por cada frontera</td><td>But, for every border</td></tr>
<tr><td>existe también un puente.</td><td>There also exists a bridge.</td></tr>
</table>

(Valdés, 1996, pp. 4–5)

These powerful lines from Valdés' bilingual book of poetry remind us that language can be a barrier, a kind of border, for many students who enter school as dominant Spanish speakers. García, Kleifgen, and Falchi (2008) have suggested that we refer to such students as emergent bilinguals because as they learn English, they become bilingual. However, in some schools students' bilingualism is not valued. As García and her colleagues (2008) point out, "When officials and educators ignore the bilingualism that these students can and often must develop through schooling in the United States, they perpetuate inequities in the education of these children" (p. 6).

The assessment measures in the No Child Left Behind Act have created an atmosphere in which competence in English is all that matters in most schools. As Baker (2006) notes, "Any mention of bilingualism or developing native language competence is missing from this federal law" (p. 199). He goes on to argue that high-stakes testing in English has transformed the curriculum to the detriment of bilingual students.

The number of Latino students who may be adversely affected by the negative approaches of education legislation has increased dramatically. In the ten-year period between 1995/1996 and 2005/2006, the number of K–12 English language learners grew by over 57 percent, from nearly 3.2 million to over 5 million. These figures are in sharp contrast to growth in the total school enrollment during that period, which was only 3.6 percent (NCELA, 2007). While the emergent bilinguals come to school from many different language backgrounds, almost 80 percent are native Spanish speakers (Zehler et al., 2003). All of these students need to become literate in English, and research shows that bilingual students do better in English reading when their first language is also developed (August & Shanahan, 2006). In this chapter we suggest that teachers need to help their students reclaim their first languages in order to grow as new language learners.

Developing Literacy in Two Languages

Research shows that students who fully develop their first language succeed at higher rates than students in short-term bilingual programs or in English only programs (Collier & Thomas, 1996; Greene, 1998; Rolstad, Mahoney, & Glass, 2005). Academic content and literacy development in the first language accelerates the learning of a second language because languages are interdependent (Cummins, 2000). When students are taught in and develop proficiency in their first language, that proficiency transfers to the second language because there is a common underlying proficiency. The concept of a common underlying proficiency helps explain why students who enter school in the United States with grade-level literacy skills in their first language succeed academically at higher rates than students who enter with limited formal schooling and little or no native language literacy. When emergent bilinguals come to school with first-language literacy or receive instruction in their first language for an extended period of time as they also learn English, they build the linguistic resources they need to develop literacy in English.

As Valdés notes, for every border there is a bridge. One way teachers, even teachers who are not bilingual, can help emergent bilinguals cross the language border is to provide them with culturally relevant bilingual books. These books enable students to use their background knowledge and their first language in order to make sense of their new language, English. By drawing on bilingual students' strengths, teachers validate who their students are. All too often, emergent bilinguals are required to leave their language and their culture at the schoolhouse door. However, when teachers use culturally relevant bilingual books, they help their students reclaim their first language and culture as they develop high levels of bilingualism and biliteracy. In addition, when teachers understand how to use and choose bilingual books, they can reclaim literature as the material for teaching reading to their students who are emergent bilinguals. In this chapter we provide monolingual English-speaking and Spanish/English bilingual teachers with specific ideas they can use to select appropriate bilingual books.

We begin this chapter by discussing ways teachers can use bilingual books. We then describe different formats for bilingual books. Next, we present a series of questions teachers can use to determine whether a book has characteristics that support reading (Freeman & Freeman, 2006, 2009). A key characteristic is that the books need to be culturally relevant. In the final section we present a set of questions teachers can use to determine whether a book is culturally relevant. As we explain the ways to use bilingual books, the different types, and how to choose them, we exemplify each point with examples from high-quality, engaging Spanish/English bilingual books.

Using Culturally Relevant Bilingual Books

Bilingual books can be used effectively in bilingual classrooms, second-language classrooms, or mainstream classrooms (Ernst-Slavit & Mulhern, 2003). One effective way is to engage students in linguistic investigations. Students can compare and contrast the structures of the two languages. For example, students might note that both Spanish and English follow the same basic sentence pattern of subject–verb–object, but in Spanish, if the subject is a pronoun it can be deleted. These comparisons help students build metalinguistic awareness.

Bilingual books can also help strengthen the home–school connection. Both English-speaking and Spanish-speaking parents can read these books to their children or listen to their children read and then discuss the books in either language (see Fain & Horn and its extension, this volume).

Bilingual books are an excellent resource for a dual-language program. Teachers could read the book in the students' first language as a preview to build background for reading the book later in their second language. Students could also read a book independently in their second language and use the first language text as a resource. In addition, during free reading time, students could choose the language they want to read in.

Despite these benefits, some teachers in bilingual programs hesitate to use bilingual books because they are concerned about keeping the languages of instruction separate. While it is true that constant translation should be avoided, since it has been shown to be ineffective, current research (García et al., 2008; Cummins, 2007) shows that bilingualism is dynamic. García (2009) suggests that instead of viewing students' languages as separate, teachers should encourage students to draw on all their linguistic resources as they develop literacy and content knowledge. For example, effective bilingual readers draw on their knowledge of cognates. Teachers can call attention to strategies like this that help students transfer their first language knowledge into their second language as they develop biliteracy.

Types of Bilingual Books and Some Cautions

Bilingual books come in different formats. In some cases there are two separate versions of a book, one in English and one in Spanish. The two books are exactly alike, including the cover and the illustrations, except that they are written in different languages. An example is *Me llamo María Isabel* (Ada, 1993a) and *My Name is María Isabel* (Ada, 1993b), chapter books by the well-known children's author Alma Flor Ada. These books tell about a girl's first experiences in school in the

United States when the teacher changes her name. Another example of two separate books is *El sancocho del sábado* (Torres, 1995a) and *Saturday Sanchocho* (Torres, 1995b). This story is about a clever grandmother who shows her granddaughter how to get all the ingredients for the Colombian stew *sancocho*, as she barters at the marketplace with only a dozen eggs.

The bilingual flip book is organized differently. A reader can read the book in one language and flip the book over to read it in the other language. *Yum! ¡MmMm! ¡Qué rico! Brotes de las Américas/Yum! ¡MmMm! ¡Qué rico! Americas' Sproutings* (Mora, 2007) is a flip book of haiku poetry and informative narratives about crops of both North and South America. As when Spanish and English are presented in separate books, the illustrations, pagination, and covers of these flip books are the same for both versions.

The majority of bilingual books are published as a single book with both Spanish and English text on the same page or on facing pages. Sometimes the text is in English on one page and in Spanish on another page. Other books have lines in one language followed by lines in the other language on the same page. The storyteller Joe Hayes has provided many books formatted with Spanish and English on the same page, including *A Spoon for Every Bite/Una cuchara para cada bocada* (2005), the tale of a conceited rich man who spends his fortune buying spoons when his poor neighbors tell him about someone who uses a different spoon for every bite. The story's twist is that the "spoons" the poor neighbor refers to are tortillas used for scooping up food.

In most cases, teachers will not have a choice in the format of the book. There will be two separate books, a flip book, or one book with both languages on the same or facing pages. The benefit of having two books or having a flip book is that the two languages are clearly separated. This avoids a situation in which students read the text that is in their stronger language and ignore the other language. However, there are also advantages of having the two languages close to one another. A reader can read primarily in one language but use the other language as a resource when comprehension starts to break down. Readers can also compare and contrast the two languages as they read.

Educators should be aware of certain formatting issues when two languages are in the same book (Ernst-Slavit & Mulhern, 2003). Often, the English title of the book on the cover and title page is much larger than the Spanish, and in a font that is clearer to read. Within the books, when both languages are on a page, the English is usually printed above the Spanish. Sometimes the Spanish is in a font more difficult to read, or in another color. As Nathenson-Mejía and Escamilla (2003, p. 107) point out,

> These differences, though they may appear to be insignificant, hinder the reading experiences of the child reading in Spanish. The placement of the Spanish below the English . . . reinforces the lower status that Spanish occupies in the dominant US culture.

An even more important consideration than formatting when looking at bilingual books is that one language is a translation. Whether the book was originally written in Spanish or in English, the translation into the other language must be a good one (Schon & Corona Berkin, 1996). In some cases, such as the books by Alma Flor Ada, the author is a proficient bilingual who wrote both versions. Too often, however, translations are literal and do not represent natural language. It is essential that translations be of the highest possible quality. Monolingual teachers using bilingual books can always ask bilingual colleagues, parents, or professionals they know about the quality of the translations of the texts they share with their students.

Choosing Culturally Relevant Bilingual Books

When choosing bilingual books, educators should carefully consider whether or not the text has characteristics that support readers. Books with the characteristics we discuss next can help teachers reclaim literature for teaching reading. In the following sections we discuss a series of questions teachers can use to determine whether or not a bilingual book has the characteristics that support reading.

The first question a teacher might ask is, "Is the language of the text natural?" Often, the first books students are given have very limited text. Even those books, however, should sound natural. The words in the texts should be something the children recognize as language people use. *Carlos* (Womersley, 1999a, 1999b), a counting book, is available in separate English and Spanish versions. The delightfully illustrated text in both languages is natural. The main character, Carlos, explains that he has five fingers, four friends, three freckles, two grandmothers, and one baby sister with no teeth.

A second, related question is, "Is the text authentic?" Authentic books are written to inform or entertain, not to teach a particular sound–letter correspondence, grammar point, or, as is often the case with Spanish, the sounds of related syllables. A good example of an authentic limited-text book is *No hay nadie como yo* (Bradman, 1999a) with the English version *There's Nobody Quite Like Me* (Bradman, 1999b). These two pattern books tell how a little girl is like her friends and even like her twin sister in many ways, but "There's nobody quite like me," or, in Spanish, *"No hay nadie como yo"* (p. 13). Books such as these connect to young readers because they validate who they are and talk about actual experiences the readers have.

A third question teachers can ask is, "Is the text predictable?" For emergent readers, bilingual books are predictable if they are like other books children have read. In *Green Corn Tamales/Tamales de elote* (Rodriguez, 1994) the nana (grandma) asks for help from the family to make tortillas. This book follows the same pattern as the Little Red Hen tale, since the children respond to Nana's request by saying they will not help. Of course, once the tamales are all made, they eagerly volunteer to help eat them.

This book also contains a predictable pattern of question and response and code switching. "Not I," said my brother Jaime. "*Yo no,*" said cousin Larry. "Not I," said *tío* José. Since many bilingual students naturally move between languages in this way with other bilinguals around them (García 2009; Gutiérrez, Baquedano-López, Alvarez, & Chiu, 1999), the responses in the book that include code switching are predictable.

Older developing readers find texts more predictable when they follow familiar patterns such as a clear beginning, middle, and end or contain an easily identifiable problem and solution. A classic story from Venezuela, *La calle es libre* (Kurusa, 1983), also available in English as *The Streets Are Free* (ibid.), presents a problem as children living in the slums on the hills outside of Caracas want a place to play because, although the streets are free, they are also dangerous. The children work together to find a solution, and eventually find an area for a park that the community helps to build. The book's problem–solution pattern makes it more predictable for readers.

The next question is, "Is the text interesting and/or imaginative?" Readers are more engaged when the texts they are given to read are engaging, and, as Guthrie (2004) has shown, engagement leads to higher levels of reading proficiency. *A Perfect Season for Dreaming/Un tiempo perfecto para soñar* (Sáenz, 2008) is a beautifully illustrated imaginative book in which a grandfather dreams about traveling armadillos, a mariachi band of coyotes, and flying pigs that fall out of a piñata. He shares only with his granddaughter his strange imaginings.

For Christmastime, *Charro Claus and the Tejas Kid* (Garza, 2008) provides an especially imaginative Santa Claus tale situated along the Texas–Mexico border. Santa Claus enlists the help of his *compadre*, a former *charro* (Mexican cowboy), to help deliver Christmas presents on Christmas Eve to the children living all along the Rio Grande.

An important question for picture books is, "Is there a good text–picture match?" As Rog and Burton (2001–2002) point out, one of the factors that influences the difficulty of texts for readers is "the degree of support offered by illustrations" (p. 348). Many of the bilingual books already mentioned accomplish this, but a good example of a book with a clear text to picture match is *Sorpresa de Navidad para Chabelita* (Palacios, 1994b), *A Christmas Surprise for Chabelita* (Palacios, 1994a). In this story, Chabelita's mother must go to live and work in a city far from home, so Chabelita lives with her grandparents. She goes everywhere with them, including the marketplace, where her grandfather talks to his friends and her grandmother buys all her fruits and vegetables. The text describing these events is especially well illustrated.

Culturally Relevant Texts

A final question teachers can ask to determine whether or not a text has characteristics that support readers is, "Is the text culturally relevant?" Culturally responsive teaching is one of six factors the Center for Research on Education, Diversity and Excellence identified as important for Latino student success (Padrón, Waxman, & Rivera, 2002). One way to engage in culturally responsive teaching is by using culturally relevant books. When readers can connect what they read to their own lives, they are more engaged and have more success in reading. Freire and Macedo (1987) makes this point powerfully by explaining that "[r]eading does not consist merely of decoding the written word or language; rather, it is preceded by and intertwined with knowledge of the world" (p. 29).

The books we have discussed have different characteristics that support readers. However, all the books we included in this chapter are culturally relevant. The books connect to students' backgrounds, ethnicity, and cultural experiences. By using culturally relevant bilingual texts, teachers help emergent bilinguals reclaim their culture and their language. Jiménez (1997) found that struggling Latino students were better able to read and understand texts that were culturally familiar. Gray (2009) found that students chose texts because they "wanted to read books related to their life, their family, and their interests" (p. 476).

Not only do students choose culturally relevant books more often than other books, but they comprehend these books better as well. In Goodman's (1982) research using miscue analysis and retellings with speakers of Navajo, Hawaiian Pidgin, Samoan, and Spanish, young readers understood better when they read books connected to their experiences. As Goodman notes,

> the more familiar the language of the text, the actions of the characters, the description of the setting, the sequence of the events—the closer the readers' predictions will match the author's expression and the easier the text will be for the reader to comprehend.
>
> *(p. 302)*

Drawing on this research and her own miscue analysis studies with Spanish-speaking students in both rural and urban settings, Ebe (2010) developed a set of questions that teachers can use to help them determine the cultural relevance of texts. Each question highlights certain features of cultural relevance for readers.

The first item asks readers whether the characters in the story are like those of their families. This question considers students' ethnicity and the connections they can make with the books and their own ethnic backgrounds. In *René Has Two Last Names/René tiene dos apellidos* (Colato Laínez, 2009), a newcomer from El Salvador is confused when his second last name is missing from the label on his desk. When the class project is to make a family tree, René shows his classmates and his teacher how important his mother's side of the family is. He validates the Hispanic custom of using both parents' names.

Me encantan los Saturdays y los domingos (Ada, 2004) or the English version, *I Love Saturdays and domingos* (Ada, 2002), is an ideal book for children from bicultural families. The little girl in the story goes to her Anglo, English-speaking grandparents' house on Saturdays and to her Latino, Spanish-speaking grand-parents' home on Sundays. The activities she does with each set of grandparents are representative of their different worlds. Many emergent bilinguals come from backgrounds like this girl's.

The second question to ask is about the setting: "Have you ever lived in or visited places like this?" In *My Very Own Room/Mi propio cuartito*, Pérez (2000) tells how a young girl living in a large city who no longer wants to share her bedroom with her several brothers is able create a room of her own in their small family home. Many emergent bilinguals live in settings like this.

In contrast to the city setting, Herrera (1995) describes a rural setting in *Calling the Doves/El canto de las palomas* as he recalls his childhood memories as a migrant child. In *Cajas de cartón* (cardboard boxes) (Jiménez, 2000) and *The Circuit* (Jiménez, 1997), Jiménez relates in a longer chapter book different migrant experiences he and his family had as they followed the crops along a circuit in California. Children who live in such settings can picture the places in the stories and are better able to understand what they are reading.

The third question is, "Could the story take place this year?" Sometimes teachers have used folk tales and historical readings from students' home countries. However, students are usually more interested in reading about the present. Gray (2009) found that students "wanted books that were connected to their lives today" (p. 476). *When My Dad Comes Home* (Vela, 2008b) and *Cuando regresa mi papá* (Vela, 2008a) describe the different activities of a Latino boy and his mother while the father is in the armed services in Iraq. The boy fondly plans how these events will be shared by all three "when my Dad comes home." A similar book about current events is *¡Sí, se puede! Yes, We Can!* (Cohn, 2002), a fictional story based on the real-life janitors' strike that took place in 2000 in Los Angeles. With the help of his teacher, the young boy in the story finds a way to support his mother, one of the key organizers.

Another question to ask is, "How close do you think the main characters are to you in age?" Readers are usually more interested in reading a book if the characters are close to them in age. For example, in *Waiting for Papá/Esperando a papá* (Colato Laínez, 2004), Beto remembers escaping from El Salvador with his mother when he was 5. His father promises to follow but, in the story, has still not been able to come to the United States when Beto celebrates his eighth birthday. This book is good for younger students. *Birthday in the Barrio/Cumpleaños en el barrio* (Dole, 2004) is a birthday book that appeals to older students. In this story, Chavi unites her Cuban American community in Miami to arrange a traditional fifteenth/*quinciñera* birthday celebration for a friend of her sister whose family cannot afford to do it for her.

Girls often want to read about other girls, and boys often want to read about other boys. The next question relates to gender: "Does the story have boy characters (for boy readers) and girl characters (for girl readers)?" *Xochitl and the Flowers/Xóchitl, la niña de las flores* (Argüeta, 2003) is the story of a Salvadoran family that moves to San Francisco. The family begin a flower business like the one they had in El Salvador by selling flowers in the streets, but Xochitl, a young girl, learns she needs the help of her neighbors for her family to establish a nursery and a more stable business. In *Playing Lotería/Jugando lotería* (Colato Laínez, 2005), a young boy's parents send him to Mexico to spend a summer with his grandmother despite his worries that he does not speak Spanish and she does not speak English. He soon helps his grandmother in her job as a caller for the game of *lotería*, picking up Spanish in the process.

The next question is, "Do the characters talk like you and your family?" *My Name Is Jorge on Both Sides of the River* (Medina, 1999) is a book of poems in both Spanish and English that depict experiences of Latino children and families in schools. In one, Jorge applies the common slang label for Anglos to his teacher, saying, "Crazy *gabacha*. Who understands her?" (p. 41). Latino children reading this poem all recognize this slang term. Similarly, Salinas (2003) uses slang in *Cinderella Latina/La cenicienta latina*. For example, the father goes to *la pulga* (the flea market), where the sign says *"Compramos chatarra y vendemos antigüedades"* (We buy junk and sell antiques).

The next question asks about genres: "How often do you read books like these?" Books are more predictable when students have read other books of the same genre. Some bilingual books are extremely imaginative autobiographies. For example, in *A Movie in My Pillow/Un película en mi almohada* (Argüeta, 2001) the author recalls the volcanoes and the delicious cornmeal *pupusas* (stuffed tortillas) of his homeland, and his grandmother's stories. He combines these memories with his adventures as a young boy in San Francisco. His memories make a kind of movie in his pillow. In *The Upside Down Boy/El niño de cabeza* (Herrera, 2006), Herrera remembers his first months in the big city of his new country. In the city, everything seems upside down. Chickens come in plastic bags, the school schedule is confusing, and his tongue feels like a rock when he tries to speak English.

Several bilingual books are folktales, a genre that many of the Latino students are familiar with because they have heard them from their parents and grand-parents. *¡El Cucuy! A Bogeyman Cuento in Spanish and English* (Hayes, 2001) and *La llorona/The Weeping Woman* (Hayes, 2006) are familiar to children from Mexico. They delight in hearing the stories read aloud and modifying them with versions they have heard from relatives. As students read additional autobiographies, folktales, or other genres, the books become easier to read because the students become more familiar with the way each genre is structured.

The final consideration for choosing culturally relevant books is "How often have you had experiences like the ones described in the story?" In *My Diary from Here to There/Mi diario de aquí hasta allá* (Pérez, 2002) the author writes about herself as a young girl leaving Mexico and about keeping a diary of memories, fears, and new experiences as she travels to her new home. In *The Bakery Lady/La señora de la panadería* (Mora, 2001), the main character, Monica, spends many hours in her grandparents' Mexican bakery and wants to become a baker herself. In *La fiesta de las tortillas/The Fiesta of the Tortillas* (Argüeta, 2006), readers connect to familiar foods as well as to the adventures of the characters in the story as a mysterious spirit of the corn invades the family's Salvadoran restaurant business and brings the family closer together. As readers engage with texts like these, they are able to connect the experiences and the themes to their own lives.

Reclaiming Bilingual Books

Culturally relevant bilingual books help both monolingual and bilingual teachers reclaim the important roles of languages in teaching reading. When teachers choose texts with the characteristics that support reading and use them in effective ways, they help their emergent bilingual students reclaim their cultural and linguistic heritage. Rather than leaving their language and culture at the schoolhouse door, Spanish-speaking students build on the language resources they bring with them as they learn to read and write in two languages. Bilingual books that are engaging for Spanish/English emergent bilinguals provide bridges to biliteracy.

References

August, D., & Shanahan, T. (Eds.). (2006). *Developing literacy in second-language learners: Report of the National Literacy Panel on language minority children and youth.* Mahwah, NJ: Lawrence Erlbaum.

Baker, C. (2006). *Foundations of bilingual education and bilingualism* (4th ed.). Clevedon, UK: Multilingual Matters.

Clark, K. (2009). The case for structured English immersion. *Educational Leadership, 66*(7), 42–46.

Collier, V. P., & Thomas, W. P. (1996). Effectiveness in bilingual education. Paper presented at the National Association of Bilingual Education, Orlando, FL.

Cummins, J. (2000). *Language, power and pedagogy: Bilingual children in the crossfire.* Tonawanda, NY: Multilingual Matters.

Cummins, J. (2007). Rethinking monolingual instructional strategies in multilingual classrooms. *Canadian Journal of Applied Linguistics, 10*(2), 221–240.

Ebe, A. (2010). Culturally relevant texts and reading assessment for English language learners. *Reading Horizons, 50*(3), 193–210.

Ernst-Slavit, G., & Mulhern, M. (2003). Bilingual books: Promoting literacy and biliteracy in the second-languaage and mainstream classoom. *Reading Online, 7*(2). Retrieved from www.readingonline.org/articles/art_index.asp?HREF=ernst-slavit/index.html

Freeman, Y., & Freeman, D. (2006). *Teaching reading and writing in Spanish and English in bilingual and dual language classrooms.* Portsmouth, NH: Heinemann.

Freeman, Y., & Freeman, D. (2009). *La enseñanza de la lectura y la escritura en español y en inglés en clases bilingües y de doble inmersión* (2nd revised ed.). Portsmouth, NH: Heinemann.

Freire, P., & Macedo, D. (1987). *Literacy: Reading the word and the world.* South Hadley, MA: Bergin & Garvey.

García, O. (2009). *Bilingual education in the 21st century: A global perspective.* Malden, MA: Wiley-Blackwell.

García, O., Kleifgen, J. A., & Falchi, L. (2008). *From English language learners to emergent bilinguals*. New York: Teachers College.

Goodman, Y. (1982). Retellings of literature and the comprehension process. *Theory into Practice: Children's Literature, 21*(4), 301–307.

Gray, E. (2009). The importance of visibility: Students' and teachers' criteria for selecting African American literature. *Reading Teacher, 62*(6), 472–481.

Greene, J. (1998). *A meta-analysis of the effectiveness of bilingual education*. Claremont, CA: Tomás Rivera Policy Institute.

Guthrie, J. (2004). Teaching for literacy engagement. *Journal of Literacy Research, 36*(1), 1–29.

Guthrie, J., & Davis, M. (2003). Motivating struggling readers in middle school through an engagement model of classroom practice. *Reading and Writing Quarterly, 9*, 59–85.

Gutiérrez, K., Baquedano-López, P., Alvarez, H., & Chiu, M. (1999). Building a culture of collaboration through hybrid language practices. *Theory into Practice, 38*, 67–93.

Jiménez, R. (1997). The strategic reading abilities and potential of five low-literacy Latina/o readers in middle school. *Reading Research Quarterly, 32*(2), 224–243.

Krashen, S. (1996). *Under attack: The case against bilingual education*. Culver City, Language Education Associates.

Nathenson-Mejía, S., & Escamilla, K. (2003). Connecting with Latino children: Bridging cultural gaps with children's literature. *Bilingual Research Journal, 27*(1), 101–115.

NCELA (2007). The growing numbers of limited English proficient students 1995/96–2005/6. Retrieved January 18, 2009 from www.ncela.gwu.edu/policy/states/reports/statedata/2005LEP/GrowingLEP_0506.pdf

Padrón, Y., Waxman, H., & Rivera, H. (2002). *Educating Hispanic students: Obstacles and avenues to improved academic achievement* (No. 8). Santa Cruz, CA: Center for Research on Education, Diversity and Excellence, University of California, Santa Cruz.

Rog, L., & Burton, W. (2001–2002). Matching texts and readers: Leveling early reading materials for assessment and instruction. *Reading Teacher, 55*(4), 348–356.

Rolstad, K., Mahoney, K., & Glass, G. (2005). A meta-analysis of program effectiveness research on English language learners. *Educational Policy, 19*(4), 572–594.

Schon, I., & Corona Berkin, S. (1996). *Introducción a la literatura infantil y juvenil*. Newark, DE: International Reading Association.

Valdés, G. (1996). *Puentes y fronteras/Bridges and borders*. Tempe, AZ: Bilingual Review Press.

Zehler, A., Fleischman, H., Hopstock, P., Stephenson, T., Pendizick, M., & Sapruu, S. (2003). *Descriptive study of services to LEP students and LEP students with disabilities: Volume I. Research Report*. Washington, DC: OELA.

Literature References

Ada, A. F. (1993a). *Me llamo María Isabel*. New York: Libros Colibri.

Ada, A. F. (1993b). *My name is María Isabel*. New York: Atheneum Books.

Ada, A. F. (2002). *I love Saturdays and domingos*. New York: Atheneum Books.

Ada, A. F. (2004). *Me encantan los Saturdays y los domingos*. Miami: Santillana.

Argüeta, J. (2001). *A movie in my pillow/Una película en mi almohada*. San Francisco: Children's Book Press.

Argüeta, J. (2003). *Xochitl and the flowers/Xóchitl, la niña de las flores*. San Francisco: Children's Book Press.

Argüeta, J. (2006). *La fiesta de las tortillas/The fiesta of the tortillas*. Miami: Santillana.

Bradman, T. (1999a). *No hay nadie como yo* (R. Aguirre, Trans.). Boston: Houghton Mifflin.

Bradman, T. (1999b). *There's nobody quite like me!* Boston: Houghton Mifflin.

Cohn, D. (2002). *¡Sí, se puede! Yes, we can!: Janitor strike in L.A.* El Paso, TX: Cinco Puntos Press.

Colato Laínez, R. (2004). *Waiting for papá/Esperando a papá.* Houston, TX: Arte Público Press.

Colato Laínez, R. (2005). *Playing lotería mexicana/El juego de la lotería mexicana.* Lanham, MD: Luna Rising.

Colato Laínez, R. (2009). *René has two last names/René tiene dos apellidos.* Houston, TX: Piñata Books.

Dole, M. (2004). *Birthday in the barrio/Cumpleaños en el barrio.* San Francisco: Children's Book Press.

Garza, X. (2008). *Charro Claus and the Tejas kid.* El Paso, TX: Cinco Puntos Press.

Hayes, J. (2001). *¡El Cucuy! A bogeyman cuento in English and Spanish.* El Paso, TX: Cinco Puntos Press.

Hayes, J. (2005). *A spoon for every bite/Una cuchara para cada bocado.* El Paso, TX: Cinco Puntos Press.

Hayes, J. (2006). *La llorona/The weeping woman.* El Paso, TX: Cinco Puntos Press.

Herrera, J. F. (1995). *Calling the doves/El canto de las palomas.* Emeryville, CA: Children's Book Press.

Herrera, J. F. (2006). *The upside down boy/El niño de cabeza.* San Francisco: Children's Book Press.

Jiménez, F. (1997). *The circuit: Stories from the life of a migrant child.* Albuquerque, NM: University of New Mexico Press.

Jiménez, F. (2000). *Cajas de cartón.* Boston: Houghton Mifflin.

Kurusa (1983). *La calle es libre (The streets are free).* Caracas, Venezuela: Ediciones Ekaré-Banco del Libro.

Medina, J. (1999). *My name is Jorge on both sides of the river.* Honesdale, PA: Boyds Mills Press.

Mora, P. (2001). *The bakery lady/La señora de la panadería.* Houston, TX: Piñata Books.

Mora, P. (2007). *¡Yum! ¡MmMm! ¡Qué rico!: Americas' sproutings: Haiku by Pat Mora.* New York: Lee & Low.

Palacios, A. (1994a). *A Christmas surprise for Chabelita.* New York: Andrews McMeel.

Palacios, A. (1994b). *Sopresa de Navidad para Chabelita.* Mexico: Bridge Water Books.

Pérez, A. I. (2000). *My very own room/Mi propio cuartito.* San Francisco: Children's Book Press.

Pérez, A. I. (2002). *My diary from here to there/Mi diario de aquí hasta allá.* San Francisco: Children's Book Press.

Rodriguez, G. M. (1994). *Green corn tamales/Tamales de elote.* Tucson, AZ: Hispanic Books Distributors.

Sáenz, B. A. (2008). *A perfect season for dreaming/Un tiempo perfecto para soñar.* El Paso, TX: Cinco Puntos Press.

Salinas, B. (2003). *Cinderella Latina/La cenicienta latina.* Oakland, CA: Piñata Publications.

Torres, L. (1995a). *El Sancocho del sábado.* New York: Farrar, Straus & Giroux.

Torres, L. (1995b). *Saturday sancocho.* New York: Farrar, Straus & Giroux.

Vela, G. E. (2008a). *Cuando regresa mi papá.* Salem, MA: Pedestal Publishing.

Vela, G. E. (2008b). *When my dad comes home.* Salem, MA: Pedestal Publishing.

Womersley, J. (1999a). *Carlos.* Boston: Houghton Mifflin.

Womersley, J. (1999b). *Carlos* (S. Espinosa, Trans.). Boston: Houghton Mifflin.

CHAPTER 13 EXTENSION

Emergent Bilingual Learners Engaging in Critical Discussions

Carmen M. Martínez-Roldán

The process of reclaiming one's language should include the use of quality children's literature in readers' native languages, as Freeman, Freeman, and Ebe propose. Reclaiming language also means creating classroom contexts where critical discussions about quality literature written in Spanish can take place—in other words, where young children can read the word and the world (Freire, 1970) in the language of their homes and families. This means that we should move beyond the widespread belief that we need to teach emergent readers first to read in primary grades and then later use reading to learn. Literature discussions with emergent bilingual readers have taught me that young children are more than willing to use reading not only to learn about the world but to critique and make sense of unfair situations around them.

Bilingual books such as *La mariposa* by Francisco Jiménez (1998) and *In My Family/En mi familia* by Carmen Lomas Garza (1996) prompted thoughtful discussions from Latino/a children in a second-grade classroom where Julia, the teacher, and myself collaborated to organize literature discussions for the children. To introduce the book *In My Family/En mi familia*, Julia read the author's note at the beginning of the story. It mentions how Garza was punished for speaking Spanish at school, and says she wrote the book so Mexican Americans could feel proud of their heritage. Julia asked the students what they thought about the author's note. Mario was the first one to respond, and did so with an intertextual connection to the book *La mariposa*. The conversation occurred in Spanish:

Transcription	Translation
Mario: A mí me recordó eso (que escribió la autora en *En mi familia*) esa (historia, *La mariposa*) porque la castigaban como en *La mariposa*, porque no lo dejaban hablar español, no más ingles.	*Mario:* That (which the author wrote in *In My Family*) reminded me of that story (*La mariposa*), because she was punished like in *La mariposa*, because they didn't let him speak in Spanish, English only.
Julia: ¿Y qué te parece eso?	*Julia:* And what do you think about that?
Helena: Mal.	*Helena:* Bad.
Mario: Mal, porque ese libro fue de verdad y en ese no podían hablar español ni en el otro tampoco, no podían hablar en español.	*Mario:* Bad, because that book was true and in that one they couldn't speak in Spanish either, they couldn't speak Spanish.

Another child, Amaury, commented that he knew how Francisco, the main character in *La mariposa*, felt, because, in his opinion, Francisco "couldn't speak in English [because he didn't know English] and he couldn't speak in Spanish, so he couldn't speak at all." In this discussion the children were not only learning about reading, including gaining insights into the characters' feelings and making connections to other books, but also developing awareness of a situation that is too close to many Latino children, one of linguistic discrimination. They began to share their own stories about being forbidden from using Spanish, such as when Dayanara talked about her cousin: "My cousin, we need to hide from her too so I can speak in Spanish because if she hears me speaking Spanish she'll go tell her mom and her mom won't let her play with me anymore." We examined those experiences and the children developed a sense of connection to the authors and to each other. Naming and evaluating such experiences is an important element in the process of experiencing a liberatory education (Freire, 1970).

In this classroom, bilingualism was an asset, something to feel proud about, as Sandy's words reflect:

Sandy: I like speaking in both languages.
Carmen: Do you?
Sandy: . . . Because my mom speaks in English and my dad speaks in Spanish, and then I have to speak to my dad in Spanish, and I have to speak to my nana in Spanish, my dad's nana.

For many children like Sandy, relatives played an important role in their decisions to become bilingual. The children valued becoming language brokers for others, as Nadine told us: "A mí me gusta ser—hablar en español y en inglés porque cuando mi abuelita se—hay unos señores que hablan en inglés y mi abuelita no los entiende y yo le ayudo" (I like to be—to talk in Spanish and English because when my grandmother—there are some men who speak in English, and my grandmother does not understand them, and I help her).

Critical readings of culturally relevant bilingual literature and subsequent discussions about the books led some of the children to reclaim their bilingualism. The Spanish-speaking children in this classroom (about half of the class) were seen as valuable resources and partners. For instance, as part of the organization of the small-group literature discussions we asked the children to write the name of a student they would like to have in their group. They had to explain why they wanted to work with this peer. Héctor, who was working at reclaiming his bilingualism and recovering his Spanish, wrote, "Ada. Why? Because she's nice and she's a great partner and she helps me speak in Spanish and we're bilingual."

A couple of years ago a teacher who works in Arizona shared with me the discussions her third-grade bilingual students had about *Super Cilantro Girl/La Superniña del Cilantro* by Juan Felipe Herrera (2003). This bilingual picture book addresses the theme of bringing immigrant families back together after they have been separated owing to deportation. Inspired by the superhero movies enjoyed during his childhood when he visited friends in Mexico and by the stories told by relatives about crossing the border, Herrera offers children a superheroine who saves her mother, who in spite of being a citizen is detained at the Mexico–US border, in Tijuana. Super Cilantro Girl is able to save her mom, in part because she makes cilantro, the green herb that is so salient in Mexican culinary art, grow all over the border until the border disappears. Cilantro works as a metaphor for Mexican culture. The aroma of the cilantro distracts the border patrol and they have to stop to smell it and even get inspired to speak some Spanish.

Commenting about this part of the story, the children in this third-grade classroom told their teacher, "Oh, Sheriff Arpaio would need lots of cilantros to become bilingual." Sheriff Arpaio, in Arizona, goes into communities searching for undocumented citizens and brings terror even to those who are citizens. That these children made the connection between this literature and a scary political situation in Arizona that affects them so deeply speaks to the importance of creating safe contexts where children, as part of their interpretive work, imagine themselves exercising some agency and empowering themselves.

Supporting emergent bilingual children as critical readers and thinkers helps move forward a transformative educational agenda for social justice. In other words, helping young bilingual children make sense of their experiences related to linguistic discrimination, and providing them with bilingual literature through which to revalue themselves as bilinguals, is essential for reclaiming reading.

References

Freire, P. (1970/1993). *Pedagogy of the oppressed*. New York: Seabury.

Herrera, J. F. (2003). *Super Cilantro Girl/La Superniña del Cilantro*. San Francisco: Children's Book Press.

Jiménez, F. (1998). *La mariposa*. Boston: Houghton Mifflin.

Lomas Garza, C. (1996). *In my family/En mi familia*. San Francisco: Children's Book Press.

PILLAR V

Reclaiming Sociocultural Contexts

14

RECLAIMING PLAY

Reading Toys as Popular Media Texts

Karen E. Wohlwend and Pam Hubbard

On a typical winter morning, kindergartners trickle into Pam's kindergarten class-room, chatting, clomping, and bundled head to toe. A closer look at the children's clothing reveals favorite media characters on Spiderman ski masks, Cinderella parkas, Transformers boots, and Shrek mittens. It's likely that an even closer look into backpacks and pockets would uncover other popular media objects that accompany the children to school: Thomas the Tank train cars, Hello Kitty lip gloss, YuGiOh cards, Polly Pocket dolls, and Snoopy pencils. Such popular media items are often banned from classrooms, but children bring toys into school anyway, stashed away in backpacks until recess, when they are quickly pocketed and toted out in the relative freedom of playgrounds. However, Pam recognized that toys and their familiar media storylines offer powerful means for integrating children's cultural resources into literacy curriculum. She allowed her students to bring toys from home into the classroom and play with toys while writing and drawing during writing workshop.

What literacy value is there in children's fascination with popular media products? And how should teachers respond when popular toys come to school? In this chapter we seek to reclaim play as a way of reading the popular media toys that are key texts in the social context of modern childhoods. We share vignettes from Pam's classroom that demonstrate how children make sense with, and make use of, toys attached to popular multimedia. An expanded writing workshop inte-grated literacy, play, and the "stuff" that children love; this revaluing of popular media toys generated books, plays, storyboards, puppet shows, and more. Drawing from Pam's kindergarten experiences and Karen's three-year ethnographic study of language, literacy, and play in early childhood classrooms, we examine how children read popular media toys as texts for story making and identity construc-tion, for literacy and for participation; that is, children use toys to creatively perform plays and inspire storytelling as well as to gain access to peer groups and to assume and assign power-laden identities. Bratz dolls, Belle and Cinderella puppets, Barbies, Hello Kitty dolls, and Spiderman action figures served as concrete meaning-holders that anchored familiar storylines as well as children's invented texts. Toys held meanings stable from day to day as children rehearsed and revised their writing, rewriting social identities in the process (Wohlwend, 2009).

Recent Research on Popular Culture, Toys, and Literacy Development

Children's play with toys supports literacy development and identity construction by providing props and proxies that suggest particular roles and inspire storytelling. Recent literacy research shows that children extend their understandings of texts when they play with toys as they read and write. For example, Rowe's research (Rowe, 2000; Rowe, Fitch, & Bass, 2003) demonstrates that providing children with toy-and-book sets encourages them to play while reading, which deepens and expands meanings through transmediation, or movement of messages from one sign system to another (Siegel, 1995). In a study of 2-year-olds in a preschool program, Rowe (2000) finds that transmediation of print into dramatic play causes children to consider new aspects of stories as they imagine dialogue and action for characters that were minimally developed in the books. "[Dramatic play] allows children to walk around in story settings. It allows them to touch, feel, and actually look at objects from the vantage points of book characters" (p. 20). Similarly, when children play with toys as they enact picture books, they explore new perspectives as they take on character identities and create dialogue in their own words. Marsh's (2006) studies of popular culture demonstrate the power of multimedia to make early literacy curriculum more engaging and relevant. Dyson's (1997, 2003) research in primary classrooms shows that young children incorporate popular media characters and texts into their writing as a way to access more powerful classroom identities in both school and peer cultures.

In this chapter we argue that bringing popular media toys into classrooms represents a readily available and powerful means for implementing a "permeable curriculum" (Dyson, 1989) that encourages children to explore, critique, and produce multimedia texts. Incorporating popular media toys into literacy curriculum enables children to draw from their popular culture repertoire with implications for their literacy development and social status in peer culture (Dyson, 2003).

A Glimpse into Pam's Kindergarten Classroom

From the moment children enter Pam's classroom, they continually select from a menu of choices to map out unique learning paths for themselves. A typical morning in this kindergarten begins with Settling In. After signing in, children fan out across the room as they take out puppets, flannelboard sets, taped books, writing folders, and journals. After about 15 minutes or so, Pam assembles the group into the Family Circle, a whole-class sharing and planning time. She explains her planned activities and adjusts the day's agenda displayed on a large pocket chart to include the activities that children suggest. Once the plan for the day is settled, Pam leads the children in shared reading of poems, songs, and a featured big book on the adjacent story easel. Literacy Centers follows, a 30-minute period of adult-supported activity at the reading table, art table, writing table, listening center, and Book Nook (big books, story easel, song and poem charts, and classroom library). After Literacy Centers, the class regroups on the circle rug in front of the rocker for a second Family Circle. Pam recaps discoveries from different groups and a few children share work samples as they transition into Writing Workshop. "Put your finger on your chin if you know what you want to write about," Pam asks the children individually about their plans for Writing Workshop as they trickle off to work on projects. Children choose their own topics and often perch favorite toys next to writing folders or journals, playing as they write to inspire stories. Pam next introduces activities for Choice Time, the final period of the morning. Children's favorite toys mix with classroom materials in the literacy centers as well as other areas: blocks, math, snacks, house corner, and the dollhouse.

Incorporating Popular Toys as Texts in Reading/Writing Workshop

A view of toys as texts recognizes that children's play with media characters, dolls, and accessories offers a window into their interests and a rich resource for reading and writing in school. Pam is always looking for a "hook" that might open another door for the children in their reading and writing. Every year evolves differently. For example, she looks for opportunities to facilitate the process of storyboarding and planning for a puppet show or for a play through one-on-one conferencing with a child, knowing that he or she will demonstrate the process to other children. Pam reflects:

> I always follow the children's interests. For example, one year I had a child who loved SpongeBob, and was making SpongeBob characters during choice time. I had taken a media and popular culture class in graduate school, and saw this as an opportunity to invite popular culture into my classroom and use it as a springboard for merging mediational means (sign systems) and print literacy. For this particular child, I introduced the concept of story-boarding to him, showing him how folding the paper and numbering the squares could serve as a helpful planning tool for his SpongeBob play. I guided him through the process and got him started, ensuring that he shared his progress with the class as his work progressed. One child opens a door for another child, and pretty soon we have many different projects occurring very enthusiastically in different places around the room.

Children and Toys in New Textual Landscapes

Pam's character-covered kindergartners illustrate that popular media images and toys aren't limited to out-of-school settings; they're imported into school on children's clothing, school supplies, books, and toys. Children are immersed in "new textual landscapes" that are increasingly focused on commercial logos, licensed images, and franchised products associated with popular media (Carrington, 2005). As consumers, children read and respond to the explosion of media and merchandising that they encounter through television shows or videos, the Internet, video games, and other products marketed directly to them.

Among children's consumer goods, a toy is a special child-oriented product specifically designed to allow children to easily recognize the ways it can be used in play (Brougère, 2006). Toys are identity texts (Carrington, 2003) which invite players to enact identity performances, ranging from imitations of adults in everyday routines to dramatizations of fantasy characters. Marsh (2005) notes that popular culture toys and products provide material objects that allow young children to strongly identify with media characters, supported by parents who talk about and purchase themed goods to decorate bedrooms and stock toy chests. As children become attached to these objects and incorporate them into daily rituals, they also identify with the characters, learning and absorbing the characters' associated traits, typical actions, and storylines.

Toys, especially those toys attached to animated television shows, video games, or films, are texts that come with embedded storylines that children not only replay but also adapt and appropriate for their own stories. Children learn the storylines and character actions for Disney Princesses, Spiderman, or Batman action figures, which are sold in large collections and playsets for children to play and replay with. On the surface, favorite toys allow children to replay memorized scripts from films, DVDs, television programs, and video games. But there are other messages that are harder to detect: exaggerated stereotypes typical of popular culture (Hilton, 1996) that are gendered, raced, and classed (Christensen, 2000). For example, many popular media toys are designed to be stereotypically gendered; the doll aisles in toy stores are awash in pink and lavender packaging to mark these toys as specifically for girls. "Two separate, opposite gender roles are created and maintained through such images and narratives of Superman and Barbie which, by being separate and markedly different, work eventually to hold a hierarchy of male power in place" (Hilton, 1996, p. 35). In this way a toy's materials and visual design also communicate messages about how it should be used and who should play with it.

Reading Toys as Gendered Identity Texts for Young Consumers

In times of corporate licensing and mass marketing, toys are not isolated objects; they're linked to other toys and media through distribution networks. Licensing agreements for media franchises are ubiquitous in media targeted to children, so that it is difficult to know which idea came first: the line of toys or the film. Fast food toys form the leading edge of blockbuster promotions with toys that match the characters in the film trailers. On the other hand, toys that catch on with children can launch a line of multimedia products: animated television series, full-length feature films, books, DVDs, and CDs. By purchasing licensed merchandise, displaying favorite dolls and clothing, and viewing television and video, children are not only playing media storylines but also learning how to participate in global markets as young consumers. For example, Disney reports that children around the world love and purchase Disney Princesses products:

> One of our most successful businesses continues to be the Disney Princess franchise, which ranges from dolls and DVDs to video games, a popular magazine and the top selling Disney Princess TV at Target stores. In fiscal 2005 the franchise generated $3 billion in global retail sales, and we expect that number to continue to grow.
>
> *(Iger, 2006)*

Licensing agreements between fast food companies and media companies create mass marketing synergies that package girlhood identities along with the burgers and fries. For example, one McDonald's–Disney collaboration featured Disney Princess and Pirates of the Caribbean toys that are aimed to promote Disneyworld vacations and to increase demand for Happy Meals. But the fast food toys also promoted notions about who young children should want to be and how they should play. The Disney Princess toys were fashion and hair accessories and makeup products that emphasized the essential characteristic of a princess: she must be beautiful (Baker-Sperry & Grauerholz, 2003). These toys (pictured in Figure 14.1) read as gendered identity texts for girls that stress the necessity of meeting a widespread cultural model of feminine beauty: the mirror, jewelry, perfume, and accessories for dress-up play are decorative objects that send a message that girls should use these toys to be beautiful. The design of the toys' materials—pastel colors, embellished designs, silky fabric, and smiling princess faces—repeat these expectations for girls as appropriate toy users.

In contrast, the Pirates of the Caribbean toys (Figure 14.2) marketed to boys during the same month were texts for action: a pocket watch with movable parts, a working compass, action figures with swinging weapons for attacking, a wind-up chattering skull, and a floatable pirate ship. The materials in the pirate toys have a masculine palate—saturated shades of primary colors—and stress grotesque images designed to repel rather than appeal to adults. In this way, toys for girls emphasize *being*; toys for boys emphasize *doing*. By design, the identity text in the toy collection for girls reads passive, pretty, "good girl" princess while the identity text in the toy collection for boys reads active, adventurous, "bad boy" pirate.

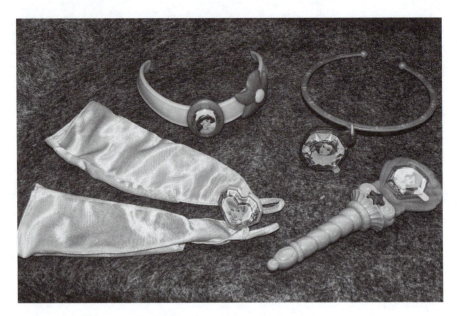

FIGURE 14.1 Happy Meal Toys for Disney Princess Promotion
(photo by Dorothy Menosky)

FIGURE 14.2 Happy Meal Toys for Pirates of the Caribbean Promotion
(photo by Dorothy Menosky)

But how do children actually read the identity texts in toys? In transactional literacy theory, readers and authors take equally productive semiotic roles as readers actively construct personal meanings, including surplus meanings unimagined by the author, through recursive interactions with a text (Goodman, 2003; Rosenblatt, 1978). In the same way, toys are subject to novel interpretations by players/readers. Manufacturers like Disney can make an expected use for a toy more likely by making it more appealing (pastel colors, big-eyed Disney Princesses in films conveying innocence and vulnerability that is repeated in the toys) but children read and reshape characters according to their own purposes.

Reading and Transacting Identity Texts in Toys

The following example of play among one group of boys in Pam's classroom demonstrated how children read identity texts in toys in complex ways. The boys transgressed the consumer expectations for girls as intended doll players to read and faithfully enact parts of a Disney Princess text, but interspersed with a karate scene.

Three boys sit on the floor of the kindergarten room in front of the three-story plastic pink and lavender dollhouse. Jacob picks up a blonde doll in a red ball gown to enact the evil queen in Snow White: "Mirror, mirror on the wall, who's the fairest of them all?" Jon, playing the role of Snow White, bounces a small doll along the carpet and intermittently calls out "Snow White! Snow White!" Bobby, who is holding a tiny plastic baby doll, asks Jon, "Do you like to be the lady??" Jon corrects him: "I'm Snow White."

A few minutes later, Bobby suggests to Jacob, "How 'bout we are both fighting? HiYA! HiYA!" The play action immediately changes from a castle scene to a fight between Bobby's baby and Jacob's queen as both boys use the dolls to slice the air with karate moves. Finally, Jon reclaims the film's storyline by switching to the role of one of the seven dwarfs and restarts the action just after Snow White bites the poison apple: "Oh-Oh! Snow White! Snow White! Snow White! Wake up! Wake up!" Jon and Jacob (suddenly also a dwarf) pretend to cry over Snow White while Bobby watches.

The recognition of reading and play as transactional acts highlights the need to focus on the relationships surrounding, rather than merely the content of, children's play with toys as texts. Like literacy, play is a semiotic system, one made up of multiple relationships between actors, actions, and language that simultaneously produce texts and contexts (Bateson, 1955/1972). In dramatic play, children must work together to maintain a *play frame*, the imagined context that is situated in the here-and-now reality of the classroom. This complex task requires players simultaneously to maintain the storyline action and roles between characters, and to maintain social relationships between players. In the vignette, Bobby was puzzled, but not by the story action or the queen's dialogue, "Mirror, mirror, on the wall," that occurred within the play frame. Instead, he could not make sense of an incongruity—or what he saw as a miscue in Jon's reading of the toy's social text—within the classroom context: that is, a *boy* taking up a woman's role in a Disney Princess story marketed to girls. Bobby's question, "Do you like to be the lady?" signals a mismatch in the here-and-now context, between Jon's intention to play the powerful role of the queen and the doll's meanings as a girl's toy reinforced by Disney's marketing practices. Bobby's follow-up suggestion "How 'bout we are both fighting?" occurs outside of the play frame and introduces a hypermasculine text from popular culture, a karate fight with appropriate shouts punctuated with hand slashes, that counters what he may see as an overly feminine play scenario. Jacob participates in the fight until Jon is able to reclaim the Snow White storyline by switching from a comatose Snow White to a grieving dwarf.

Play relationships are multiple and dynamic, as are the shared meanings that they support. In addition to explicit talk that organizes play, every action during play carries an implicit message that also affects the play frame and its meaning (Schwartzman, 1978). Play actions that are consistent with children's agreed-upon text or context sustain and build shared meanings, while play actions that are incongruous with the imagined characters or contexts challenge or alter the direction of play. Jon and Jacob were fans of the Disney Princess films and frequently used the dollhouse, dolls, and accessories to act out the stories. Although Bobby and other children seem puzzled by their willingness to act out female roles, Jon and Jacob answered their questions without hesitation and appeared to have no qualms about violating the toys' implicit expectations for girls as the only appropriate players. The boys were also able to convince other children to transcend the expected texts in toys through their abilities to nimbly negotiate play meanings and to generate inventive and engaging play themes.

Teachers as well as students learn through playful explorations with toys. Many of our "aha" moments as teachers involved artifacts that didn't use print-based reading. For example, when Pam introduced a piano keyboard into one play center, several children explored the toy by tapping out invented music. However, across the room two boys were busily scribbling away on a sheet of paper.

After working together for some time, the boys ran to the keyboard and asked the children playing with it to play the song they had written (the paper had little music-like notes all over it). The children looked at them blankly, and the boys kept insisting, but to no avail. Later in the day, the paper and a little rolled-up and taped paper tube were lying by the rocking chair to be shared. The boys got in the chair side by side and one boy held up the song while the other played the "flute" they had made while they sang and played the Pokémon theme song. There were no "words" on the page—just wonderful little approximated music notes and a flute. This example didn't involve "traditional" literacies, but was the most wonderful example of meaning making and what we see as teachers when we really open our eyes and look beyond what we know.

Addressing Teacher Concerns

Literacy education in elementary grades has typically not provided opportunities for children to read, respond to, or produce multimedia texts; popular culture materials and toys are especially suspect (Marsh, 2006). Some teachers and school administrators object to the messages in toys and video games and discourage children from bringing Barbie dolls, Pokémon cards, or SpongeBob SquarePants toys to school, believing that the popular culture toys are inappropriate or too frivolous for school. However, New Literacies Studies (New London Group, 1996) indicate that such prohibitions distance children from important linguistic and cultural resources.

> It may be the case that this resistance would weaken if educators were clearer about the important role such narratives play in children's identity construction. Marginalizing these texts, or banning them outright, serves only to ask of children that they cast off aspects of their identities as they move from home to school.
>
> *(Marsh, 2005, p. 39)*

In this section we address some of the concerns and questions that teachers express when considering whether to allow popular culture toys in their classrooms.

Isn't Play with Media Toys Inappropriate in the Classroom?

Many teachers resist integrating popular culture into curricula, in part from perceptions of popular media as overtly sexual or violent and inappropriate for innocent children, or as frivolous activity that is not academically rigorous (Marsh, 2006). The well-intentioned aim to shelter children from inappropriate material is rooted in middle-class beliefs about taste and propriety (Pompe, 1996) that are situated in teaching discourses of nurture and child innocence (Cannella, 2001). As a result of teacher lack of interest in the mainstays of children's culture, we know little about the ways that young children actually read, play, and make social use of their beloved media toys. It's likely that the absence of popular media toys in early childhood classrooms particularly disadvantages working-class children:

> The promotional, mass-market toys sold in Toys R Us and most available to and popular with working-class children are the toys most likely to be excluded from the culture of the classroom. So-called quality toys, the materials that conscientious, affluent parents will have provided for kids when

they have taken expert advice to heart (and had the time to follow through on it by providing recommended toys), will be precisely the kinds of things the child will encounter in preschool and kindergarten. The familiarity of the material objects will be just one of the many advantages that will bear on the child's future success in the classroom. Promotional toys, on the other hand, are likely to meet a cool reception by teachers. . . . In [teachers'] attempts to censor mass culture, the children most in need of comfort, security and involvement in school are the ones most disadvantaged.

(Seiter, 1992, p. 246)

Toys and children's media are cultural artifacts deserving of our attention in schools. Seiter (1993) situates gender stereotypes within the growing attention being paid to children as consumers and childhood culture. Children's culture thrives on exaggeration and parody of adult culture. Play with media toys represents an important mechanism for children to confront limitations in prepackaged scripts and to imaginatively improvise their way out of restrictive roles in stereotypical characters. Contemporary mass culture of childhood can be found in toys, advertisements, and television programs for children, and children use media toys to decipher important structures in adult culture. "In some cases, children's toys and television characters copy themes of adult culture but present them in exaggerated versions unacceptable to adults. Gender roles are a notorious example of this" (Seiter, 1998, p. 300). Children's involvement, as consumers, with toys is a two-way relationship in which companies manufacture and produce toys but also respond to consumer desires (Tobin, 2004). Children exercise agency through their decisions to purchase particular toys, or to exercise what the toy industry terms "pester power" by influencing their parents to purchase products.

Won't Parents or Administrators Object?

Some teachers who want to include play or popular culture in their curriculum fear opposition from parents or principals who object to such play as frivolous, to SpongeBob as vulgar, or to Barbie as stereotypically gendered. We argue that popular culture is omnipresent in children's worlds and serves as an important linguistic and cultural resource. Those of us who feel uncomfortable introducing popular culture texts can at least allow children to access it in schools by providing a permeable curriculum and by allowing, or even encouraging, children to bring toys to reading and writing workshops. Marsh's (2005) research on parents' perspectives on literacy, popular culture, and media in classrooms demonstrates that many parents support children's engagement with media toys at home. By inviting children to bring toys into her classroom, Pam used an approach that inherently accommodated parents; children brought toys that she could assume parents approved of and had purchased for them. When Jenna asked to bring her Zhu Zhu pet hamster to school, Pam encouraged her to do so. When Jenna's mother worried that the toy would disrupt the kindergarten, Pam reassured her that the toy would provide opportunities for literacy play. And it did. The children played with the automated hamster as it scurried around on the tables; Jenna read an informational book about hamsters to her toy pet; and the next day, several children wrote and shared stories about hamsters. Pam captured hamster-inspired literacy in digital photos that she emailed to Jenna's mother to demonstrate why this kind of play was meaningful for the class. Pam notes, "So whenever I have a parent that is unsure about this, I provide concrete examples of the natural occurrences that arise as a result of inviting toys into the class."

Pam takes a similar proactive approach to educating administrators. A new vice-principal visiting her classroom once stopped and did a double-take when he walked by two boys playing with Transformers. He looked puzzled but said nothing and walked on. Although Pam wondered what he thought, she waited for a teachable moment. It came a few days later when the two boys ran up to Pam, asking, "How do you fold that paper again?" They wanted to create storyboards (a process that Pam had demonstrated to facilitate children's playwriting) for a Transformers play. When the boys were ready to perform their play, Pam invited the vice-principal, and the children explained how the project evolved from their play with favorite toys.

Won't Some Children Who Don't Have Popular Toys Feel Left Out?

Some teachers prohibit toys from classrooms in an effort to create a more equitable or harmonious classroom; they aim to forestall squabbles over coveted possessions or to prevent children who have many toys from displaying wealth. The archetype is the early childhood staple "Show and Tell" in which a child stands before the class to show off the latest and greatest toy. However, as previously noted, children's culture is highly connected to children's media products, so that children's status on the playground and in the classroom is affected by their ability to participate through popular culture texts.

In a year-long study of young children's recess play, Karen found that children's knowledge of the texts that ground popular toys is an important tool to access play groups. In other words, it was not necessary to own or hold a particular valued toy; displaying an insider's knowledge of popular toys was enough to be accepted into play groups. For example, one excluded child on the playground was able to join play groups by offering play suggestions based upon his expert knowledge of a range of Pokémon characters, their relative powers, and their transformed characters. Popular media play themes and materials act as important tools for friendship building, peer acceptance, and gaining access to play groups (Wohlwend, 2004). Children can gain social status among peers by demonstrating knowledge connected to favorite films or TV shows and by sharing popular toys with friends. Children's friendships are key components in the classroom social history that influence who can take up key leadership roles and literate identities in school (Christian & Bloome, 2004).

Future Steps in Rethinking Toys and Revaluing Play in Schools

We've outlined first steps for incorporating play and integrating media toys into literacy workshops. But it's only a beginning. To reestablish the primacy of a meaning-based literacy curriculum that recognizes the value of play, toys, and peer culture, we need to:

- *Engage in literacy teaching that values play as a multimodal meaning-making system.* Play is more than a device to induce children to do literacy tasks as in the typical recommendation to infuse literacy materials into dramatic play centers. In fact, some play researchers question whether this common teaching strategy substitutes low-level imitations of teacher-modeled literacy tasks for the richer real-world identity performances that children invent themselves (Trawick-Smith & Picard, 2003). We need to value play itself as a potent way to read, write, reread, and rewrite the world (Wohlwend, 2008). This includes encouraging children to play with favorite toys as an integral part of story-telling and writing. Consider adding popular media toys to classroom libraries for dramatic play.
- *Provision the environment and create regular opportunities for child-directed play.* In addition to a rich variety of art materials, picture books, toys, and props for pretending and exploring, Pam provided daily blocks of sustained time for children to collaborate, negotiate, and direct their own play as part of reading and writing workshops as well as during free play periods.
- *Advocate for reintegrating play into elementary curricula as a tool for twenty-first-century literacy learning.* Current efforts to reestablish play in schools focus on its benefits for physical fitness, psychological need, or social skills development and overlook its connection to enactment and design knowledge consistent with video and graphic productions in new literacies. To understand children's intentions and meanings, we need to attend to their interests and purposes in play. Play is an important avenue through which to blend out-of-school literacies with school literacy practices.
- *Recognize that play opens opportunities to reproduce as well as challenge stereotypes.* We need to be prepared to mediate play that is exclusionary by talking with children, showing excluded children how to gain access to a play group by suggesting a logical role or action for their character, or by joining a play scenario to demonstrate inclusive play practices. We can also help raise children's consciousness by encouraging children to walk around in a character's shoes to experience what another person might be feeling, and to imagine alternatives to stereotypical roles and storylines.

- *Contribute through our own teacher research to an emerging body of literacy research on social context and children's popular culture.* This reconceptualization of toys as texts aligns with calls on several fronts in literacy research: literacy development as participation in early literacy apprenticeships (Rowe, 2008), children's inventive uses of literacy materials and tools (Bomer, 2003), and multimodal literacy (Kendrick & McKay, 2004; Siegel, 2006).

- *Be aware of growing digital opportunities to integrate popular toys with school literacy.* International researchers are examining young children's out-of-school literacies and identity work with new forms of play, such as online play in social networks such as Club Penguin and Webkinz. The proliferation of online digital doll sites for young girls (e.g., http://Barbie.everthinggirl.com, http:// disney.go.com/princess/#/home/) that allow users to play with toys and animate avatars (Richtel & Stone, 2007) suggests that these mergers of new literacies and media toys will be increasingly important spaces for children to read, write, and play in.

References

Baker-Sperry, L., & Grauerholz, L. (2003). The pervasiveness and persistence of the feminine beauty ideal in children's fairy tales. *Gender & Society, 17*(5), 711–726.

Bateson, G. (1955/1972). A theory of play and fantasy. In G. Bateson (Ed.), *Steps to an ecology of mind* (pp. 177–193). San Francisco: Chandler.

Bomer, R. (2003). Things that make kids smart: A Vygotskian perspective on concrete tool use in primary literacy classrooms. *Journal of Early Childhood Literacy, 3*(3), 223–247.

Brougère, G. (2006). Toy houses: A socio-anthropological approach to analysing objects. *Visual Communication, 5*(1), 5–24.

Cannella, G. S. (2001). Natural born curriculum: Popular culture and the representation of childhood. In J. A. Jipson & R. T. Johnson (Eds.), *Resistance and representation: Rethinking childhood education* (pp. 15–22). New York: Peter Lang.

Carrington, V. (2003). "I'm in a bad mood. Let's go shopping": Interactive dolls, consumer culture and a "glocalized" model of literacy. *Journal of Early Childhood Literacy, 3*(1), 83–98.

Carrington, V. (2005). New textual landscapes, information, and early literacy. In J. Marsh (Ed.), *Popular culture, new media and digital literacy in early childhood.* New York: RoutledgeFalmer.

Christensen, L. (2000). Unlearning the myths that bind us. In *Reading, writing, and rising up: Teaching about social justice and the power of the written word* (pp. 39–56). Milwaukee, WI: Rethinking Schools.

Christian, B., & Bloome, D. (2004). Learning to read is who you are. *Reading and Writing Quarterly, 20*(4), 365–384.

Dyson, A. H. (1989). *Multiple worlds of child writers: Friends learning to write.* New York: Teachers College Press.

Dyson, A. H. (1997). *Writing superheroes: Contemporary childhood, popular culture, and classroom literacy.* New York: Teachers College Press.

Dyson, A. H. (2003). *The brothers and sisters learn to write: Popular literacies in childhood and school cultures.* New York: Teachers College Press.

Goodman, K. S. (2003). Reading, writing, and written texts: A transactional socio-psycholinguistic view. In A. Flurkey & J. Xu (Eds.), *On the revolution of reading: The selected writings of Kenneth S. Goodman* (pp. 3–45). Portsmouth, NH: Heinemann.

Hilton, M. (1996). Manufacturing make-believe: Notes on the toy and media industry for children. In M. Hilton (Ed.), *Potent fictions: Children's literacy and the challenge of popular culture* (pp. 19–46). London: Routledge.

Iger, B. (2006). Walt Disney Company annual meeting of shareholders. Retrieved November 8, 2006, from http://media.disney.go.com/investorrelations/presentations/060310_transcript.pdf

Kendrick, M., & McKay, R. (2004). Drawings as an alternative way of understanding young children's constructions of literacy. *Journal of Early Childhood Literacy, 4*(1), 109–128.

Marsh, J. (2005). Ritual, performance, and identity construction: Young children's engagement with popular cultural and media texts. In J. Marsh (Ed.), *Popular culture, new media and digital literacy in early childhood* (pp. 28–50). New York: RoutledgeFalmer.

Marsh, J. (2006). Popular culture in the literacy curriculum: A Bourdieuan analysis. *Reading Research Quarterly, 41*(2), 160–174.

New London Group. (1996). A pedagogy of multiliteracies: Designing social futures [Electronic Version]. *Harvard Educational Review, 66*, 60–93. Retrieved from http://bert.lib.indiana.edu:2174/harvard96/1996/sp96/p96cope.htm

Pompe, C. (1996). "But they're pink!"—"Who cares!": Popular culture in the primary years. In M. Hilton (Ed.), *Potent fictions: Children's literacy and the challenge of popular culture* (pp. 92–125). London: Routledge.

Richtel, M., & Stone, B. (2007, June 6). Doll web sites drive girls to stay home and play. *New York Times.* Retrieved from www.nytimes.com/2007/06/06/technology/06doll.html?_r=1&oref=slogin&pagewanted=all

Rosenblatt, L. (1978). *The reader, the text, and the poem.* Carbondale, IL: Southern Illinois University.

Rowe, D. W. (2000). Bringing books to life: The role of book-related dramatic play in young children's literacy learning. In K. A. Roskos & J. F. Christie (Eds.), *Play and literacy in early childhood: Research from multiple perspectives* (pp. 3–25). Mahwah, NJ: Lawrence Erlbaum.

Rowe, D. W. (2008). The social construction of intentionality: Two-year-olds' and adults' participation at a preschool writing center. *Research in the Teaching of English, 42*(4), 385–386.

Rowe, D. W., Fitch, J. D., & Bass, A. S. (2003). Toy stories as opportunities for reflection in writers' workshop. *Language Arts, 80*, 363–374.

Schwartzman, H. B. (1978). *Transformations: The anthropology of children's play.* New York: Plenum.

Seiter, E. (1992). Toys are us: Marketing to children and parents. *Cultural Studies, 6*(2), 232–247.

Seiter, E. (1993). *Sold separately: Children and parents in consumer culture.* Piscataway, NJ: Rutgers University Press.

Seiter, E. (1998). Children's desires/mother's dilemmas: The social contexts of consumption. In H. Jenkins (Ed.), *The children's culture reader* (pp. 197–317). New York: New York University Press.

Siegel, M. (1995). More than words: The generative power of transmediation for learning. *Canadian Journal of Education, 20*, 455–475.

Siegel, M. (2006). Rereading the signs: Multimodal transformations in the field of literacy research. *Language Arts, 84*(1), 65–77.

Tobin, J. (2004). *Pikachu's global adventure: The rise and fall of Pokémon.* Durham, NC: Duke University Press.

Trawick-Smith, J., & Picard, T. (2003). Literacy play: Is it really play anymore? *Childhood Education, 79*(4), 229–231.

Wohlwend, K. E. (2004). Chasing friendship: Acceptance, rejection, and recess play. *Childhood Education, 81*(2), 77–82.

Wohlwend, K. E. (2008). Play as a literacy of possibilities: Expanding practices, materials, and spaces. *Language Arts, 86*(2), 127–136.

Wohlwend, K. E. (2009). Damsels in discourse: Girls consuming and producing gendered identity texts through Disney Princess play. *Reading Research Quarterly, 44*(1), 57–83.

CHAPTER 14 EXTENSION

Reading Tags as Texts

Debbie Smith

As I pictured Wohlwend and Hubbard's description of kindergartners arriving at school, bundled in winter clothing and Disney-driven identities, it was as if I were reading a description of my Arizona high school students. Like Hubbard, I read my students' identities in the color and style of clothes they wore—in my case, they were typically blue and baggy to represent their gang, the CRIPs—and in their language—my students used specific vocabulary like "roll call" and "slobs" that required I create a glossary to keep track. One student's quickly gestured hand sign would be answered with a second silent sign of mutual understanding and acknowledgment of belonging to a group. Dallas Cowboys caps and tattoos, and objects such as cell phones, mp3 players, and iPods, were just some of the tools— or toys—my adolescent students used in order to construct meaning in their world.

Like Hubbard, I learned to allow my adolescent students to bring their toys to school, thereby legitimizing typically forbidden items as part of school life and reclaiming my students' sociocultural context as part of reading in my classroom. At the beginning of my career, as a remedial reading and writing teacher in a traditional high school setting, my students' worlds trickled into my classroom through the topics of the books they read and about which they wrote. However, it wasn't until I taught in an alternative setting, where many of my students were gang members, that I discovered how critical students' cultures and literacies outside the school are for reading in the classroom. For example, my students taught me how tags serve as legitimate texts and can support marginalized students' entry into reading instruction.

My students, CRIP members who ranged in age from 13 to 18, were initially so reluctant to read that I wasn't sure if they knew how to handle books, much less read them. One of the boys, whose street name was Smurf, told me, "If we wanted to read, we'd have stayed in school," and another student called Juice told me, "Miss, we know how to read, we just don't want to read."

They claimed they didn't read, but I soon became aware of what I thought was "doodling" that they constantly created on paper, books, and any available surface. One day, as I watched, Smurf "doodled" something and then reread what he had written. He reoriented the paper and wrote something else. I started asking questions and learned that the doodles were tags. A tag is one type of graffiti found on walls, buildings, fences, street signs, and bridges. In schools, tags are readily found in the bathroom, inside lockers, and on notebooks, shoes, and desks.

I thought, "Well, if this is something they enjoy and they are writing, maybe I need to incorporate tagging into the classroom." I placed a large piece of butcher paper on the wall where my students could freely tag. The butcher paper was immediately filled. Although I recognized a certain beauty in the stylized marks, I couldn't read the tags. My students read them effortlessly and voraciously, and responded to them orally and with more tagging. Soon the students taught me that "periods" placed between words let readers know where one word ends and another begins. Quotation marks around letters or words emphasize the importance of that letter or word. Most important, I learned that the tag represents who the author is and to what gang they belong. My reading education continued as my students and I drove through town and they taught me how to make meaning from various tags in their community.

Back in the classroom, the butcher paper full of tags became a discussion board. When we dialogued about the tags, we were legitimately reading and responding. On one occasion, when Angela misread a tag, Smurf, the author, quickly corrected her and showed her how it should be read. I emphasized to the students that reading tags is reading and therefore they were readers.

I started writing the daily schedule or other announcements using the same style and characteristics the students used in their tags. The students used CRIP conventions. They crossed out "b" (because it stands for the rival "Bloods" gang) and "r" (because the Bloods' gang color is red) in their school writing. They didn't use the letters "ck" together because that stands for "CRIP killer," so they spell "back" as "bacc," with the "b" crossed out. I developed projects that focused on the students' lives outside of school, and they used gang-style fonts in all their work. Fairy tales were rewritten with a gangster slant so that Jack and the Bean Stalk became Lil Boy Blue and the Marijuana Plant. My class was writing and reading because tagging was central to my students' identities.

I still struggled to encourage the students to read beyond tags and to engage with books, because I wasn't satisfied with the breadth of their reading or writing. I kept observing. I listened to my students reference articles they read in *Lowrider* magazine. The magazine company agreed to send me enough copies for the class, and when they arrived, my students were so excited to get their very own that I felt like Santa on Christmas Day. They immediately thumbed through the magazine and read. The class was quiet for a while and then slowly the students began to talk. They described cars they had seen in the neighborhood in relation to the cars they were reading about. They talked about rims, sound systems, and the accessories they dreamed of for their cars. They alternated between reading and talking for the rest of our time together that day. We reread the *Lowrider* magazine on several occasions. One time, our discussion focused on the role women play in the magazine and how such images might affect the four girls in the class. Interestingly, the girls were not offended by the pictures in the magazine. They felt that if the girls in the pictures wanted to be used that way, it was their choice. The boys explained to me the difference between a "bitch" and the women in their real lives.

I bought more magazines that focus on hip-hop culture or deal with topics like marijuana and tagging; these included *The Source*, *Vibes*, and *Rap Pages*. I learned that not only did I need to bring into my class the reading materials that were part of my students' world, but I needed to honor their concept of reading.

Eventually, we moved from magazines to short stories and poems. Literature study involved the whole class having different copies of poems or short stories and reading what they wanted to and sharing when they needed to. Sometimes I read to them from books. Other times, one student would read a poem or story out loud for the class and a discussion would begin. Eventually, the discussions advanced to their thoughts about what they read in relation to their world experiences. At times, they constructed tags to express the meaning they made of the reading.

The main question I'm asked when I share my experiences teaching gang members who were allowed to read and write tags is: Aren't you hindering your students' abilities to be successful in the "real world" by allowing their language into the classroom? In fact, bringing students' outside-of-school literacy into the classroom doesn't prevent them from learning the skills they need to progress in the "real" world. Instead, as they learned about audience and purpose, they were motivated to learn the skills and vocabulary of more conventional language. For example, my students were asked to write the mayor of the city about how valuable the alternative high school program was to them. A discussion evolved about whether the students should use their gang style and words to write the letter. They realized that they couldn't use their "gang language" because it would simply turn off the mayor and not achieve their purpose, which was to encourage him to support their school. When my students and I made a presentation about our experiences to teachers at a conference, we asked each other, "Who is our audience and what do we want to accomplish?" The students learned that their language, how they spoke, and how they dressed affected how the audience would listen to their message. Although they often selected one student to dress more gangsta style as an illustration for the audience, their presentation language, both oral and written, was conventional.

Reading Wohlwend and Hubbard's chapter about kindergartners and their toys brought my students to mind. Adolescents' toys and concerns are different, yet they are deeply revered artifacts of their sociocultural context and central to their identities. When the adolescent worlds of tagging and rap, like the early childhood worlds of SpongeBob and Cinderella, enter our classrooms, we effectively reclaim the reading community.

Note

If you're interested in learning more about Smurf, Juice, and other CRIP members who were Debbie's students, read Smith, D., & Whitmore, K. F. (2006). *Literacy and advocacy in adolescent family, gang, school, and juvenile court communities: "CRIP 4 LIFE."* Mahwah, NJ: Lawrence Erlbaum.

15

CRITICAL LITERACY GOES DIGITAL

Exploring Intersections between Critical Literacies and New Technologies with Young Children

Vivian Vasquez and Carol Felderman

> *Ben:* ¡Hola! ¡Mi nombre es Ben y esto es como empezó! Nuestra clase tuvo una reunión sobre las excursiones del año. Scarlett fue la que preguntó si íbamos a ir al Acuario de Baltimore este año. Nuestra maestra nos dijo que no podíamos ir porque cuesta demasiado dinero.
>
> *Scarlett:* Decidimos de tener una reunión con [El Director de la escuela]. Le mandamos una carta por correo electrónico y llevamos una copia a su oficina. El nos dio una cita para el viernes. Pensamos que la reunión era buena. Entonces empezamos a preparar todo el trabajo duro que íbamos hacer todo este año. Otra vez hicimos carteles y enseñamos a nuestros compañeros como hacerlos. Esta vez más clases participaron. No podemos esperar para ver lo que va a pasar mañana.
>
> *Ben:* Hi! My name is Ben and this is how it began! Our class had a meeting about the trips of the year. Scarlett was the one that asked if we were going to go to the Baltimore Aquarium this year. Our teacher told us we could not go because it costs too much money.
>
> *Scarlett:* We decided to have a meeting with [the principal]. We sent him a letter via email and took a copy to his office. He gave us an appointment for Friday. We believe that the meeting was good. Then we started to prepare all the hard work. We cannot wait to see what will happen tomorrow.

In this chapter we explore a group of second graders' use of podcasting as a communicative tool for representing social action projects they took on in their classroom. Throughout the year, their teacher, Carol Felderman, attempted to frame her teaching from a critical literacy perspective while building curriculum based on their interests. The opening exchange comes from the "100% Kids" podcast show #2. The podcast was an online radio show hosted by the children. In their exchange, Ben and Scarlett referred to a year-long project their class took on to problematize and create a solution for an administrative decision to cancel a school event for which many of the children had great passion. The show was often recorded in English and Spanish because of the large number of families in the school whose first language was Spanish. This kind of social action work, which focused on topics of interest to children, was a far cry from the prepackaged, one-size-fits-all programs that are prevalent in classrooms across the United States. The podcasting work also offers a demonstration of what happens when technology is used in creative ways beyond simply using it to produce electronic workbooks or learning spaces. Although rooted in a curricular project, the children's and teacher's understanding of and reaction to their sociocultural contexts was a way to reclaim that context as organic, vital, specific to their setting and experience, and fundamental for reading in the classroom.

Extending Children's Repertoire of Literacy and Communications Practices

While describing pedagogies of responsibility and place, Comber, Nixon, and Read (2007) note that in the teaching of literacy, our role as teachers includes extending the repertoires of literacy and communications practices available to our students. They define a "pedagogy of responsibility" as "classroom practice that is informed and structured by teachers' commitment to engaging with questions of diversity and democracy" (p. 14) with their students. Place-based pedagogies, they say, foreground the local and the known and are opportunities for teachers "to structure learning and communication experiences around the things that are most meaningful to their students: their own places, people and popular cultures, and concerns" (p. 14). They ask how technology, such as sending a message or text using a cell phone, creating a video, and participating in online spaces such as electronic art galleries for children, provides new and interesting ways for children to communicate their ideas, questions, and understanding of the sociocultural contexts in which they live. Comber and her colleagues further note:

> Literacy teaching cannot, and we believe it should not, be a content-free zone. We know that there is great potential for students to expand their literate repertoires when they become deeply engaged in acquiring new knowledge about things that matter.
>
> *(p. 14)*

Regarding things that matter, there is a line in the 2006 movie *Cars* (Anderson, 2006) where Sally, one of the main characters, reflects on a time when roads and roadways moved with the land rather than cutting through it. She lamented that back then, "[c]ars didn't drive on the road to make great time, they drove on the road to have a great time." In pedagogies of responsibility and place as described by Comber and her colleagues (2007), the journey matters. This chapter focuses on a journey by a group of second graders into the world of podcasting and the transformative effects that resulted from the experience. Rooting the work in reclaiming the sociocultural contexts of the children involved engaging with new technologies as tools for supporting their critical reading development.

New Technologies and Critical Literacy

Critical literacy has been a topic of contestation for some time. This, in part, is due to the belief that it should look, feel, and sound different, and accomplish different sorts of life work depending on the context in which it is being used as a theoretical and pedagogical framework (Comber & Simpson, 2001; Vasquez, 2001a, 2001b, 2004). Vasquez (2004) refers to this framing as a way of being when she argues that critical literacy should not be an add-on but a frame through which to participate in the world. As such, there is no such a thing as a critical literacy text. The world—the sociocultural contexts of life—as texts can be read from a critical literacy perspective. What this means is that the issues and topics that capture learners' interests as they participate in the world around them can and should be used as texts to build school experiences that have significance. Key tenets that comprise this perspective are as follows:

- Critical literacy involves having a critical perspective (Vasquez, 2004).
- Students' cultural knowledge and multimodal literacy practices should be utilized (Comber, 2001).
- The world is a socially constructed text that can be read (Frank, 2008).
- Texts are never neutral (Freebody & Luke, 1990).
- Texts work to position us in particular ways, therefore we need to interrogate the perspective(s) of others (Meacham, 2003).
- What we claim to be true or real is always mediated through Discourse (Gee, 1999).
- Critical literacy involves understanding the sociopolitical systems in which we live and considering the relationship between language and power (Janks, 1993).

Critical literacy practices can contribute to change and the development of political awareness (Freire & Macedo, 1987; Freebody & Luke, 1990). Text design and production can provide opportunities for critique and transformation (Janks, 1993; Larson & Marsh, 2005). The last tenet is where new technologies and social media have a strong role in reclaiming sociocultural contexts of school and life. Text design and production refer to the creation or construction of texts and the decisions that are part of that process. This includes the notion that it is not sufficient to simply create texts for the sake of practicing a skill. If children are to create texts, they ought to be able to let those texts do the work intended. For instance, if children write surveys, these ought to be done with real-life intent for the purpose of dealing with a real issue. If children write petitions, they ought to be able to send them to whomever they were intended for. Helping children understand real-life functions of text is an important component of growing as a critically literate individual (Luke & Freebody, 1999).

There are growing accounts of critical literacy work in classrooms (Comber, 2001; Morgan, 1997; O'Brien, 2001; Vasquez, 2001a, 2004). Very limited in the literature, however, are accounts of the ways new technologies intersect with critical literacies. This chapter is an attempt to fill that gap.

Social Media

"Social media" is an umbrella term used to refer to the integration of technology and social interaction. Social media tools, such as podcasting and blogging, allow people to connect electronically using the World Wide Web. In this chapter we are particularly concerned with the question: What can new technologies and social media afford our work with critical literacy as a means to reclaim reading? This question rings especially true in the area of text design (creating texts) or redesign (taking existing texts, critiquing their construction, and then creating new texts), and production (making texts available more broadly within and across sociocultural contexts). We refer to texts as broadly construed and not limited, for instance, to print-based or image-based text.

We want to be clear that the use of new technologies and social media does not constitute engagement with critical literacies. Simply using new technology in the classroom does not mean one is engaging in critical literacies. However, new technologies and social media can be used as tools to carry out critical literacy work. Such tools can be used in the production and distribution of texts both locally and globally as a way of (re)claiming sociocultural con-texts (i.e. that which goes along with or subsumes the text) in reading.

A Journey into Podcasting

A podcast is an online radio show whereby a podcaster, the person(s) doing the podcast, records either audio or video of themselves and/or others, using a digital recorder, and then posts it to a place on the Internet (a blog site or website) for others to hear or view. The second graders took on the role of podcaster during the spring of 2007 in Carol's classroom. The second-grade classroom is located in a school with over 800 students. According to the school website, the students represent over 40 countries of origin and over 20 different languages spoken at home, although the most dominant of these is Spanish. The neighborhood is located about 25 minutes outside of Washington, DC, in a neighborhood that is experiencing increased gang activity and where most of the children are on free or reduced lunch. On average there were 20 students in the class. Fifty percent of the children were English language learners. There was one student identified with learning disabilities and another eight in the referral process for identification as learning disabled.

The exchange at the start of this chapter represents the children's use of podcasting as a tool for talking about projects they were doing or for sharing their thinking on topics or issues that were important to them, both locally, such as advocating for certain privileges, and globally, such as global warming or environmental issues. The exchange is part of a multi-episode discussion on problematizing the cancellation of a long-standing expectation for all the second graders to go to the Baltimore Aquarium at the end of the school year.

Some of the children had anticipated this end-of-the-year trip from the time they were in kindergarten. The trip was especially important for the children who, owing to financial constraints at home, were counting on trips like this as their only opportunity to go to places like an aquarium. Being told the trip was cancelled was very problematic and resulted in Carol's class taking social action to reverse this decision by organizing a series of fund-raising events over the course of the year. They used the Internet to research what they could learn from going to the aquarium as a way of building an argument for why this was a good learning experience. They calculated costs for the trip, including how many other second-grade classes were interested in attending, entrance fees, and busing, to determine how much money they would need to raise to make the trip happen. They met with the principal on two occasions to understand how such decisions are made, by whom, and for what purpose, as well as to share with him their position regarding why they felt the trip was worthwhile. They also wanted to discuss with him a plan of action for reinstating the trip. In the end, after hosting many fund-raising events, including popcorn sales and a bingo night, the children were successful in raising enough funds for the entire second grade to go to the Baltimore Aquarium. Supporting children as agents with advocacy in their worlds is a way of helping them—and ourselves—reclaim the sociocultural contexts of school and reading.

New Technical Stuff and New Ethos

Lankshear and Knobel (2007) suggest that one of the questions we need to ask ourselves is what new technologies can afford the work that we do. Specifically, what new things can we do, in terms of literacy teaching and learning, with the use of this new technology? What can we do differently in our teaching as a result of new technology? Lankshear and Knobel note that alongside new technical *stuff* comes a new ethos. New technical stuff refers to living in a digital culture, or digitality, and what that affords: connectivity, social networking and instant information. The new ethos stuff refers to a shift of mindset, or way of thinking about technology use, as a result of the new technical stuff.

In terms of podcasting, which is the focus of this chapter, the question is: What does podcasting afford the work done by the second graders? Said differently: What sorts of possibilities for connecting with the world outside the classroom are made available through the use of this social networking tool, and specifically, how might this tool be used in carrying out students' critical literacy work? Finally, how might this social media tool work to position children differently, creating space for them to participate differently?

Podcasting with Second Graders: Getting Started

Carol's second-grade students were born into a world that is technologically very different from the world into which we were born. It was not surprising, therefore, that many of the children came to school with knowledge of and experience with the new technological and new ethos stuff described by Lankshear and Knobel (2007). Their interest in podcasting was therefore not a surprise.

The children first started asking questions about podcasting when they heard Carol's voice in a segment she did for the Critical Literacy in Practice Podcast (www.clippodcast.com), which Vivian hosts. Carol shared their curiosity with Vivian, who then sent her some Internet links of children who were podcasting, such as Halloween Boy (Sage, 2007) and the children of Selsted School (Bilodeau, 2006). The Halloween Boy podcast is created by an 8-year-old boy who shares topics that are interesting to him, such as stories that he retells or has made up himself, and tips, such as how to make good bubbles. *Save Our School: The Children of Selsted* is the story of a small school in England that was earmarked for closure. The students and parent community wrote, performed, and sold copies online of a song, "Save Our School," to keep their school open. Their song was picked up and played by podcasters across the globe, resulting in the raising of enough funds to keep the school doors open. Hearing other children's voices through the Internet generated more interest and conversation and led to the children's desire to start a podcast of their own.

"100% Kids": Creating a Focus

After a number of discussions regarding what their podcast should be about, the children decided on creating a show that focused on sharing the ways they made a difference in their school and beyond by contributing to change in some way. They wanted to share experiences such as the Baltimore Aquarium project that focused on issues of fairness and injustice—not to take the moral high ground but to make accessible to potential listeners, both kids and adults, how they made change in different spaces and places. Following further conversation, they decided to call their show "100% Kids" (Vasquez & Felderman, 2007) to indicate that they would generate the show's topics and be the primary voices listeners heard. Some of the topics they addressed in their show included: equity and fairness, animal rights, global and environmental issues, and identity and positioning.

Podcasting and Identity Work

Once the children had decided on a focus for the show, the next step was to inform their families about the project and have them sign permission forms. With the consent of all the parents, the podcast project was quickly on its way. The next step was for the children to come up with radio names or show names. Carol talked with the children about issues related to safety as the primary reason for taking on different roles and identities online. This was an effective way of helping the children to understand that anyone can take on a different identity online, which is why we always need to be careful about whom to believe and trust, and mindful of when we need to be cautious. The children were not naive concerning the existence of other people online who might not have their best interests in mind. Carol spoke with them about not blindly trusting people they met on the Internet, including those who might comment on their podcast. We took extra precautions and monitored comments about the podcasts so that any inappropriate ones were deleted. In the case of "100% Kids," other than some spam email, all of the comments were productive and supportive.

Following the creation of radio names, we sat down with the children to determine what segments to include in their show, and why. They wanted an introduction piece to prepare their audience for listening to the show and an art piece that represented the salient issues from the show on the podcast homepage. When possible, they wanted to include a song or two in connection to the topic(s) to be discussed. They also decided on including a news or current events segment, a dedication piece, and finally an acknowledgment section.

The act of choosing radio names was very exciting as children realized that it was an opportunity to construct new identities. Gee (2003) talks about new technology, like podcasting, as opening up possibilities for new forms of interacting that are quite motivating and compelling. For some, the act of renaming themselves into a different existence was transformative, and once shy and hesitant children for whom the curriculum was difficult to access took on new roles in the classroom. This fits Nixon and Gutierrez's (2007) notion of identity play whereby children are able to extend the ways in which they express themselves and tell their stories. As they played with language for publication in the online space, they developed an authorial stance or point of view from which they communicated their ideas. In doing so they developed new identities as meaning makers.

Mary, a very shy, withdrawn 7-year-old who was identified as having multiple learning issues, was one such child. When Vivian first met her, she deliberately shied away, barely spoke, and did not have much to do with the other children, especially their podcasting. In her journal, Carol wrote:

Mary developed many difficulties with learning, speech, and hearing. She came to my class with an IEP [Individual Education Plan] for social skills and speech and language which barely touched on how much more there was to learn about her struggles with learning. She mostly liked to be alone and work alone which stood out to me. I also could not understand what she said and this dilemma was true for many of the students in the class as well. Her classmates said, "What?!" when we introduced ourselves in the first days [of school]. She tried hard, but much of what came out of her was not understandable. The kids wanted to know about her favorite foods and colors, so their questioning was in her best interests, but still hurt Mary because she was trying so hard to make herself understood.

While Mary's classmates could not understand her, she could not always understand them either. Mary has partial hearing loss and uses an amplifying unit so that she can better hear and understand what someone is saying in whole-group sessions. I wore a microphone on days when I knew I would not be able to speak as loudly as possible. Mary was given a seat on the rug next to me if we were in a circle, or if we were in a group lesson she had a place in the front. Still, I watched Mary just escape into her own world as lessons went too fast or if she was tired from the night before or from the amount of focus she needed to keep in order to comprehend what was going on. Mary had plenty of struggles to manage throughout the year.

While the children busily worked away at putting together a show, Mary sat or stood along the periphery of the classroom doing other things. As she noticed how involved her classmates were in their scriptwriting and rehearsing, her interest was piqued and slowly she began watching more closely. We watched as she listened in on some of their conversations. Eventually she listened, with the other children, to a couple of shows and became more and more interested. The first thing she did was to give herself a radio name, Queen, a nickname her mom called her. This was a name that apparently made her feel good, safe, and wanted.

The first recording session with Queen lasted about 15 minutes. Before we started, we talked with her about the equipment we were using and reassured her that we could record as many times as she wanted. Queen's debut performance consisted of one line, "We hope you like our painting of the world," which would be part of the art section of the podcast where there was a brief discussion regarding the piece of art used in the show notes.

It took six or seven takes and approximately 25 minutes of editing to produce what amounted to Queen's 2.5 seconds of audio. If this had been another task, she would have given up on it or not participated at all, but Queen hung in there. We explained to her that we could cut out the pieces she wasn't happy with and leave in the pieces she liked. Knowing that these editing tools were available, in the words of Gee, "lowered the consequences of failure" (2003, p. 21) and created a space for Mary to take on this new challenge.

Several shows later a different Queen emerged as she physically and emotionally moved from the periphery of the classroom to the center where her classmates were. No longer was she recording with Vivian in private; she wanted to record with the other children. Soon after, Queen could be heard participating in the online banter and ad-libbing done by some of the children while recording segments for the show. In subsequent episodes, Queen could be heard singing songs, which she helped create with her classmates, and saying things like "You go, girl" or "That's right, girl." In her identity as Queen, Mary was able to position herself as part of a group. No program of study or mandated curriculum could have helped her with this! For Queen, the experience of podcasting was transformative, as it was for some other children in the class.

Putting Together a Show

From Monday to Thursday the children generated ideas for the show. Carol did not limit the amount of time spent on crafting the scripts. The new technology created new "hybrid textual spaces" (Marsh, 2005, p. 6) in which the various elements and content areas of the second-grade curriculum collided and merged. As time went on, it became more and more obvious that this work cut across different curricular areas. Some days they worked for 30 minutes and other days they spent the whole morning working on the show. We compared the literacies produced through the children's podcasting work against a representative example of the Standards of Learning for Virginia public schools (Virginia Department of Education, n.d.), which describe the commonwealth's expectations for student learning and achievement in grades K–12 (see Table 15.1). The literacies that the children came away with from creating the podcasts far exceeded what is mandated through the standards. Attention to recognizing and (re)claiming their sociocultural contexts led to more engaging, far-reaching, and meaningful curriculum (even in terms of standards).

The children wrote, read, revised, reread, and performed, and then revised again, their various scripts until they had crafted a text they felt was meaningful to share with an audience. They often asked for each other's opinions. They worked collaboratively in small groups, drawing on each other's knowledge of particular topics or events and researching particular bits of information. They talked to one another and other adults from home or at school, and they read books from their classroom and the library, as well as gathering information from the Internet. Families played a role by helping with translating some of the episodes to Spanish.

As the children moved, according to their interests and desires, to doing different parts of the show, they mentored and ushered each other along. In a way, they were doing what Gee refers to as "debugging their experiences" (2003, p. 21), thereby learning from the experiences of others as they took on new roles or exchanged roles in the production of the show. Knowledge was shared and distributed among the children, and groups were often cross-functional. This

TABLE 15.1 Comparison of Literacies Produced in Podcasting against State Standards

Virginia Standards of Learning	*Literacies Produced through Podcasting*
Oral Language: 2.3 The student will use oral communication skills. a) Use oral language for different purposes: to inform, to persuade, and to entertain. b) Share stories or information orally with an audience. c) Participate as a contributor and leader in a group. d) Summarize information shared orally by others.	• Use oral language to inform, persuade, entertain, question and make meaning of the world. • Share stories and report events with a local and global audience as indicated by a cluster map which provides information regarding where listeners are located. • Participate as a contributor and leader. • Research and summarize information gathered from various resources including information shared orally by others.
Writing: 2.11 The student will write stories, letters, and simple explanations. a) Generate ideas before writing. b) Organize writing to include a beginning, middle, and end. c) Revise writing for clarity. d) Use available technology.	• Research and generate ideas before writing. • Engage in multiple genres of writing, including story narratives, reports, jokes, songs, and persuasive texts. • Organize writing to include a beginning, middle, and end. • Revise writing for clarity, to help with the flow between segments in the show, and to ensure a smooth transition between segments. • Use available technology, including the Internet, recording equipment, and digital cameras.

Source: The Virginia Standards of Learning are available at www.doe.virginia.gov

meant that children did not always work with the same group of classmates and had no problems with creating and re-creating new groups, depending on which part of the show they were interested in developing. Children like Queen, for whom the curriculum was not accessible at the start of the year, were able to take on different identities in the podcasting world that created space for them to participate in ways they had not done previously.

Putting together a show wasn't always easy, but the children took on the challenge without hesitation. On Fridays we recorded the show one segment at a time. The children were quick to learn that using a digital recorder meant we could do as many takes as needed and that we could edit out extraneous errors and misreadings. After recording on Friday, Vivian edited the pieces together over the weekend and released the show on the following Monday. Not only were

Mondays spent listening to the show as a group, but they were also a time to critique the audio and make adjustments to the upcoming episodes. During their critique of the show the children came up with ways of revising it, such as incorporating a jokes segment to give their audience a break from the deep issues and topics discussed in other segments.

We Did It and So Can You!

Soon it was our last time to gather together as podcasters and we gathered to listen to the final episode of "100% Kids." The children's friends and some of their family members listened, and when it was over, Serita's mother approached us to say thank you for having done the show with the children. "My family doesn't live together because we cannot. Her father, he lives in Colombia. He waits for this [the "100% Kids" podcast] each week so he can hear [Serita]." Apparently, the release of each episode was the highlight of the week for him. He listened to the show at an Internet café in Colombia along with other family members. The family had been divided and lived in different countries as a way to create a better life for themselves. It was an extraordinary surprise to discover that the children's podcast had this kind of impact.

"We did it and so can you!" was a sentiment the children shared repeatedly in show #8 as a way of reminding their listeners to act on their beliefs, especially if those beliefs contribute to more equitable ways of being in the community and beyond. We hoped this experience would be transformative in some ways for the children and we were surprised when it was also transformative for families like Serita's.

For the children, producing, designing, and redesigning podcast episodes and segments created a space in which to understand that texts are socially constructed and that literacy is most definitely not a neutral technology. The children learned they could individually contribute to a shared experience. They learned about ways they are positioned within certain social systems and the discursive practices or ways of being, doing, speaking, and acting that shaped the topics and issues in their podcasts. They learned about the ways in which they position others through the choices they make. They learned to use what the technology afforded them to reach people beyond the physical limitations of their school site. Throughout the process, we drew from their cultural and linguistic resources and in the end the experience was transformative, as many of them learned that they could understand, act upon, and influence the sociocultural contexts in which they lived. These exciting outcomes were part of reclaiming reading via critical and digital engagements.

References

Anderson, D. K. (Producer). (2006). *Cars* [DVD].

Bilodeau, A. (Producer). (2006, October 16). *Save our school: The children of Selsted Primary* [Audio podcast]. Retrieved from www.bazmakaz.com/clip/2006/10/16/save-our-school-_-clip-15/

Comber, B. (2001). Critical inquiry or safe literacies: Who's allowed to ask which questions. In S. Boran & B. Comber (Eds.), *Critiquing whole language and classroom inquiry*. Urbana, IL: National Council of Teachers of English.

Comber, B., and Simpson, A. (Eds.). (2001). *Critical literacy at elementary sites*. Mahwah, NJ: Lawrence Erlbaum.

Comber, B., Nixon, H., & Reid, J. (2007). *Literacies in place*. Newtown, NSW: Primary English Teaching Association.

Frank, B. (2008). Critical literacy. Paper session presented at the meeting of International Literacy Educators Research Network. Mississauga, Ontario.

Freebody, P., & Luke, A. (1990). Literacies programs: Debates and demands in cultural context. *Prospect: Australian Journal of TESOL, 5*(3), 7–16.

Freire, P., & Macedo, D. (1987). *Literacy: Reading the word and the world*. London: Bergin & Garvey.

Gee, J. P. (1999). *Discourse analysis: Theory and method*. New York: Routledge.

Gee, J. P. (2003). *What video games have to teach us about learning and literacy*. New York: Palgrave Macmillan.

Janks, H. (1993). *Language and position*. Johannesburg: University of Witwatersrand Press.

Lankshear, C., & Knobel, M. (2007). *A new literacies sampler*. New York: Peter Lang.

Larson, J., & Marsh, J. (2005). *Making literacy real*. Thousand Oaks, CA: Sage.

Luke, A., & Freebody, P. (1999). A map of possible practices: Further notes on the four resources model. *Practically Primary, 4*(2), 5–8. Retrieved from www.alea.edu.au/freebody.htm

Marsh, J. (Ed.). (2005). *Popular culture, new media and digital literacy in early childhood*. New York: RoutledgeFalmer.

Meacham, S. J. (2003, March). Literacy and "street credibility": Plantations, prisons, and African American literacy from Frederick Douglass to 50 Cent. Paper presented at ESRC Seminar Series Conference, University of Sheffield.

Morgan, W. (1997). *Critical literacy in the classroom*. New York: Routledge.

Nixon, A. S., & Gutierrez, K. D. (2007). Digital literacies for young English learners: Productive pathways toward equity and robust learning. In C. Genishi & A. L. Goodwin (Eds.), *Diversities in early childhood education: Rethinking and doing* (pp. 121–135). New York: RoutledgeFalmer.

O'Brien, J. (2001). Children reading critically: A local history. In B. Comber & A. Simpson (Eds.), *Negotiating critical literacies in classrooms* (pp. 41–60). Mahwah, NJ: Lawrence Erlbaum.

Sage (Producer). (2007, August 2). *Halloween boy* [Audio podcast]. Retrieved from http://quirkynomads.com/wp/2007/08/02/halloween-boy/

Vasquez, V. (2001a). Constructing a critical curriculum with young children. In B. Comber & A. Simpson (Eds.), *Negotiating critical literacies in classrooms* (pp. 55–68). Mahwah, NJ: Lawrence Erlbaum.

Vasquez, V. (2001b). Classroom inquiry into the incidental unfolding of social justice issues: Seeking out possibilities in the lives of learners. In B. Comber & S. Cakmac (Eds.), *Critiquing whole language and classroom inquiry* (pp. 200–215). Urbana, IL: National Council of Teachers of English.

Vasquez, V. (2004). *Negotiating critical literacies with young children*. Mahwah, NJ: Lawrence Erlbaum.

Vasquez, V., & Felderman, C. (Producers). (2007). *One hundred percent kids* [Audio podcast]. Retrieved from www.bazmakaz.com/100kids

Virginia Department of Education. (n.d.). *Virginia standards of learning*. Retrieved from www. doe.virginia.gov

CHAPTER 15 EXTENSION

The Reading–Writing Connection in Video Production

Chuck Jurich and Richard J. Meyer

For the past three years Chuck has sponsored an after-school video club for students in grades 4 and 5. Video and other forms of social media, such as the podcasts that Vasquez and Felderman describe, provide unique opportunities to examine the intersection of technology, reading and writing, identity exploration, and critical literacy. Videos produced in the club may address perceived injustices in the authors' lives and, in turn, imagine how the students would like the world to become. Through writing scripts, creating characters, role-playing, and video editing, students export their real identities into virtual and projected identities (Gee, 2007) onto the screen or other digital media. When students write these texts, they seriously consider how the videos will be read by their audiences; they read (and perform) like writers and write like readers; and they address sociocultural issues from school and community contexts. We present one student production to demonstrate how reading during video production informed and influenced writing and supported reclaiming reading in school.

Video Production

Children in the club produce video texts in a three-stage process: *pre-production* (scriptwriting, prop creation, scene locating and building), *production* (acting and shooting video), and *post-production* (video and sound editing). In each stage the "text" is substantially transformed from script to performance to video. How students read these protean texts contributes greatly to how they are revised and re-authored along the way. In order to read and write in video production, students have to work with a variety of text modes, including speech, print, image, sound, video, real-world objects, and virtual digital clips. In addition, video making involves multiple authors—scriptwriters, directors, camera operators, actors, editors, and more—and the final composition is arguably more collaborative than any text students write in most classrooms. While video is not a new medium, *video production*, particularly in the elementary school, is rare. Most schools already have the technologies required to make videos, such as video cameras, tripods, computers, and video editing software; however, they usually lack the personnel to teach students how to use the tools effectively in order to produce video texts.

Video work brought the social facets of reading and writing to the forefront of composing. Video productions were completed through a system of cooperation, negotiation, compromise, and perpetual revision. Therefore, in the club no video was completed by a single person, and students rarely worked alone, preferring— even needing—to write, read, and edit in pairs; this collaborative work is consistent with twenty-first-century thinking (see Meyer & Altwerger, this volume). As a result, students go into video production assuming that the work will be collaboratively constructed, with input and criticism from everyone involved. They also understand that the videos are created to be shared.

Video production is a way for students to construct characters and situations that comment on their lives. Real life is complicated, and stories must be simplified for the screen in order for readers/viewers to understand them. Generally following the patterns of traditional film narratives, student productions first establish the ordinary world in which the characters live. The main character is easy to sympathize with and we know we should dislike their nemesis. A conflict is overtly introduced and the leading player experiences a series of escalating trials and difficulties (usually in threes) before the conflict is at last resolved in a happy, if not too neat, ending. Using their reading knowledge as a guide, students recognize in their productions endings that are unsatisfying ("that shouldn't happen to that character") or unrealistic ("that is impossible!") and learn to compose increasingly complex video texts with subtleties.

Lessons from "Monkey-Girl"

One fourth-grade student named Summer started work on an unusual script in which the main character was part monkey and part girl—a "monkey-girl." She was taunted by her peers, had no friends, and felt she was doomed to be alone and miserable forever. Monkey-Girl's father, a single parent, was depicted as very caring but overly busy and fairly incompetent in helping her through her issue. The five-and-a-half-minute video took nearly two months to complete and involved a relatively slim crew of just five people. As was typical for such compositions, some students performed multiple production roles. Summer herself was the scriptwriter, co-director, an actor, as well as the "marker" (person who documents on a dry erase board what scene, shot, and take the crew is on and displays it in front of the camera before each shot). Much of the time spent to produce the film took place in post-production work involving video editing, voice overdubs, and adding sound and music. A cut of the video was shown to the rest of the video club, and while feedback was positive, the editors were quick to revise a few sequences and make subtle yet significant changes in sound; such reading, rewriting (revising), and reperforming were common.

Summer's film addressed the idea of visual differences in people and the consequences of being different, something she was aware of as a Native American. She could have made the main character realistically foreign but for difference to be immediately read, she had to be obvious and visually over-the-top. After reading a draft of her provocative script, I informed Summer that I had access to a monkey suit. Her eyes lit up. She hadn't solved how Monkey-Girl would be visually constructed. Now, the character could clearly have attributes of both monkey (monkey suit, references to eating bananas for lunch) and girl (a human face, wearing glasses, talking). When the actress put on the suit for the first time, the club members were impressed by the look but there were issues. "She looks like a bear, or maybe a giant mouse!" one student commented. Summer took the costumed actress down the hall for fresh opinions, asking any available students or teachers, "What animal is she?" A consensus could not be found and the crew decided that a tail was needed. At the next session, a wiry brown one appeared. The tail was changed again, halfway through filming, for a much fatter and more pronounced one. The old tail was put on Monkey-Girl's father, complicating his genetic makeup and turning him into a more complex character.

Readers of the video understood that Monkey-Girl was ambiguously human and monkey-like. Visually, the video opened with Monkey-Girl in a playground, literally swinging from monkey bars. In a later shot, Monkey-Girl sat by herself picking things off her tail and eating them. On the other hand, she was shown to live in a house, walked on two legs, and went to school like any ordinary girl. Monkey-Girl herself declared on two occasions that she was not "full monkey" but only "half"; however, the bullies' actions indicate that even part monkey is too much, and clearly being full human is best. Dad's advice, that "they make fun of you because they want to be just like you," rang hollow, just as the scriptwriter intended it to sound. Though we were led to believe through his modest tail that he was part monkey himself, the father saw her issue as simple and petty jealousy among children and not a larger systemic issue that dealt with discrimination and being of "mixed species."

Monkey-Girl had a somewhat unsatisfying ending. One of the bullies came to her house and simply apologized for her behavior, saying, "I've been so rude." Monkey-Girl replied that she forgave her. The transformation happened in the bully, not the character we followed closely. Some students responded to the critique of the ending by saying it was the bully who had the problem so it made sense that she apologized. Monkey-Girl's contribution was forgiveness. In the next shot, presumably after playing together, they hugged goodbye and the ex-bully blurted out, "Ahh! I got fur in my mouth!"—an accident in the performance that was kept in the final cut. Monkey-Girl corrected her, saying, "It's not fur, it's hair." The decision by the editors to use this improvised clip was an interesting one because it ended the video on a funny note but also highlighted that the differences between the two characters were still present.

Video production is sustained by the multiple streams of feedback that come from those who are viewing/reading the video in progress. The process is highly social and collaborative. Scripts are read out loud to gauge whether dialogue feels natural; directors read scripts before filming to see if they make sense; revisions are made; acting is done in multiple takes and evaluated moments afterwards; and video is imported into the computer with a sea of eyes appraising which clips are suitable and which are not. Video editors (readers) often have the most significant role when they examine, arrange, and modify the clips with a careful eye on story, clarity, and style. The technology of video making allows for substantial changes (revisions) to happen quite quickly. Reading video on a computer monitor or projected on a screen allows for multiple people to view/read the texts at once and for immediate discussion and criticism. Students develop a language for talking about visuals—the major mode of video making—and become even better at critically reading videos. A contemporary form of reading and writing, video production provides a wonderful opportunity for children to explore the intersection of technology and the sociocultural issues, concerns, contexts, and questions in their lives.

References

Gee, J. P. (2007). *What video games have to teach us about learning and literacy* (revised and updated ed.). New York: Palgrave Macmillan.

In Closing

16

RECLAIMING JOY

Spaces for Thinking and Action

Richard J. Meyer and Kathryn F. Whitmore

As we read and reread the chapters and extensions in this book, even as various initiatives were being issued from state and federal legislatures, we found ourselves immersed in discussions of joy. We relished the chance to dig deeply into Ken and Yetta Goodman's theory and engage intellectually in a conversation about how reading works. We wondered at the brilliance evident in the examples of children's and family members' transactions with texts in so many of the chapters. And we wanted to cheer for the many stories of teachers accomplishing what they know to be best for children (and themselves) throughout this book.

At times, though, we'd stop our discussions and look at each other as though we'd been caught reading contraband, and then a flood of emotions would follow. How dare we be joyful when teachers and children are under attack by the very sources that should be supporting them? What about the many teachers who are not sufficiently supported, daring, secure, or informed to respond to the terrible conditions in which they teach? We thought about how the work within this book could be read, explored, interrogated, and expanded by researchers, teachers, and our students, regardless of whether we taught in elementary, middle, secondary, preschool, or in higher education settings.

There were moments when hope completely evaporated and Kozol's description of work he did in New York City resonated:

> When I'm taking notes during a visit to a school and children in a class divert themselves with tiny episodes of silliness, or brief epiphanies of tenderness to one another, or a whispered observation about something they find amusing—like a goofy face made by another child in the class—I put a little round face with a smile on the margin of my notepad so that I won't miss it later on. In all the 15 pages that I wrote during my visit in this classroom in the Bronx, there is not a single small round smiling face.

I couldn't find a single statement made by any child that had not been prompted by the teacher's questions, other than one child's timid question about which "objective" should be written on the first line of a page the class had been asked to write. . . . I found no references to any child's traits of personality or even physical appearance. . . . The uniform activities and teacher's words controlled my own experience perhaps as much as they controlled and muted the expressiveness of children.

(2006, pp. 623–624)

Kozol presents an increasingly common narrative of life in school, a narrative reminiscent of prison settings and other oppressive metaphors.

The work presented in this book is part of our effort to participate in the crafting of multiple counternarratives, along with teachers, children, researchers, and other supporters of progressive education. Counternarratives (plural) are stories of work in classrooms, schools, and communities that challenge, interrogate, and offer multiple other possibilities, rather than the dismally sad current stories. Counternarratives are stories of success, growth, intensity, passion, sorrow, grief, flight, and more—much more—that are crafted locally, celebrated locally, and eventually incorporated (we hope) into new views of teaching, learning, curriculum, language, and sociocultural contexts as they relate to reading.

Complicating Joy

We argue in this chapter that joy is not a simple feeling of euphoria or pleasure; it is also found in moments of intensity when dealing with something powerful and important. Such moments of joy may be responses to negative ideas or occur during disheartening events, when there is a growing awareness, understanding, consciousness, and conscientization of the participants in the event. Two examples may help to clarify what we mean by the idea of a complicated notion of joy.

Vianca and Joy

Vianca was a sixth grader in a classroom in which Rick did research for a year. He explained to the children on the first day what his one expectation was:

You've got to tell the truth. Your truth. No matter what we do, you've got to tell the truth. And your truth can be different from my truth or anyone else's in this room. It can be different from mine or your teacher's or your best friends'. We have to be able to disagree.

Of course, few of the children believed or perhaps even understood what Rick meant until they began to read things they'd never read in school. They read Chicano/a poets because the class was 98 percent Hispanic. They read about economic poverty because everyone in the school received free lunch, and they read about being different, excluded, marginalized, and bracketed. The children consumed these works with rage, anger, questions, challenges, and resonation. All of these emotions are signifiers of joy. The last one (resonation) was evidenced as they spoke and wrote about their own lives and the lives of those they loved. Vianca was quite taken with Harjo's (1994) writing and crafted this poem:

> My happiness ends here.
> My happiness ends in the class.
> No matter what we have to do in
> class we have to live.
> The things we have to do in class
> are already prepared, set in my table.
> So it will be there for all the students
> in the class.

Teresita and Joy

Teresita was also a sixth grader. One day she offered Kathy, who was a researcher in her classroom, a lengthy story she wrote at home and brought to school to share with her ELL teacher. The story described Teresita's "very sad day" when she left her mother on one side of the Rio Grande River and crossed with her father and brother to the other side and into the United States. The conclusion of her story was as follows:

> Then we went back home so we got our bag and went to the river call El Rio Grande. When we got there then I said, "Goodbye, Mom, and don't forget that I love you." She said, "I would not forget that you love me, and I love you, Teresita."
> Then we hug each other and crying.
> My dad said, "Let go because the boat driver want to go." Then I said again, "Goodbye, Mom." Then I got in the boat crying. Then we cross the river I was still crying. I stop crying when we got out the boat to go to California. That was my very sad day.

Vianca's profound understanding of the ways in which curriculum, language, teaching, and learning, and even sociocultural contexts, are controlled in school was a joyful moment because once she knew and could express the shortcomings of her own schooling, she and Rick could act upon it. The comfort and release that Teresita experienced when she expressed her very sad story on paper and shared it with her teacher and Kathy, both of whom cared very much for her, was joyful as well. It was a means by which Kathy and Teresita's teacher could express their sorrow at Teresita's loss and their happiness that she was in their lives. The pieces of writing became points of origin for these girls to explore and interrogate issues of identity, schooling, and themselves as writers who could cause profound responses in readers.

We call for reclaiming this kind of joy in schools: joy nuanced by a broad spectrum of emotions and rooted in real-life issues and understanding.

Joyful and joyous moments are present in all the previous parts of this book, in children's reading of and acting upon their worlds, and in teachers' hard work to value and revalue who their students are and what they know. The search for joy is a search for spaces in which students and teachers engage in twenty-first-century activity, free from the influences of greed and outdated means of measuring what occurs in classrooms. Joy cannot be measured. Joy in assessment needs to include stories, events, experiences, processes, multiple modes, and relationships. The active search for and cultivation of a complicated view of joy is political work. As we pointed out in the introduction, most teachers didn't become teachers to be political activists, yet every action that teachers take is political. Complying is political. Undermining is political. Looking for cracks in which to teach like those you've read about in this book is political.

(Re)(e)volutionary Teachers' Joy

Rick presented at a one-day workshop recently, showing the work of Vianca and her sixth-grade colleagues. The attending teachers laughed along with silly stories that some of the children wrote, cried along with stories of families shattered by the border, and interrogated whether or not children should be allowed to write their truths about gangs, economic poverty, and drugs in their community. Understanding our students' lives has recently been trumped by test scores, scripted curriculum, and calls for compliance and homogeneity. The important focus on individuality and the ways in which uniquenesses are the *stuff* of composing curriculum have been stripped away from many teachers, students, and schools by reified and simplistic views of learning, teaching, language, and curriculum, and the dismissal of sociocultural contexts in which students live.

At the conclusion of the one-day workshop in which Rick explored these issues with teachers, there was an eerie silence as all those present realized that they would return to school newly aware or more deeply informed, but still unsure of what to do. Rick said:

> Our growing awareness is a form of joy. It's a complicated joy in which we see problems that face us in a new, and perhaps too bright, light. Once you know the way things are, you have to act on your truths and your under-standings or you will suffer from the stressful energy it takes to repress our own consciousness. The joy is in the knowing and in the potential for action.

"So what do we dooooo?" came a voice from the back of the room of 65 teachers.

"We do what we can," Rick replied. "We find spaces to invite children in, to value them and their families, and we keep talking to each other. We never, never, never let our voices be silenced, because that will be our doom."

Rick sensed the dissatisfaction with this response. It wasn't neat and tidy; things weren't fixed. "I know how this feels," he said. "You want an answer and you hate that the answer is you and your work with children and your relationships with your students, their families, each other, and the community. It seems too big."

Silence.

Rick said:

> Well, Anne Lamott [1995] is a writer some of you may know. When she was young, she had to do a report on birds, but kept putting it off until the weekend before it was due. She ran to her father, who was also an author, and explained her problem. He found a place for her to write, they worked together to find some books, and then he told her to write. She was worried that she'd never finish by Monday. Finally her father told her that she'd get it done by going "bird by bird." Change is an evolutionary process for teachers; we'll get it done bird by bird.

After the workshop, one teacher approached Rick and said, "I wrote this. The workshop was good. Hard, but good." She handed a note to Rick, asked him to keep it, and was gone:

> Education—where are we going with it? What are we doing to kids as we teach under the influence of NCLB? I, as a teacher, feel like a prisoner in my teaching. Forced to teach kids to read 40 words in 1 min. What is this? There isn't time just to enjoy reading—no time to immerse children in stories. What am I doing to kids? I want to teach kids to love learning, not in one minute either. At the beginning of the summer, I ask the Lord to forgive me for what I've done to his children and at the beginning of the school year, I ask for forgiveness for what I'm going to do to them. Why don't we teachers revolt against all this?
>
> *(Anonymous teacher's feedback after a workshop)*

The workshop was over but the joy was still there as teachers lingered to talk about some of their experiences and ideas for action. The conversations would continue, they promised each other. Perhaps they did; perhaps not. The point is that the talk had begun and the awareness was raised, so that was a joyful moment.

The Search for Twenty-First-Century Joy

Why don't we revolt? Because it's not in teachers' natures to do so in the United States; we don't have any historical points of reference to initiate such actions.

It's not in our teaching DNA to revolt, which does not mean we can't, but would we ever? Perhaps if things got so grossly out of hand that children were being physically hurt or our jobs were being eliminated in large numbers, then we might act the way that teachers in Mexico, Haiti, Korea, and other countries have (Freidberg, 2005), taking to the streets to raise awareness to stir support and action. At the time of this writing, a 1-million-teacher march is being planned, and by the time you read this, you will know what happened with and because of it. Even the planning of such an event suggests the urgency and desperation some teachers feel. Planning to act, especially with others who are like-minded, is another form of the complicated joy we pose here. Acting upon our worlds in almost any way that seeks constructive and just ends is joyous work.

Nearing the end of this book, we sense the need to leave it to you, our readers, to reclaim reading. One hope we have is that the five pillars around which we've organized this book will serve you in that work. As teachers and researchers we may situate ourselves so that we are supported by these five pillars; by doing that, we will be informed, grounded, and strong. We will be articulate as we confront those with whom we disagree and find points during the school day when we can teach, students can learn, and researchers can research in and for the twenty-first century.

We can do things bird by bird; little by little we can find spaces for joyous moments for ourselves and our students. Little by little, we can move our classrooms and research closer to the actions described by the authors of the chapters and their extensions in *Reclaiming Reading*. We offer below some ideas that may help begin, extend, or continue the work to cultivate joy.

Learn, Use, and Study Miscue Analysis

We draw upon theory to respond to questions addressed to us as well as to frame our teaching and research, so it is important to be articulate about that theory. Miscue analysis is a joyful path to understanding how reading works, assessing what readers do and what they understand about how reading works, and recognizing the types of mediation (instruction) that will best move them forward in their learning. Miscue analysis as a means of reclaiming reading includes the reading miscue inventory, over-the-shoulder miscue analysis, and eye movement miscue analysis. The natural extension from the data that we collect using miscue analysis is retrospective miscue analysis. This direct connection between assessing and using assessment information to teach is severely lacking in the current test-and-report-and-suffer-the-consequences climate.

Rely upon Authentic Materials

Readers need real texts with which to transact for purposes that accomplish something in their lives. Reclaiming reading means remembering the value of real books and expanding definitions of "text" to include twenty-first-century modes of making meaning; this includes considering the plethora of texts that are available: on the web, through digital means (such as moviemaking), in the toy box, and on shelves.

Talk about Reading and Talk about Texts

Reading is a social process, and reclaiming reading means remembering that readers need to talk, interact, respond, and engage. Classrooms that are liberatory and holistic are busy. Learners and teachers are active as they co-construct meaning for the texts they read.

Celebrate the Diversity of Languages and Cultures

Children need to know the importance and power that they can access when they know more than one language and are part of multiple cultures. If they are fortunate enough to come from a home in which a non-dominant language is spoken, that needs to be honored, celebrated, and viewed as a point of origin for teaching and learning. Classroom libraries that represent multiple languages and cultures enrich children's and teachers' lives. In places where such celebration and such libraries are forbidden, joy turns to pain, sorrow, and marginalization.

Create Democracy through Critical Literacy

Supporting children in their reading of the world helps them understand power, position, and agency, and contributes to their being informed and caring citizens. Issues that initiate questions about power and privilege in the world can be found in very local contexts by selecting reading materials and curriculum that invite learners to think and even act. Our commitment to multiple points of view demands that we invite students, colleagues, researchers, families, and other community members into our discussions.

The work yet to be done, *bird by bird* and piece by piece, will reclaim reading for the purposes for which it was truly intended: to know, to understand, to grow, and to act upon the world with an informed sense of agency.

Your Piece of the Action

In this final section of the book we present some questions to help you consider what you've learned and how you will apply and extend it in your own setting. It is our hope that you can find like-minded souls with whom to address these questions and other more personal and local questions that arose from your reading. We hope that these (and your own) questions will help you interrogate your practice with the ultimate goal of joy, both within the process and as you reach some tentative findings.

Reclaiming Learning

Learning to read is a sociopsycholinguistic transactional process, which means that it is social, involves thought, is based in language, and is unique to each learner. That said, some questions to consider about learning to read are as follows:

- What do I believe about learning to read?
- What do my students believe about learning to read?
- How do I work to revalue those who don't consider themselves to be readers?
- How can I systematically study and present my work with those learning to read?

Reclaiming Teaching

The chapters and extensions in this book provide many examples of informed teachers (informed about the reading process, pedagogy, assessment, language, culture, and more) making decisions about what to teach readers, when to teach it, and how to teach it. Some questions to consider in our teaching of reading are:

- How does my teaching demonstrate my understanding of the reading process as meaning making?
- How do I decide what to teach, when to teach it, and how to teach it?
- How do I ensure that learning to read and reading to learn occur simultaneously and are not artificially separated?
- How does my pedagogy ensure that readers use reading to act upon their worlds, evoke genuine questions, and lead to further reading, writing, and actions?

Reclaiming Curriculum

Once a teacher defers to a specified curriculum package, she or he has also deferred decisions and theoretical commitments about teaching, learning, language, and sociocultural contexts to others (publishers, district-level decision makers, legislators). With that in mind, you might ask:

- What evidence is there that the enacted reading curriculum serves the learners?
- In what ways does or can the reading curriculum support students in reading their worlds, posing real problems, and addressing and acting upon their problems?
- How do I construct invitations full of choices for learners?
- How can I reclaim curricular decisions about reading instruction by joining with others to strengthen our collective voice?

Reclaiming Language

Language is a tool for making meaning, and everything that occurs in classrooms and research should ultimately and immediately be about the making of meaning. Questions growing from the language pillar in this book include the following:

- In an increasingly multilingual society, how do my reading theory, instruction, and practice include, represent, portray, and rely upon the linguistic strengths that my students bring to school?
- How do we discuss books, reading, language, and ideas in ways that honor learners' identities and perspectives?
- In the teaching and learning of reading, how do I engage learners in the many modes they have at their disposal: dance, song, arts, photography, movie-making, etc.?

Reclaiming Sociocultural Contexts

Perhaps the most egregious insult to reading teachers and learners in the current legislative and policy climate is the marginalization of the rich sociocultural capital that lies within the communities that schools serve. Writing about her personal experience in school, Gutiérrez explains this sad phenomenon:

> I came to kindergarten so excited and ready to learn. I came prepared with my *maleta* (suitcase) full of so many wonderful things, my Spanish language, my beautiful culture, and many other treasures. When I got there, though, not only did they not let me use anything from my *maleta*, they did not even let me bring it into the classroom.
>
> *(Gutiérrez & Larson, 1994, p. 33)*

Questions to consider when interrogating this pillar in practice include:

- How can I welcome everyone's *maleta* at the door and in the classroom reading activity?
- How can the cultural artifacts that are important to my students permeate the reading activities in which they engage (including toys, technology, cultural activities and artifacts, etc.)?
- What evidence do I have that each learner's unique life is present, represented, and included in the reading activities and invitations in which we engage?

Finally, we close this book with a wish and a short poem. We wish for the truly complicated types of joy that are imaginable: the joy that arouses our curiosity, is rooted in our passions, and demands our full attention. It is this kind of work that makes life matter, brings life meaning, and makes classrooms places rich in joy and the hopes and dreams that are realized from it. A poem by Esparanza closes this book. She reflected upon changes during her sixth-grade year, noting her own growing consciousness, much like ours and, we hope, yours:

I used to have a brain
Without words
But now
I do

References

Freidberg, J. (2005). *Grain of sand/Granito de arena*. Seattle: Corrugated Films.

Gutiérrez, K., & Larson, J. (1994). Language borders: Recitation as hegemonic discourse. *International Journal of Education Reform, 3*(1), 22–36.

Harjo, J. (1994). *The woman who fell from the sky: Poems*. New York: W. W. Norton.

Kozol, J. (2006). Success for all: Trying to make an end run around inequality and segregation. *Phi Delta Kappan, 87*(8), 624–626.

Lamott, A. (1995). *Bird by bird: Some instructions on writing and life*. New York: Anchor Books.

CONTRIBUTORS

Peggy Albers
Professor
Georgia State University
Decatur, GA

Bess Altwerger
Professor
Towson University
Towson, MD

Jane Baskwill
Assistant Professor
Mount Saint Vincent University
Halifax, Nova Scotia, Canada

Rose Casement
Professor
University of Michigan-Flint
Flint, MI

M. Ruth Davenport
Professor
Eastern Oregon University
La Grande, OR

Michelle Doyle
Teacher
Pot Spring Elementary
Timonium, MD

Corey Drake
Associate Professor
Iowa State University
Ames, IA

Ann Ebe
Assistant Professor
Hunter College
New York, NY

Carol Felderman
Adjunct Professor
American University
Washington, DC

David Freeman
Professor
University of Texas at Brownsville
Brownsville, TX

Yvonne Freeman
Professor
University of Texas at Brownsville
Brownsville, TX

Andrea García
Associate Professor
Hofstra University
Hempstead, NY

Kristen Gillaspy
Literacy Coach
White Knoll Middle School
West Columbia, SC

Carol Gilles
Associate Professor
University of Missouri
Columbia, MO

Jeanne Gilliam Fain
Assistant Professor
Middle Tennessee State University
Murfreesboro, TN

Kenneth S. Goodman
Professor Emeritus
University of Arizona
Tucson, AZ

Yetta M. Goodman
Regents Professor Emerita
University of Arizona
Tucson, AZ

Jerome C. Harste
Professor Emeritus
Indiana University
Bloomington, IN

Robin Horn
Teacher
Chandler Unified School District
Chandler, AZ

Pam Hubbard
Teacher
Weber Elementary School
Iowa City, IA

Chuck Jurich
Doctoral Candidate
University of New Mexico
Albuquerque, NM

Edward Kastner
Digital Art and Photography Teacher
Wydown Middle School
Clayton, MO

Koomi Kim
Associate Professor
New Mexico State University
Las Cruces, NM

Allen Koshewa
Teacher
Davis Elementary
Portland, OR

Tasha Tropp Laman
Associate Professor
University of South Carolina
Columbia, SC

Carol Lauritzen
Professor
Eastern Oregon University
La Grande, OR

Prisca Martens
Professor
Towson University
Towson, MD

Carmen M. Martínez-Roldán
Associate Professor
University of Texas at Austin
Austin, TX

Richard J. Meyer
Professor
University of New Mexico
Albuquerque, NM

Kathryn Mitchell Pierce
Writing Specialist
Wydown Middle School
Clayton, MO

Lori Norton-Meier
Associate Professor
University of Louisville
Louisville, KY

Debra Peters
Teacher
Smithton School
Columbia, MO

Renita Schmidt
Associate Professor
Furman University
Greenville, SC

Kathy G. Short
Professor
University of Arizona
Tucson, AZ

Debbie Smith
Educator
Spotsylvania VA

Yoo Kyung Sung
Assistant Professor
University of New Mexico
Albuquerque, NM

Lisa Thomas
Teacher
Peter Howell Elementary
Tucson, AZ

Katie Van Sluys
Associate Professor
DePaul University
Chicago, IL

Vivian Vasquez
Associate Professor
American University
Washington, DC

Dorothy Watson
Professor Emeritus
University of Missouri
Columbia, MO

Kathryn F. Whitmore
Professor
The University of Iowa
Iowa City, IA

Jennifer L. Wilson
Assistant Professor
University of South Carolina
Columbia, SC

Karen E. Wohlwend
Assistant Professor
Indiana University
Bloomington, IN

INDEX